Illuminate
Publishing

WJEC/Eduqas
A Level
Law
Book 2

Book 2

Sara Davies • Karen Phillips • Louisa Draper-Walters

Published in 2018 by Illuminate Publishing Ltd
PO Box 1160, Cheltenham, Gloucestershire GL50 9RW

Orders: Please visit www.illuminatepublishing.com
or email sales@illuminatepublishing.com.

British Library Cataloguing in Publication Data.

A catalogue record for this book is available from the British Library.

ISBN 978-1-911208-46-4

Printed by Cambrian Printers, Aberystwyth

03.18

The publisher's policy is to use papers that are natural, renewable and recyclable
products made from wood grown in sustainable forests. The logging and manufacturing
processes are expected to conform to the environmental regulations of the country
of origin.

This material has been endorsed by WJEC and Eduqas and offers high quality support
for the delivery of WJEC and Eduqas qualifications. While this material has been through
a WJEC and Eduqas quality assurance process, all responsibility for the content remains
with the publisher.

WJEC and Eduqas examination questions are reproduced by permission from WJEC and Eduqas.

Editor: Julia Sandford-Cooke (WordFire Communications)
Design and layout: Kamae Design
Cover design: Kamae Design
Cover image: Nagel Photography / Shutterstock.com

Acknowledgements
Crown copyright information is reproduced with the permission of the Controller of HMSO and
the Queen's Printer for Scotland.

Dedication
In memory of Dr Pauline O'Hara, who was an inspiration to us and many Law students.

Contents

Introduction

How to use this book

The contents of this textbook are designed to guide you through the WJEC or Eduqas Law specification and lead you to success in the subject. It has been written by senior examiners who have pinpointed what is required of candidates, in terms of content, to achieve the highest marks. In addition, common errors have been identified, and support and advice given in how to avoid these errors, which will help lead to success in your AS/A Level examination. It contains a range of specimen exam questions for each specification, along with sample answers and examiner commentaries.

The guide covers:

- Eduqas AS Level components 1 and 2
- Eduqas A Level components 1, 2 and 3
- WJEC AS Level units 1 and 2
- WJEC A Level units 3 and 4.

This textbook covers the knowledge content that is required for each topic within the various specifications. There is also a selection of learning features throughout the topics.

Key terms: Important legal terms are emboldened in the main text and accompanied by a definition in the margin. They have also been compiled into a glossary at the end of the book for ease of reference.

Grade Boost: This gives you an insight into the examiners' mind and provides advice on things you should include to achieve the higher marks.

Stretch and Challenge: These activities provide opportunities to research a topic further and give you advice on wider reading. These are usually additional cases, current affairs or areas under reform, knowledge of which should really impress your examiner.

Cases and Key Cases: Examples of cases are highlighted to clarify the points of law they illustrate.

Exam Skills: This gives advice and guidance on how to prepare for your exams.

Summary: At the end of each topic there is a handy summary to help you structure your revision.

The **Exam practice and techniques** section provides you with both an opportunity to practise your own examination skills and an insight into the quality of answer that is expected to achieve a high grade. This section shows you examples of Grade A answers as well as a Grade C/D answers. A detailed commentary explains how the candidate achieved their marks, and key tips suggest how these answers can be improved. The marks that would have been given to a candidate are split into the Assessment Objectives, so you can see how the exam answer has been marked.

AS/A Level qualifications

The book is intended to support you in the A Level study of both Eduqas and WJEC. Additional content required for AS and some A Level specifications for both Eduqas and WJEC can be found in Book 1 (ISBN 978 1 911208 45 7).

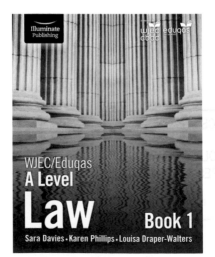

The content coverage section below explains exactly what can be found in each book. References to the WJEC specifications are represented by the letter **W** and references to the Eduqas specifications are represented by the letter **E**. Content that is only relevant to specific parts of either the Eduqas or WJEC specifications is colour coded:

WJEC WJEC only (purple)

EDUQAS A LEVEL Eduqas A Level only (blue)

Book 1	Book 2
The Nature of Law and the Welsh and English Legal Systems	**Law of Contract**
E1.1.1 W1.1 Law making Law reform	**E2.1.3 W3.8** Express and implied terms
E1.1.2 W1.2 Delegated legislation	**E2.1.4 W3.9** Misrepresentation and economic duress
E1.1.3 W1.3 Statutory interpretation	**Law of Tort**
E1.1.4 W1.4 Judicial precedent	**E2.2.4** Torts connected to land
E1.2.1 W1.5 Civil courts	**E2.2.5** Vicarious liability
E1.2.2 W1.6 Criminal process Juries	**E2.2.6** Defences: Tort
E1.2.3 W1.7 Legal personnel: Barristers and solicitors Judiciary Magistrates	**Criminal Law**
	E2.3.3 W3.14 Fatal offences against the person
E1.2.4 W1.8 Access to justice and funding	**E2.3.4 W3.15** Property offences
Law of Contract	**E2.3.5 E2.3.6 W3.16 W3.17** Capacity and necessity defences
E2.1.1 W3.6 Rules of contract	**E2.3.7 W3.17** Preliminary offences of attempt
E2.1.2 W3.7 Essential requirements of a contract	
E2.1.3 E2.1.5 W3.10 Discharge of contract	
E2.1.4 E2.1.6 W3.11 Remedies: Contract	
Law of Tort	
E2.2.1 W2.1 Rules of tort	
E2.2.2 W2.2 Liability in negligence	
E2.2.3 W2.3 Occupier's liability	
E2.2.4 E2.2.7 W2.4 Remedies: Tort	
Criminal Law	
E2.3.1 W3.12 Rules of criminal law	
E2.3.2 W3.13 General elements of criminal liability	
E2.3.3 W3.14 Offences against the person	
Human Rights Law	
E2.4.1 E 2.4.2 W3.1 Rules, theory and protection of human rights law	
E2.4.3 W3.2 Specific provisions of the ECHR	
E2.4.5 E2.4.6 W3.5 Reform of human rights	
E2.4.4 W3.3 Restrictions of the ECHR	

Which qualification are you studying for?

You may be studying for either Eduqas qualifications or WJEC qualifications. This book covers the examination requirements for both. Most of the content is very similar in all the specifications, and the questions and mark schemes only differ slightly. For more information, look at the examination guidance section of this book and the examination papers and mark schemes of the qualification for which you are studying and discuss them with your teacher.

WJEC AS/A Level examination content

Wales

In Wales, most candidates will be studying for the WJEC AS in their first year followed by the A Level in their second year. In most cases, AS exams will be sat at the end of the first year and these will be combined with the A Level exams sat at the end of the second year to achieve the full A Level qualification. For the full WJEC specification content, go to www.wjec.co.uk.

- The AS is less challenging and worth 40% of the full A Level qualification.
- The AS is a stepping stone to the full A Level qualification, so ideas introduced at AS will be developed on the full A Level papers.
- A full WJEC A Level has four units or examinations. This content is covered across both books 1 and 2.
- A WJEC AS Level has two units or examinations. This textbook includes enough topics to help you prepare for the exams.

	Unit 1	Unit 2	Unit 3	Unit 4
WJEC AS Level	The Nature of Law and the Welsh and English Legal Systems	The Law of Tort	n/a	n/a
	80 marks available (25% of full A Level qualification)	60 marks available (15% of full A Level qualification)	n/a	n/a
	1 hour and 45 minutes	1 hour and 30 minutes	n/a	n/a
WJEC A Level	Units 1 and 2, above, plus units 3 and 4		The Practice of Substantive Law	Substantive Law Perspectives
			100 marks available (30% of full A Level qualification)	100 marks available (30% of full A Level qualification)
			1 hour and 45 minutes	2 hours

The overall weightings are 40% for AS and 60% for A2.

- **Unit 1:** The Nature of Law and the Welsh and English Legal Systems (25%).
- **Unit 2:** The Law of Tort (15%).
- **Unit 3:** The Practice of Substantive Law (30%).
- **Unit 4:** Substantive Law Perspectives (30%).

Key terms and legal authority

Students often say that studying law is like learning a whole new language. In fact, you will need to become familiar with some Latin terms, such as *ratio decidendi*. If you are to get into the top mark bands, you need to use appropriate legal terminology. Key terms are highlighted throughout the book. Many of the shorter exam questions will require you to explain the meaning of a term, or describe a concept. Extended-response essays should always start with an explanation of the key term in the question. The rest of your answer should focus on ideas and debates related to that key term.

In order to support the points you make, you should include **legal authority**. This can be a case, statute or legislation, for example *Donoghue v Stevenson (1932)* or **s1 Theft Act 1968**.

Eduqas AS/A Level examination content

England

In England, most candidates will be studying for the Eduqas AS or A Level. For the full Eduqas specification content, go to www.eduqas.co.uk.

The Eduqas AS Level is half of the content of the full A Level but is equally challenging as the full A Level.

- A full Eduqas A Level has three components or examinations. This content is covered over both books 1 and 2.
- A full Eduqas AS Level has two components or examinations. This textbook includes enough topics to help you prepare for the exams.

	Component 1	Component 2	Component 3
Eduqas AS Level	The Nature of Law and the English Legal System	Understanding Substantive Law	n/a
	60 marks available (50% of qualification)	60 marks available (50% of qualification)	n/a
	1 hour and 30 minutes	1 hour and 30 minutes	n/a
Eduqas A Level	The Nature of Law and the English Legal System	Substantive Law in Practice	Perspectives of Substantive Law
	50 marks available (25% of qualification)	75 marks available (37.5% of qualification)	75 marks available (37.5% of qualification)
	1 hour and 30 minutes	2 hours and 15 minutes	2 hours and 15 minutes

AS Level Law with Eduqas is a stand-alone qualification and is weighted at 40% of the overall A Level. Each component is worth 50% of the qualification.

A Level Law with Eduqas is a linear course and the components are weighted as follows:

- **Component 1:** 25%.
- **Component 2:** 37.5%.
- **Component 3:** 37.5%.

Assessment in Eduqas and WJEC Law

Assessment is covered in more detail in the examination section at the end of this book. However, before you start to study, it will help you to understand the key skills that you are being tested on. These consist of the following:

- **Assessment Objective 1 (AO1):** Describing what you know.
- **Assessment Objective 2 (AO2):** Applying your knowledge.
- **Assessment Objective 3 (AO3):** Analysing/evaluating this knowledge.

All mark schemes offer marks for the different skills and examiners are trained to look for and recognise them.

- **AO1:** You must demonstrate **knowledge and understanding** of legal rules and principles.
- **AO2:** You must **apply** legal rules and principles to given scenarios in order to present a legal argument using appropriate legal terminology.
- **AO3:** You must **analyse and evaluate** legal rules, principles, concepts and issues.

CONTRACT LAW
Express and implied terms

Spec reference	Key content	Assessment Objectives	Where does this topic feature on each specification/exam?
WJEC A Level **3.8:** Express and implied terms, conditions, warranties and innominate terms, exclusion and limitation clauses **Eduqas A Level** **2.1.3:** Express and implied terms	• Obligations under a contract: difference between representations and terms • Express terms: incorporation of express terms, parole evidence rule • Implied terms: terms implied by fact, terms implied by statute: implied terms under the Consumer Rights Act 2015, Consumer Contract Regulations 2013 • Exclusion clauses in both consumer and business-to-business contracts: incorporation of exclusion clauses, Unfair Contract Terms Act 1977 • Other terms: conditions, warranties, innominate terms	**AO1** Demonstrate knowledge and understanding of legal rules and principles **AO2** Apply legal rules and principles to given scenarios in order to present a legal argument using appropriate legal terminology **AO3** Analyse and evaluate legal rules, principles, concepts and issues	**WJEC A Level:** Unit 3 and 4 **Eduqas AS Level:** Component 2 **Eduqas A Level:** Component 2 and 3

The difference between representations and terms

The **terms** of a contract set out the obligations under a contract. Terms can be **express** or **implied**. Terms can also be classified according to their importance, as **conditions**, **warranties** and **innominate** terms.

Terms need to be distinguished from mere **representations**, which have no liability attached to them because they have just induced a party to enter into the contract. These are usually made orally before the contract has been made. Sometimes, these representations can be terms, and whether they are a representation or a term depends on the intention of the parties.

However, if a representation has been false and has wrongly induced the other party to enter the contract, this is a **misrepresentation** and it will attach liability to the party making it.

Incorporation of express terms

Whether a **precontractual** statement is a **representation** or a **term** will depend on the intention of the parties. Whatever the case, if the parties wish it to be part of the contract, it must be **incorporated**. This is straightforward if it is written into the contract but can prove more complicated if it is not. To combat this, the courts have developed some guidelines, as follows.

The importance of the statement

Bannerman v White (1861)

In a transaction for the purchase of hops, White asked whether the hops had been treated with sulphur. Bannerman said that the hops had not been treated, believing this to be the truth. However, it was discovered that sulphur had been used. White sued because he would not have entered into the contract if he had known beforehand that sulphur had been used.

*The court agreed that the statement about the sulphur was incorporated into the contract because **had it not been for that statement**, White would not have entered into the contract.*

The knowledge and skill of the person making the statement

If the person making the statement has expert knowledge or skills, clearly the courts will be more willing to interpret it as a term rather than a representation.

Dick Bentley Productions Ltd v Harold Smith (Motors) Ltd (1965)

*The **claimant**, Dick Bentley Productions, was looking for a 'well-vetted' Bentley car. The **defendant**, a car dealer, stated that he had one for sale that had recently had its gearbox and engine replaced, and since then had only done 20,000 miles.*

*After the car had been purchased, problems began to emerge and it also emerged that the car had in fact done 100,000 miles since the replacements. The court **held** that the statement was a term because the claimant relied on the expertise of the car dealer in good faith.*

The timing of the statement

The more time that elapses between the statement being made and the contract being concluded, the less likely the courts will be to consider the statement a term.

Routledge v McKay (1954)

This case concerned the sale of a motorbike. Both parties were private individuals with no specialist knowledge. The seller believed the motorbike had been manufactured in 1942 but it turned out to have been manufactured in 1930. The claim that the date of manufacture was a term failed because the interval between the statement being made and the contract concluded suggested that the statement was not a term.

Agreements in writing

There is a presumption that any statement made before the contract which was then **not** incorporated into a written contract was a mere representation and not a term. If the parties intended it to be a term, it would have been included in the written documents.

KEY TERMINOLOGY

claimant: the person bringing the action. Until April 1999, this person was called the plaintiff.
defendant: the person defending the action (e.g. the person accused of a crime).
held: decided; the decision of the court.

STRETCH AND CHALLENGE

Research *Duffy v Newcastle United Football Co Ltd (2000)*, which concerned the opportunity for season ticket holders to buy their seats. Discuss the following questions:
1. Why was the promotional material not deemed to constitute terms?
2. Why did the fans argue that they should have been deemed terms?

Interpretation of express terms

When determining the meaning of an express term, judges often have to discover the parties' intentions. This has been the subject of some debate in the courts in recent years.

KEY CASE

Arnold v Britton (2015)
This case concerned leases for holiday chalets in a caravan park in Swansea. The term in question concerned the amount that needed to be paid for the service charge and maintenance of the caravan site.

In its decision, the Supreme Court laid down some guidance on how terms should be interpreted, favouring a **literal** interpretation of contracts.

- Commercial common sense should not be used to undervalue the language of the contract.
- A court is more likely to move away from the natural meaning of the words if the drafting is bad.
- Just because a contract has worked out badly for one party, it does not justify departing from the wording of the contract.
- In construing a contract, the courts can only take into account facts and circumstances known to both sides at the time the contract was made.
- If an event occurs which the parties had not contemplated, but it is clear what their intention would have been had they done so, the court can give effect to that intention.

This is the most recent decision in relation to the interpretation of contracts and it seems that a literal approach is favoured over business sense.

This approach contrasts with Lord Neuberger's comments in the slightly earlier case of *Marley v Rawlings (2014)*, where a more **purposive** approach was favoured. Lord Neuberger stated that the court must identify the intention of the parties by identifying the meaning of the relevant words in light of:

1. the natural and ordinary meaning of those words

2. the overall purpose of the document

3. any other provisions in the document

4. the facts known or assumed by the parties at the time that the document was executed

5. common sense.

STRETCH AND CHALLENGE

Research some cases that have come before the court concerning the interpretation of terms. Discuss whether a **literal** or a more **purposive** approach was taken in each.
1. *Martinez v Ellesse International SpA (1999)*
2. *Pink Floyd Music Ltd v EMI Records (2010)*
3. *Investors Compensation Scheme Ltd v West Bromwich Building Society (1998).*

Implied terms

Terms implied by fact

An implied term is not laid down in the contract but is assumed by both parties to have been included had they thought about it. The leading case on this is the Supreme Court decision in *Marks and Spencer v BNP Paribas (2015)*.

The Supreme Court judgement in *Marks and Spencer v BNP Paribas (2015)* clarified the law in relation to whether to imply a term into a contract. The Supreme Court suggested that the following guidelines should be used:

1. A term can only be implied if, without the term, the contract would lack commercial or practical coherence.

2. A term may also be implied if it is strictly necessary for **business efficacy**. The requirement for necessity is quite important, as this is a more stringent requirement than the previous approach, which required the proposed term to be 'reasonable and equitable'.

3. A term should also satisfy the test of **business necessity**. It must be so obvious that it goes without saying. This is what was previously known as the '**officious bystander test**'.

The **business efficacy** test and the **officious bystander** tests have been used in determining whether a term should be implied since *Equitable Life Assurance Society v Hyman (2000)*, where it was held that the term also had to be:

• capable of clear expression
• compatible with any express terms of the contract.

The officious bystander

In *Shirlaw v Southern Foundries (1926)*, the officious bystander test was clarified by MacKinnon LJ:

'That which, in any contract, is left to be implied need not be expressed in something as obvious that it goes without saying so that, if while the parties were making their bargain, an officious bystander were to suggest some express provision for it in the agreement, they would testily suppress him with a common "Oh, of course!".'

Business efficacy

This is a term which one side alleges must be implied to make the contract work.

The Moorcock (1889)

*The Court of Appeal held that a contract to use the defendant's jetty to unload the claimant's boat contained an implied term that the boat would be moored safely at the jetty. It held that such a term would be necessary for business efficacy, otherwise the claimant 'would simply be buying an opportunity for danger'. The term had been breached because the boat was permitted to be moored when the water level was too low, and therefore the actions for **damages** for **breach of contract** were successful.*

This was further clarified in *Reigate v Union Manufacturing Co (1918)* by Sutton LJ:

'A term can only be implied if it is necessary in the business sense to give efficacy to the contract: i.e. if it is such a term that it can confidently be said that if at the time the contract was being negotiated someone had said to the parties, "What will happen in such a case?", they would both have replied "Of course so and so will happen, we did not trouble to say that, it is too clear."'

This is still the law, despite attempts to unify it into one test of reasonableness in the case of *Attorney General of Belize v Belize Telecom (2009)*.

Consumer Rights Act 2015: Implied terms

There are certain terms which the law says have to be included, regardless of whether the parties want them or intended to include them.

The law surrounding this used to be governed by the *Sale of Goods Act 1979*, the *Unfair Terms in Consumer Contracts Regulations 1999* and the *Supply of Goods and Services Act 1982*. However, these Acts have now been repealed and the law is now contained in the *Consumer Rights Act 2015*.

The *Consumer Rights Act 2015* protects consumers against unfair terms, prevents companies excluding liability for negligence and also implies that certain terms automatically go into consumer contracts.

Supply of goods

This includes physical goods, as well as digital content such as downloads, software and pre-installed content.

Section 9: Satisfactory quality

This is the expectation that the goods will not be faulty or damaged, and this is judged by what a **reasonable** person would consider satisfactory. There is also the consideration that it includes 'all the other relevant circumstances'. This means any statement about the specific characteristics of the goods made by the trader in an advert or on a label, so the goods can be unsatisfactory if this was drawn to the consumer's attention before the contract was made.

Section 9(3) outlines the aspects that should be considered when judging satisfactory quality:

- Fitness for all the purposes for which goods of that kind are usually supplied.
- Appearance and finish.
- Freedom from minor defects.
- Safety.
- Durability.

Section 10: Fit for purpose

This section provides that goods should be fit for the purpose they are supplied for as well as any specific purpose made known to the retailer.

This term does not apply if the consumer did not rely, or it is unreasonable for the consumer to rely, on the skill or judgement of the trader.

Section 11: As described

This means that the goods must match any description, models or samples shown at the time of purchase. This term obviously does not apply if any differences were brought to the attention of the consumer prior to purchase.

Bringing a claim

Sections 19–24 set out the remedies that apply if the statutory rights for goods contained in *s9–11* are not met. A consumer must bring the claim against the retailer, not the manufacturer.

Date of purchase	**Section 20** gives the consumer a **legal right to reject** goods that are of unsatisfactory quality, unfit for purpose or not as described to get a **full refund**, but this is limited to within **30 days of purchase.**
30 days	**Section 23** provides that the consumer has to give the retailer one opportunity to **repair** or **replace** any goods outside the 30 days. If the attempt to repair is unsuccessful, the consumer can claim a refund or a price reduction.
6 months	If a fault is discovered **within six months** of purchase, it is presumed to have been there since purchase, unless the retailer can prove otherwise. If the fault is discovered **after six months**, the burden is on the consumer to prove that the product was faulty at the time of delivery. The consumer then has **six years** to take a claim to the small claims court.

Under **s28**, the retailer is responsible for the goods until they are in the possession of the consumer. This means that the retailer is liable for the service provided by the courier it employs.

If a retailer **fails to deliver the goods within 30 days**, the consumer has the right to terminate the purchase and get a **full refund**, even if the timing of the delivery was not essential.

As well as those statutory remedies available under the **Consumer Rights Act 2015**, the consumer can still pursue other **common law** and **equitable** remedies as an alternative or in addition. These could include:

- damages
- specific performance
- a right to treat the contract as ended.

Supply of services

This includes services for dry cleaning, entertainment, work done by professionals (including solicitors, estate agents and accountants), building work, fitted kitchens, double glazing and home improvements.

Section 49: Reasonable care and skill

The legislation does not provide a definition of what 'reasonable care and skill' means. It is thought that whether a person has met the standard of reasonable care and skill will depend on whether they have met industry codes of practice or standards.

Supply of services under the Consumer Rights Act 2015 includes work provided by tradespeople on home improvements

Section 50: Binding information

Any information that is given to the consumer before the service is provided and that is relied upon by the consumer is binding. This applies to information that is given both orally and in writing.

Section 51: Reasonable price

Where the price is not agreed beforehand, the service must be provided for a reasonable price. The explanatory notes to the legislation give an example:

'If a homeowner engages a plumber to fix an urgent leak, they may not take the time to discuss the price before fixing the problem. The price might not be in the contract if the plumber did not know the problem before they arrived to fix it. If the leak was fixed in ten minutes and with only a £50 replacement part, £1,000 is unlikely to be a reasonable price to pay.'

Section 52: Reasonable time

Unless a timescale has been agreed, the legislation states that the service must be carried out within a reasonable time frame after the contract has been agreed.

Bringing a claim

If the service does not satisfy the criteria in **s49–52**, statutory remedies are available.

- **Section 55**: The trader should either redo the element which is inadequate or perform the whole service again at no extra cost.
- **Section 56**: Where repeat performance is not possible, the consumer can claim a price reduction. This could be up to 100% of the cost and the trader should refund the consumer **within 14 days** of agreeing that a refund is due.

Consumer Rights Act 2015: Unfair terms

This legislation also provides guidance on consumer rights in relation to unfair terms contained in contracts. The protection offered by this **statute** is far greater than the protection offered by the **Unfair Contract Terms Act 1977**, which is discussed in page 17.

Section 62

This stipulates that an unfair term under the Act is not binding on the consumer. A term is unfair if, contrary to the requirement of **good faith**, it causes a significant imbalance in the parties' rights and obligations under the contract to the detriment of the consumer.

Key terms of a contract should be assessed for **fairness** unless they are **prominent** and **transparent**, or if they are terms that relate to the main subject matter of a contract, or if the assessment is of the price payable under the contract. A term would be regarded as prominent and transparent if it is 'expressed in plain and intelligible language and (in the case of written terms) is legible'.

Schedule 2

This outlines the so called 'grey list' of terms which may be regarded as unfair. These can include but are not limited to:

- fees and charges hidden in the small print
- something that tries to limit the consumer's legal rights
- disproportionate default charges
- excessive early termination charges.

Consumer Contracts (Information, Cancellation and Additional Charges) Regulations 2013

These Regulations cover online shopping and bring into UK law the **Consumer Rights Directive** from the EU. It also supersedes the **Distance Selling Regulations**.

The Regulations require traders to give certain information before entering into a contract and covers all contracts entered into after 13 June 2014. They cover the sale of goods online, over the phone, from a catalogue or face to face somewhere that is not the business premises of the trader (e.g. the consumer's home), and aim to protect consumers from unfair practices.

Key information a trader should provide include the following:

1. A description of the goods, services or digital content, including how long any commitment will last on the part of the consumer.

2. The total price of the goods, service or digital content or how the price will be calculated.

3. How the consumer will pay for the goods or services and when they will be provided.

4. All additional delivery charges and other costs.

5. Details of who pays the cost of returning items if there is a right to cancel.

6. Details of any right to cancel. The trader also needs to provide, or make available, a standard cancellation form to make cancelling easy.

7. Information about the seller, including their geographical address and contact details and the address and identity of any other trader for whom the trader is acting.

8. Information on the compatibility of digital content with hardware and other software that the trader is aware of.

Cancelling goods

Cancellation rights under the Regulations are more generous than if goods or services were bought from a shop.

Date of purchase	The **right to cancel** starts the moment the consumer places their order and ends **14 days** from the day the goods are received.
14 days	The consumer has a **further 14 days** to **return the goods** to the trader.
28 days	The trader has **another further 14 days** to give a refund from the date they receive the goods back or the consumer providing evidence of having returned the goods.

The exceptions to the rules on cancellations are for:

- CDs, DVDs or software if the seal has been broken on the wrapping
- perishable items
- tailor-made or personalised items.

Cancelling services

The consumer has 14 days to cancel, though they must pay for any service they have used up to the point of cancellation.

In relation to **digital content**, the consumer must acknowledge that, once a download has started, they will lose their right to cancel. Retailers must supply digital content within the 14-day cancellation period **unless** the consumer has given their consent for a longer period.

Exclusion clauses

An **exclusion clause** is when one party to the contract attempts to exclude all liability or to limit liability for breaches of the contract. The law has tried to control the use of these clauses, by common law and by statute, as they are unfair to the consumer.

Common law

Generally, the use of exclusion clauses is disapproved of, especially where they are made by a party with considerably stronger bargaining power than the other. To regulate exclusion clauses, the courts ask two questions:

1. **Has the clause been incorporated into the contract?** This can be done by signature, reasonable notice or through previous course of dealing.

2. **Does the clause cover the alleged breach?**

Incorporation by signature

If the contract has been signed at the time of making the contract, it is assumed that the contents become terms of the contract, regardless of whether the parties have read the terms, so long as there is no evidence of fraud or misrepresentation.

L'Estrange v Graucob (1934)

This case concerned the rental of a vending machine. The claimant had signed the contract without reading it, not realising there was a clause within the contract which excluded liability for the product. The claimant had no form of redress when the machine became faulty as she was deemed to be bound by the contract by signing the contract.

Incorporation by reasonable notice

If a party gives separate written terms at the time the contract is made, those terms only become part of the contract if the consumer has had reasonable notice that they exist.

Parker v South Eastern Railway (1877)

A cloakroom ticket had details of the cloakroom opening hours and also the words 'See back'. On the back was a limitation clause which claimed that the company was only liable for £10 for the loss of any property left with them. When the claimant tried to claim for his lost £24 bag, his action failed because he was deemed to have had reasonable notice of the limitation clause.

In deciding whether reasonable notice had been given, the courts will look at the **time** the notice was given. That is, it should be given at the same time the contract was made, or before.

Olley v Marlborough Court Ltd (1949)

The terms of the contract, including exclusion clauses, were on the back of a hotel door, which guests would not have seen until they got to their room, by which time the contract had already been completed. This was deemed to be too late to be classed as 'reasonable notice'.

The **form** in which the notice is given is also important. It should be the case that any notice of exclusion clauses is given in a document that the claimant would reasonably expect to contain contractual terms.

Chapelton v Barry UDC (1940)

Exclusion clauses were printed on the back of a ticket that was given in return for the purchase of a deckchair on a beach. This was deemed to be more like a receipt and therefore a reasonable person would not expect it to contain contractual terms.

In recent times, the courts have held that the more unusual or onerous a term, the greater the degree of notice is required to incorporate it.

STRETCH AND CHALLENGE

The concept of notice was discussed in the more recent case of *O'Brien v MGN (2001)*, which concerned a newspaper competition involving scratchcards. Research this case, and discuss whether reasonable notice of the rules was given to consumers.

Incorporation by a previous course of dealing

If two parties have previously made contracts with each other, and those contracts contained an exclusion or limitation clause, then it is assumed that those same exclusion clauses apply to subsequent transactions, even if they had not been incorporated in the usual way.

Spurling v Bradshaw (1956)

The parties had been doing business together for several years and on the occasion in question did not receive the documentation containing the exemption clauses until the contract had been concluded. The claimant lost his action on the basis that, although reasonable notice had not been given on this occasion, the parties had had enough dealings in the past to warrant the clause incorporated on this occasion.

If it is decided that an exemption or limited clause has been incorporated correctly, the courts will decide if the clause covers the breach. If the words of the clause are ambiguous then the courts will interpret them in a way which is least favourable to the party relying on them. This will help protect the consumer from deliberately vague and ambiguous language in contracts. This is known as the **contra proferentem rule**.

Unfair Contract Terms Act 1977

Statutory control for exclusion and limitation clauses lies in the **Unfair Contract Terms Act 1977** for non-consumer contracts only. There is protection for consumers in the **Consumer Rights Act 2015** as outlined on page 12.

The purpose of the **Unfair Contract Terms Act 1977** is to provide an element of control over exclusion and limitation clauses, and applies only to liability arising in the course of a business and in relation to liability from one business to another. Its main provisions are as follows.

Section 2: Exclusion of liability for negligence

- **Section 2(1)**: A business cannot exclude or restrict liability for death or personal injury arising from negligence.
- **Section 2(2)**: A business can exclude or restrict liability for other types of loss if it is **reasonable** to do so. The test for **reasonableness** is laid down in **s11**.

Section 3: Exclusion of liability for breach of contract

Subject to the **s11 reasonableness** test, a business cannot:

- exclude or restrict liability for breach of contract
- provide substantially different performance to that reasonably expected
- provide no performance at all.

Section 6: Exclusion of liability in contracts for sale of goods

Clauses that are implied by statute, such as those in the **Consumer Rights Act 2015**, cannot be excluded.

Section 11: Reasonableness test

The court should ask itself whether the term in question is a:

'fair and reasonable one to be included having regard to the circumstances which were, or ought reasonably to have been, known to or in the contemplation of the parties when the contract was made'.

Schedule 2

Factors to take into consideration when applying the reasonableness test are as follows:

1) The strength of the bargaining positions of the parties, taking into account alternative suppliers available to the purchaser.

2) Whether the customer received an inducement to accept the term, for example, whether they were given the opportunity to pay a higher price without the exclusion clause.

3) Whether the customer knew or ought to have known of the term and whether such terms are in general use in a particular trade.

4) Where exclusion relates to non-performance of a condition, whether it was reasonably practicable to comply with the condition.

5) Whether the goods were made or adapted to the special order of the customer.

One of the first cases to be brought before the courts under the *Unfair Contract Terms Act 1977* was *George Mitchell (Chesterhall) Ltd v Finney Lock Seeds Ltd (1983)*.

George Mitchell (Chesterhall) Ltd v Finney Lock Seeds Ltd (1983)
The claimant was a farmer who purchased 30lbs of cabbage seeds from the defendants for £192. The claimant planted the cabbage seeds over 63 acres and invested a lot of time on the crops. The seeds only produced a small green leaf not fit for human consumption. The contract contained a clause which limited liability to the price of the seeds. The claimant had lost £60,000 plus interest on the defective seeds.

The Court of Appeal held that the clause was unreasonable as the buyer would not have been aware of the fault whereas the seller would have been.

Importance of terms

When a term of a contract has been breached, it is important to distinguish what type of term has been breached. Contractual terms can either be **conditions**, **warranties** or **innominate terms**.

Conditions

A **condition** is a term of a contract which is so important to the contract that a failure to perform the condition would render the contract meaningless. If a condition has been breached, the claimant is entitled to the fullest range of remedies: damages or repudiation or both.

Any term implied by statute is also regarded as a condition, in terms of the effect of its breach.

Warranties

A **warranty** is a term of a contract which is minor. If a warranty has been breached, the injured party can sue for damages but not repudiation (rejection of the contract). Warranties are regarded as obligations that are secondary to the major purpose of the contract.

Innominate terms

An **innominate term** is a term of a contract which cannot be identified as either warranty or condition, and so is identified as innominate until the contract has been breached. The idea is that a contract will only be repudiated (rejected) in the event of a breach if it is fair to both sides.

It is uncertain what the **remedy** will be until the extent of the breach has been considered and the judge declares the appropriate remedy.

KEY CASE

Warranties
Bettini v Gye (1876)

KEY TERMINOLOGY

remedy: an award made by a court to the innocent party in a civil case to 'right the wrong'.

KEY CASES

Innominate terms
Hong Kong Fir Shipping Co Ltd v Kawasaki Ltd (1962)
Schuler AG v Wickman Machine Tool Sales Ltd (1973)
Reardon Smith Line v Hansen Tangen (1976)

Summary: Express and implied terms

Express terms

▶ Incorporated by:
  • being written into the contract, or
  • making a statement prior to the contract's conclusion
▶ Guidelines:
  • How much importance is placed on the statement
  • Knowledge and skill of the person making the statement
  • Timing of the statement

Implied terms: By fact

▶ Leading case: *Marks and Spencer v BNP Paribas (2015)*
▶ The term:
  • is **implied** if, without it, the contract would lack commercial or practical coherence
  • must be necessary for **business efficacy**: *The Moorcock (1889)*
  • must satisfy the **officious bystander test**: *Shirlaw v Southern Foundries (1926)*

Implied terms: By law

▶ *Consumer Rights Act 2015:* **Sale of goods**
  • **Section 9**: Satisfactory quality
  • **Section 10**: Fit for purpose
  • **Section 11**: As described
▶ *Consumer Rights Act 2015:* **Supply of services**
  • **Section 49**: Reasonable care and skill
  • **Section 50**: Binding information
  • **Section 51**: Reasonable price
  • **Section 52**: Reasonable time

Unfair terms: By law

▶ *Consumer Rights Act 2015:* **Unfair terms**
  • **Section 62**: Any term that is unfair under the Act is not binding

▶ *Consumer Contracts (Information, Cancellation and Additional Charges) Regulations 2013*

- Outlines key information that should be provided to consumers entering into contracts online, over the phone or from a catalogue
- The consumer has the right to cancel within **14 days** after ordering

Exclusion clauses: Common law

▶ Exclusion clauses must be incorporated:

- by signature
- by reasonable notice
- by a previous course of dealing

▶ The exclusion clause has to cover the breach:

- *contra proferentem* rule

Exclusion clauses: Statute

▶ *Unfair Contract Terms Act 1977* applies only to non-consumer contracts

- *Section 2*: Exclusion of liability for negligence
- *Section 3*: Exclusion of liability for breach of contract
- *Section 6*: Exclusion of liability in contracts for sale of goods
- *Section 11*: Reasonableness test

Misrepresentation and economic duress

Spec reference	Key content	Assessment Objectives	Where does this topic feature on each specification/exam?
WJEC A Level **W3.9:** Misrepresentation and economic duress **Eduqas A Level** **E2.1.4:** Misrepresentation and economic duress	• Fraudulent misrepresentation: the meaning of fraudulent misrepresentation and the remedies available • Innocent misrepresentation: the meaning of innocent misrepresentation and the remedies available • Negligent misrepresentation: the meaning of negligent representation and the remedies available • Misrepresentation Act 1967: statutory misrepresentation under s2, the limitation of liability under s3 and the remedies available • Economic duress: meaning of economic duress, distinction with duress to the person and any available remedies	**AO1** Demonstrate knowledge and understanding of legal rules and principles **AO2** Apply legal rules and principles to given scenarios in order to present a legal argument using appropriate legal terminology **AO3** Analyse and evaluate legal rules, principles, concepts and issues	**WJEC A Level:** Unit 3; Section B. Unit 4; Section B **Eduqas A Level:** Component 2; Section A. Component 3; Section A

What is a misrepresentation?

A representation is a statement made at the time of the contract being made and can be incorporated into the contract.

If the representation is falsely made, however, it can be a **misrepresentation** and can cause the contract to be voidable.

Legal definition

A misrepresentation is:

- a **statement of material fact** (*Bisset v Wilkinson (1927), Edgington v Fitzmaurice (1885)*)

- made by **one party to a contract to the other party** (*Peyman v Lanjani (1985)*) to the contract

- during the negotiations **leading up to the formation of the contract** (*Roscorla v Thomas (1842)*)

- which was intended to operate and **did operate as an inducement** (*JEB Fasteners Ltd v Marks Bloom & Co Ltd (1983), Attwood v Small (1838)*) to the other party to enter the contract

- but which was **not intended to be a binding obligation** (*Couchman v Hill (1947)*) under the contract, and which was **untrue or incorrectly stated**.

STRETCH AND CHALLENGE

Research the following cases and discuss their influence on representation.
1. *Bisset v Wilkinson (1927)*, *Edgington v Fitzmaurice (1885)*
2. *Peyman v Lanjani (1985)*
3. *Roscorla v Thomas (1842)*
4. *JEB Fasteners Ltd v Marks Bloom & Co Ltd (1983)*, *Attwood v Small (1838)*
5. *Couchman v Hill (1947)*

Fraudulent misrepresentation

Where fraudulent misrepresentation is alleged, fraud must also be proved. *Derry v Peak (1889)* showed that, if a person makes a false statement which they do not believe to be true at the time, this is a fraudulent misrepresentation. The claimant will sue for damages under the tort of deceit. However, this case has now been overturned by statute, as codified in the *Companies Act 2006*.

The damages will be awarded according to the tort of deceit and are also available under *s2(1) Misrepresentation Act 1967*. The equitable remedy of **rescission** is also available (that is, to void the contract as if it had never happened).

The defendant is responsible for all losses, including any consequential loss, providing a causal link between the fraudulent misrepresentation and the claimant's loss.

Negligent misrepresentation

There are three requirements:

1. The party making the statement must be in possession of the particular type of knowledge for which the advice is required.
2. There must be sufficient proximity between the two parties that it is reasonable to rely on the statement.
3. The party to whom the statement is made relies on the statement and the party making the statement is aware of that reliance.

Damages will be applied according to the standard tort measure of negligence or under *s2(1) Misrepresentation Act 1967*. The equitable remedy of rescission is also available.

KEY TERMINOLOGY

rescission: to unmake a contract or transaction, to return the parties to the position they would be in if it had never happened.

KEY CASE

Hedley Byrne v Heller & Partners (1964)
An advertising agency checked a prospective client's creditworthiness with its bank. The bank sent a letter apparently stating that the client would be safe to work with, so the agency sued the bank when it lost money after the client went into liquidation. The court held that damages may be recovered for a negligent misrepresentation where advice has been sought, a financial loss has been incurred and where there is a special relationship between the parties.

STRETCH AND CHALLENGE

Read Lord Denning's judgement in *Esso Petroleum Co Ltd v Mardon (1976)*. Do you agree with his judgement?

Innocent misrepresentation

Any misrepresentation not made fraudulently was historically classed as an innocent misrepresentation, regardless of how it was made.

Since the emergence of the **Hedley Byrne** principle and the passing of the *Misrepresentation Act 1967*, the only misrepresentations that can be claimed to be made innocently are those where a party makes a statement with an honest belief in its truth, for example, where the party merely repeats inaccurate information, the truth of which they are unaware.

The main remedy for innocent misrepresentation is the equitable remedy of rescission. Damages are also available under *s2(1) Misrepresentation Act 1967*.

STRETCH AND CHALLENGE

Consider what type of misrepresentation is involved in the following examples:
1. Mo is selling his motorcycle to Anisha. Anisha asks what capacity the engine is. Mo, after looking at the registration documents, tells her that it is a 600cc. Unknown to Mo, the documents are incorrect.
2. Sundus, a salesperson, tells Bryn that a carpet can be cleaned with bleach, without checking the manufacturer's specification which would have revealed that it cannot.
3. Harry, who has no qualifications at all, tells prospective employers at an interview that he has a degree in marketing.
4. Michelle recently purchased 'beefburgers' from her local supermarket, only to later discover in the newspaper that that brand actually contained horsemeat.

Misrepresentation under statute

Section 2(1) Misrepresentation Act 1967

This states:

'Where a person has entered into a contract after a misrepresentation has been made to him by another party thereto and as a result thereof he has suffered loss, then if the person making the misrepresentation would be liable to damages in respect thereof had the misrepresentation been made fraudulently, that person shall be so liable notwithstanding that the misrepresentation was not made fraudulently unless he proves that he had reasonable grounds to believe and did believe up to the time the contract was made that the facts represented were true.'

In other words, a party who has been a victim of a misrepresentation has an action available without having to prove either fraud or the existence of a special relationship under the **Hedley Byrne** criteria. The burden of proof is reversed, so that the person making the statement has to prove that they were not negligent.

Section 2(2) Misrepresentation Act 1967

Under *s2(2) Misrepresentation Act 1967*, the judge has the discretion to decide which remedy to apply. Rescission will therefore not be available if the judge has decided that damages are a more appropriate remedy.

Economic duress

A contract may be set aside because extreme coercion has rendered it commercially unviable (economic duress). Five conditions need to be satisfied for there to be a finding of duress:

1. Pressure was exerted on the contracting party: *North Ocean Shipping Co v Hyundai Construction Co (1979) (The Atlantic Baron)*.

2. The pressure was illegitimate: *Atlas Express Ltd v Kafco (Importers and Distributors) Ltd (1989)*.

3. The pressure induced the claimant to enter the contract: *Barton v Armstrong (1975)*.

4. The claimant had no choice but to enter the contract: *Universe Tankships v International Transport Workers' Federation (1983)*.

5. The claimant protested at the time or shortly after the contract was made: *North Ocean Shipping Co v Hyundai Construction Co (1979) (The Atlantic Baron)*.

Exam Skills

This topic could feature on the WJEC A Level units 3 and 4 exams and Eduqas A Level components 2 and 3 exams.

Ensure you are able to **analyse** and **evaluate** misrepresentation and economic duress, but also be able to **apply** the legal rules and principles of misrepresentation and economic duress to given scenarios.

Misrepresentation and economic duress

Summary: Misrepresentation and economic duress

Misrepresentation

▶ Definitions:

- a false statement in a contract that can cause the contract to be voidable
- a statement of material fact made by one party to a contract to the other party during the negotiations of the contract which was intended to operate and did operate as an inducement to the other party to enter the contract, but which was not intended to be a binding obligation under the contract, and which was untrue or incorrectly stated

Fraudulent misrepresentation

▶ Fraud must be proved: *Derry v Peak (1889)* but overturned by *Companies Act 2006*

▶ Remedies:

- Damages according to tort measure of deceit
- Damages under *s2(1) Misrepresentation Act 1967*
- Equitable remedy of rescission

Negligent misrepresentation

▶ **Hedley Byrne** principle: *Hedley Byrne v Heller & Partners (1964)*

▶ Three requirements:

1. Knowledge   **2.** Proximity   **3.** Reliance

▶ Remedies:

- Damages according to tort measure of negligence
- Damages under *s2(1) Misrepresentation Act 1967*
- Equitable remedy of rescission

Innocent misrepresentation

▶ *Misrepresentation Act 1967*: only claims where a party believes their untrue statement to be true

▶ Remedies:

- Equitable remedy of rescission
- Damages under *s2(1) Misrepresentation Act 1967*

Misrepresentation under statute

▶ *Section 2(1) Misrepresentation Act 1967*

- No need to prove fraud or special relationship under the *Hedley Byrne* criteria
- Person making statement must prove they were not negligent
- *Howard Marine and Dredging Co Ltd v A Ogden and Sons (Evacuations) Ltd (1978)* and *Spice Girls Ltd v Aprilla World Service (2002)*

▶ *Section 2(2) Misrepresentation Act 1967*: Judge decides remedy

Economic duress

▶ Extreme coercion renders contract commercially unviable (economic duress)

▶ Five conditions:

1. Pressure on contracting party: *North Ocean Shipping Co v Hyundai Construction Co (1979) (The Atlantic Baron)*

2. Illegitimate pressure: *Atlas Express Ltd v Kafco (Importers and Distributors) Ltd (1989)*

3. Pressure induced claimant to enter contract: *Barton v Armstrong (1975)*

4. Claimant had to enter contract: *Universe Tankships v International Transport Workers' Federation (1983)*

5. Claimant protested quickly: *North Ocean Shipping Co v Hyundai Construction Co (1979) (The Atlantic Baron)*

25

Torts connected to land

Spec reference	Key content	Assessment Objectives	Where does this topic feature on each specification/exam?
Eduqas A Level 2.2.4: Torts connected to land	• Trespass to land: unlawful entry; intention; defences of lawful authority including licence, right of entry • Public nuisance: class of persons, role of Attorney General; when individual can sue • Private nuisance: unlawful interference/physical damage, interference with health and comfort, unreasonable user, relevance of locality and utility; abnormal sensitivity; duration; effect of malice • Specific defences to nuisance: prescription; statutory authority • Rylands v Fletcher: dangerous things; accumulation; escape; non-natural user; damage • Specific defences of consent, act of stranger, statutory authority, act of God, default of claimant	**AO1** Demonstrate knowledge and understanding of legal rules and principles **AO2** Apply legal rules and principles to given scenarios in order to present a legal argument using appropriate legal terminology **AO3** Analyse and evaluate legal rules, principles, concepts and issues	**Eduqas A Level:** Component 2; Section B. Component 3; Section B

EDUQAS A LEVEL

Trespass to land

Trespass to land is a **tort** that can be defined as the unjustifiable interference with land which is in the immediate and exclusive possession of another.

The essential elements of trespass to land

There are four essential elements:

1. There is direct interference with the land.
2. The interference must be voluntary.
3. There is no need for the defendant to be aware they are trespassing.
4. There is no need for the claimant to experience harm or loss.

KEY TERMINOLOGY

tort: a civil wrong committed by one individual against another, such as injury caused by negligence.

1. Direct interference

Trespass requires direct interference with land, such as physical entry, throwing something onto the land or, if given the right to enter the land, remaining there when the right has been withdrawn.

For instance, if a person plants a tree that overhangs a neighbouring property, it is indirect interference and likely to be a private nuisance rather than trespass. However, if someone cuts down a tree and throws the branches into their neighbour's garden, that is direct interference and is likely to be a trespass.

KEY CASE

Southport Corporation v Esso Petroleum (1954)
A small oil tanker ran aground in poor weather conditions, due to carrying a heavy load and having a steering fault. Oil was deliberately discharged to free the tanker. The oil drifted onto the claimant's land. The claimant brought an action for nuisance, negligence and trespass. The Court of Appeal decided by 2 to 1 that the defendants were liable for negligence, not trespass. Denning LJ stated that the defendants were not liable for trespass because:
'(t)his discharge of oil was not done directly on to their foreshore, but outside in the estuary. It was carried by the tide on to their land, but that was only consequential, not direct. Trespass, therefore, does not lie.'

2. Voluntary interference with land

It can only be trespass if the person has voluntarily entered the land. In *Stone v Smith (1647)*, it was held that a person who was forcibly carried or thrown onto land by others was not trespassing.

3. Awareness of trespassing is not needed

An innocent trespass is still a trespass. Mistake is no defence in trespass.

KEY CASE

Conway v George Wimpey & Co (1951)
One of the defendant's lorry drivers had given a lift to the claimant, who worked for another company. Both were working on an aerodrome. This was expressly prohibited by company rules. The claimant claimed that, while dismounting from the lorry, he was injured due to the negligence of the driver.
The Court of Appeal held that, because there was no proof that the defendant knew or must have known that passengers from other companies were being given lifts, the claimant was a trespasser while on the lorry and, as a result, the defendants were not under any duty of care to him. Therefore, the Court of Appeal held that a person could be liable for trespass even if they were mistaken about the ownership of land or wrongly believed they had permission to enter the land.

4. No need for the claimant to experience harm or loss

Trespass to land is actionable **per se (in itself)**. This means that there is no need for the defendant to have caused the claimant any damage or loss.

Trespass above or below the land

Cuius est solum, eius est usque ad coelum et ad inferos is Latin for 'who owns the land owns to the heavens and down to hell'. It is controversially used to explain the common law principle that ownership of land includes the air above it and the ground below it. This principle has been restricted through precedent and statute.

Lord Hope in *Star Energy Weald Basin Limited v Bocardo SA (2010)* stated that the phrase 'still has value in English law as encapsulating, in simple language, a proposition of law which has commanded general acceptance'.

Trespass in airspace

In *Bernstein v Skyviews and General Ltd (1977)* the defendants had flown over the claimant's land to take an aerial photograph of his property which they then offered to sell to him. The High Court stated that there was no trespass because the claimant did not have an unlimited right to all the airspace above his land but only the right to that airspace as was necessary for the ordinary use and enjoyment of his land and buildings.

Griffiths J said: 'The problem in this case was to balance the rights of a landowner to enjoy the use of his land against the rights of the general public to take advantage of all that science now offered in the use of airspace. The best way to strike that balance in our present society was to restrict the rights of an owner in the airspace above his land to such height as was necessary for the ordinary use and enjoyment of his land and the structures upon it, and to declare that above that height he had no greater rights in the airspace than any other member of the public.'

Trespass below the surface of land

In *Star Energy Weald Basin Limited v Bocardo SA (2010)*, the Supreme Court held that the defendant had trespassed when, from adjacent land, it had vertically drilled oil wells that were 244 to 853 metres below the surface of the claimant's land.

However, since *s43 Infrastructure Act 2015*, land that is 300 metres or more below the surface ('deep-level land') can be exploited for 'the purposes of exploiting petroleum or deep geothermal energy' without liability for trespassing.

One of the reasons why fracking is controversial is because the Infrastructure Act 2015 allows companies to drill into land without liability for trespass, even if they do not have the landowner's permission

Trespass ab initio

Ab initio is Latin for 'from the beginning'. This is a form of trespass that occurs when a person who has entered land with the authority given by law, rather than with the permission of the person possessing the land, subsequently commits an act which is an abuse of that authority. The authority is cancelled retrospectively and the entry is deemed to have been a trespass from the beginning.

This type of trespass action was often used in cases against the police when they had exceeded the authority given to them with a search warrant while seizing stolen goods during a search of premises. Such an action often meant damages were assessed on the tortious nature of the police's whole conduct, rather than just the abuse of authority. However, precedent and statute law have increased the power of the police when searching premises so such actions are rarely successful today and, therefore, some textbooks regard *trespass ab initio* as having little relevance to English and Welsh law today.

Actions for *trespass ab initio* are more common in other common law jurisdictions such as the USA.

Defences to trespass to land

The following are the main defences to trespass to land.

1. Legal authority (or justification by law)

A person is not liable for trespass if they have legal authority permitting them to be on that land. Here are four examples:

1. The *Countryside and Rights of Way Act 2000* gives the public certain rights of access to land, provided that they comply with certain statutory restrictions.
2. The *Police and Criminal Evidence Act 1984* gives the police certain rights to enter land to make arrests and to search premises.
3. Rights of way established under the common law. Rights of way are recorded on 'definitive maps' prepared by a local authority.
4. Common land, which is land where, although it might be owned by someone else, certain people have rights of access through custom for a particular purpose, such as to graze livestock or cut peat for fuel.

2. Consent (licence) including contractual licence

A licence to enter land can be received with either the express or implied consent of the person possessing the land. Implied consent can be given in a number of ways. For instance, at the front of a house is a pathway to the front door, and the door has a letterbox and a doorbell. This gives implied consent for persons to walk on the path and come to the front door to deliver a letter or ring the bell to attract the attention of those who live there.

A contractual licence to enter land covers situations when a purchaser receives permission to be on land as part of a purchase. For instance, if you buy a cinema ticket to see a film, you receive a contractual licence to go into the cinema.

A person becomes a trespasser once express or implied permission is withdrawn or if a person exceeds the limits of the permission. The defence of consent (or licence) can no longer be used once permission is withdrawn.

For instance, although there may be implied permission for someone to come to up to a front door and deliver a letter, there is no implied permission for that person to go into the back garden or enter the property.

Even if there is a contractual licence, this can be withdrawn. If, having bought a cinema ticket, you are asked to leave the cinema, you will become a trespasser if you stay. In *Wood v Leadbitter (1845)*, a man was removed from a racecourse despite having bought a ticket. It was held that his contractual licence could be revoked, making him a trespasser.

(Of course, if having paid, you are asked to leave, you might have a remedy under the law of contract!)

3. Necessity

Necessity has two forms: private and public necessity.

Private necessity would involve an act needed to protect your own property against the threat of harm. **Public necessity** would involve an act to protect the wider public against harm.

The case law of necessity when applied to trespass is uncertain. The general rule seems to be that there must be an actual danger and the acts of the defendant must be reasonable in the light of all the facts.

KEY CASE

Rigby v Chief Constable of Northamptonshire (1985)
The police had fired a CS gas canister into a shop to force out a dangerous suspect. The gas canister caused the shop to catch fire. The police had not arranged for adequate firefighting equipment to be available so the shop was burned out. A claim was brought for negligence, under the rule in *Rylands v Fletcher (1868*, see page 40), and trespass.
The High Court held that the police were liable for negligence for failing to provide adequate firefighting equipment. However, the judge rejected liability for trespass, arguing that the defence of necessity was available in an action for trespass because there was no negligence on the part of the police in creating or contributing to the necessity. They did not create the suspect.
The judge also rejected liability under the rule in *Rylands v Fletcher (1868)* because the rule applies only to an 'escape' and 'probably' does not apply to the intentional or voluntary release of a dangerous thing.

GRADE BOOST

Note that American case law is relatively more decided than English law on the defence of necessity. Take care when selecting information from the internet that you know which country case law applies to.

Remedies to trespass to land

- Damages and injunctions are the usually remedies for trespass to land.
- Orders for Possession: these are a court order and covered by the *Civil Procedure Rules Part 55*. They are issued by a court following a successful 'possession claim against trespassers'. The order will instruct the defendants to leave the land by a particular date.
- Self-help (sometimes known as 'abatement'): this involves the common law right of a land owner or occupier to remove the trespasser themselves. This 'remedy' consists of a person using 'reasonable force' to remove trespassers. It is not available if the trespass is on a residential property.

Possession claim against trespassers

The *Civil Procedure Rules Part 55.6* state:

'Where, in a possession claim against trespassers, the claim has been issued against "persons unknown", the claim form, particulars of claim and any witness statements must be served on those persons by:

(a)

(i) attaching copies of the claim form, particulars of claim and any witness statements to the main door or some other part of the land so that they are clearly visible; and

(ii) if practicable, inserting copies of those documents in a sealed transparent envelope addressed to 'the occupiers' through the letter box; or

(b) placing stakes in the land in places where they are clearly visible and attaching to each stake copies of the claim form, particulars of claim and any witness statements in a sealed transparent envelope addressed to "the occupiers".'

Trespass in criminal law

Trespass originates in civil law. After Parliament grew concerned about many incidents of trespass by protestors, hunt saboteurs, squatters and those attending open-air raves, it created several statutory offences involving trespass, such as the offences of aggravated trespass and squatting in a residential building.

Aggravated trespass

Under **s69 Criminal Justice and Public Order Act 1994**, a person commits the offence of aggravated trespass if they trespass on land and, in relation to any lawful activity which persons are engaging in or are about to engage in on that or adjoining land, does anything there which is intended by them to have the effect of:

- intimidating any of those persons to deter them from engaging in that activity
- obstructing that activity, or
- disrupting that activity.

Offence of squatting in a residential building

Under **s144 Legal Aid, Sentencing and Punishment of Offenders Act 2012**, a person commits a criminal offence (of squatting) if they:

- are in a residential building as a trespasser, having entered it as a trespasser
- know or ought to know that they are a trespasser
- are living in the building or intend to live there for any period.

Public nuisance

A public nuisance 'materially affects the reasonable comfort and convenience of life of a class of Her Majesty's subjects' (**Attorney General v PYA Quarries Ltd (1958) per Romer LJ**).

Archbold's definition: 'A person is guilty of a public nuisance (also known as common nuisance), who (a) does an act not warranted by law, or (b) omits to discharge a legal duty, if the effect of the act or omission is to endanger the life, health, property or comfort of the public, or to obstruct the public in the exercise or enjoyment of rights common to all Her Majesty's subjects.'

(Source: PJ Richardson (ed), *Archbold: Criminal Pleading, Evidence and Practice* (2015) paras 31–40)

A public nuisance differs from a private nuisance on the basis of who is affected by the nuisance. It affects a representative cross-section of a class of society in a neighbourhood.

Public nuisance is a crime. Under **s17(1)** and **s1 Magistrates' Courts Act 1980**, public nuisance is an offence which is triable either way.

There is no requirement of intention or recklessness in the offence of public nuisance. The fault element is one of foreseeability of the risk of the type of nuisance. The defendant is liable if they knew or ought to have known of the risk of the type or kind of nuisance that in fact occurred.

This type of foreseeability was established in the key case **Wagon Mound (No 1) (1961)** and reiterated in **Cambridge Water Co v Eastern Counties Leather plc (1994)**.

KEY CASE

Wagon Mound (No 1) (1961)
The defendant's vessel, *The Wagon Mound*, leaked furnace oil at a wharf in Sydney Harbour. Some cotton debris became entangled in the oil and sparks from some welding works ignited the oil. The fire spread rapidly, destroying some boats and the wharf.
In this case, a test of remoteness of damage was substituted for the direct consequence test. The test is whether the damage is of a kind that was **foreseeable**. If a foreseeable type of damage is present, the defendant is liable for the full extent of the damage, whether or not the extent of damage was foreseeable. The Privy Council found in favour of the defendant, agreeing with the expert witness who provided evidence that the defendant, despite the furnace oil being innately flammable, could not reasonably expect it to burn on water.

KEY TERMINOLOGY

foreseeable: events the defendant should be able to have predicted could happen.

Cambridge Water Co v Eastern Counties Leather plc (1994)
The defendant owned a leather-tanning business. Small quantities of solvents were spilled over a long period of time, seeping through the floor of the building into the soil below. These solvents made their way to the borehole owned by the claimant water company. The borehole was used for supplying water to local residents. The water was contaminated beyond a level that was considered safe and Cambridge Water had to cease using the borehole. Cambridge Water brought actions based on negligence, nuisance and the rule in **Rylands v Fletcher (1868**, see page 40).

Eastern Counties Leather was not liable as the damage was too remote. It was not reasonably foreseeable that the spillages would result in the closing of the borehole.

The foreseeability of the type of damage is a prerequisite of liability in actions of nuisance and claims based on the rule in **Rylands v Fletcher (1868)** in the same way as it applies to claims based in negligence.

R v Goldstein (2006)
The defendant had enclosed some salt in an envelope together with a cheque. It was intended as a joke both because of the age of the debt he was paying and as a reference to a recent anthrax outbreak in the USA which he had discussed with the intended recipient. The salt leaked out of the envelope in a sorting office, creating an anthrax scare and the evacuation of the sorting office.

The House of Lords held that there was no public nuisance because it was not proved that the defendant knew or reasonably should have known that the salt would escape from the envelope in the sorting office and cause a nuisance.

It is the same type of foreseeability as in private nuisance. Note that the term 'fault element' is often referred as the **mens rea** in criminal law.

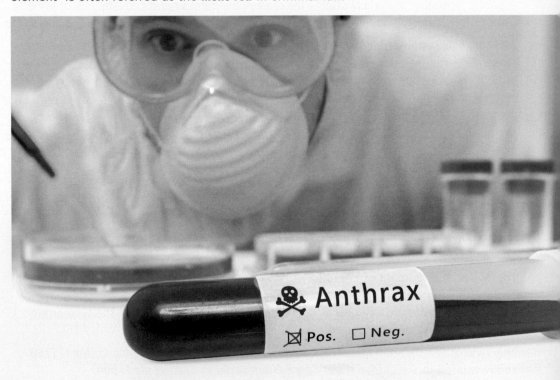

Attorney General v PYA Quarries Ltd (1958)
An injunction was obtained to prevent the defendant from emitting quantities of stones, splinters, dust and vibration from their quarry, which was disturbing local residents. The defendants unsuccessfully appealed to the Court of Appeal to have the injunction removed. The injunction was granted as the result of a 'relator action'. This is when an injunction is sought to stop a person committing a public nuisance. Relator actions are brought in the name of the Attorney General. They are very rare today.

In relation to *Attorney General v PYA Quarries Ltd (1958)*, Romer LJ stated:

'The sphere of the nuisance may be described generally as "the neighbourhood"; but the question whether the local community within that sphere comprises a sufficient number of persons to constitute a class of the public is a question of fact in every case. It is not necessary, in my judgement, to prove that every member of the class has been injuriously affected; it is sufficient to show that a representative cross-section of the class has been so affected.'

Denning LJ stated:

'I decline to answer the question how many people are necessary to make up Her Majesty's subjects generally. I prefer to look to the reason of the thing and to say that a public nuisance is a nuisance which is so widespread in its range or so indiscriminate in its effect that it would not be reasonable to expect one person to take proceedings on his own responsibility to put a stop to it, but that it should be taken on the responsibility of the community at large.'

A class of people

The facts of the case will determine if the persons affected by a nuisance amount to **a class of people**.

Class of people: Local communities

In *R v Ruffell (1991)*, the defendant had pleaded guilty to causing a public nuisance. The nuisance had consisted of an 'acid house' party. A side road to the site had been blocked by traffic. Very loud music played all night and the woodlands around the site were littered with human excrement.

The class of people affected by the nuisance were the local residents.

The defendant unsuccessfully appealed to the Court of Appeal against the custodial sentence imposed in the Crown Court.

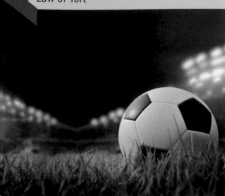

Class of people: Group with a common interest

In **R v Ong (2001)**, the defendant and others were planning to interfere with the floodlights during a Premier Division football match between Charlton Athletic and Liverpool. They pleaded guilty to conspiracy to commit a public nuisance (and another offence).

The class of people that would have been affected by the nuisance were the football spectators.

The defendants unsuccessfully appealed to the Court of Appeal against the custodial sentences imposed in the Crown Court.

Class of people: Impact on the community

In **R v Lowrie (2004)**, the defendant, who had made a number of hoax calls to the emergency services, pleaded guilty to causing a public nuisance.

The class of people that would have been affected by the nuisance were those who were in genuine need of help from the emergency services but could not get help because the emergency services had been diverted by the hoax calls.

The defendant appealed unsuccessfully to the Court of Appeal against the custodial sentence imposed.

Sending abusive letters

In **R v Rimmington (2006)**, the House of Lords held that sending racially offensive materials to members of the public was not a public nuisance. The reasoning was that sending individual letters to individual people did not constitute a nuisance affecting a class of people.

The House of Lords also stated that common law offences such as public nuisance should not be used for conduct covered by a statutory offence unless there was a good reason. Rimmington could have been prosecuted under the **Malicious Communications Act 1988**.

Making obscene telephone calls

In **R v Johnson (1997)**, the Court of Appeal held that making obscene telephone calls to several women in a geographic area was a public nuisance. However, the House of Lords indicated in **R v Rimmington (2006)** that such behaviour is unlikely to amount to a public nuisance as they were separate calls made to separate people rather than to a class of people.

Making obscene telephone calls can now be prosecuted under statutory provisions such as the **Communications Act 2003**.

Law Commission Report No 358

The Law Commission indicated in 2015 that:

- prosecutions for public nuisance were still occurring despite relevant statutory provisions
- some nuisance telephone call cases were still being prosecuted as a public nuisance. Both of the above cases indicate that limitations on prosecution imposed in **Rimmington (2006)** were not being 'reflected in practice'.

STRETCH AND CHALLENGE

Read the Law Commission's report, 'Simplification of Criminal Law: Public Nuisance and Outraging Public Decency' (Law Com No 358, 2015; www.lawcom.gov.uk/wp-content/uploads/2015/06/lc358_public_nuisance.pdf). You need only read the parts concerning public nuisance. You will find that the report gives a good insight into public nuisance.

What criticisms does the Law Commission make of the law on public nuisance?

How does the Law Commission suggest that the law on public nuisance could be reformed?

Civil actions against public nuisance

Civil actions can be brought against those committing a public nuisance in three ways. The remedies sought will be damages and a prohibitory injunction.

1. **By a realtor action**. These are brought in the name of the Attorney General on behalf of a private citizen who has persuaded the Attorney General to agree to the action. Such actions are rare. Possible reasons for this include the following:

• There are statutory bodies, such as local authorities, who will usually bring the actions.

• The Attorney General is unlikely to agree to a realtor action unless there is special damage and, if there is special damage, private citizens can bring actions in their own name without the permission of the Attorney General.

• Most nuisance which the affects the citizen can be prosecuted under statutory provisions rather than public nuisance.

• The Attorney General will often receive no applications for a realtor action in any particular year.

2. **By a local authority** under *s222 Local Government Act 1972*.

3. **By an action for tort by a private citizen** who can show that they have suffered special damage beyond that experienced by the others of 'Her Majesty's subjects'.

Private nuisance

A private nuisance is an interference with a person's enjoyment and use of their land. It is a civil action.

When courts and law reports refer to a 'nuisance', they are usually referring to a private nuisance and not a public nuisance.

When statute law refers to a 'nuisance', it usually means both public and private nuisance unless otherwise stated.

Types of private nuisance

Private nuisances are of three kinds:

1. **Nuisance by encroachment on a neighbour's land**. For example, the roots from a tree in a garden grow under the ground and into a neighbour's garden, damaging the foundations of the neighbour's house.

2. **Nuisance by direct physical injury to a neighbour's land.** For example, driving a car over a neighbour's garden, damaging their garden.

3. **Nuisance by interference with a neighbour's quiet enjoyment of their land.** For example, playing Justin Bieber music all night, every night, and stopping a neighbour from sleeping.

Lord Lloyd in *Hunter and Others v Canary Wharf Ltd (1997)* and *Hunter and Others v London Docklands Corporation (1997)* stated that just because something is an annoyance does not mean it is actionable in private nuisance. For example, a building interfering with television signals is an annoyance but is not actionable as a private nuisance.

Noisy music that disturbs your neighbours could be regarded as a private nuisance

Hunter and Others v Canary Wharf Ltd (1997)
The claimants sought damages for private nuisance in respect of interference with the television reception in their homes caused by the construction of Canary Wharf. The House of Lords stated by a majority decision that no action lay in private nuisance for interference with television caused by the mere presence of a building. Lord Lloyd stated:

'The annoyance caused by the erection of Canary Wharf and the consequential interference with television reception must have been very considerable. But, unfortunately, the law does not always afford a remedy for every annoyance, however great.'

Characteristics of a private nuisance

A private nuisance has three key elements.

1. The claimant must have an interest in the land

A claimant must have an interest in the land affected by the nuisance in order to make a claim of private nuisance. In effect, an 'interest in land' means a person must own or have a right over the land. Owners, leaseholders or tenants have an interest in the land and can make a claim of private nuisance. Visitors, family members and lodgers do not have an interest in the land and cannot make a claim of private nuisance. In effect, a person who is in exclusive possession of the land is regarded as having an interest in the land.

Foster v Warblington UDC (1906)
The claimant was an oyster merchant who for many years had occupied oyster beds artificially constructed on the foreshore. The claimant excluded everybody from the oyster beds, and nobody interfered with his occupation of the oyster beds or his removal and sale of oysters from them. However, he could not prove ownership of the oyster beds.

Despite this, the claimant could bring an action in the private nuisance caused by the defendants discharging sewage into the oyster beds because he was in exclusive possession of the land.

Malone v Laskey (1907)
A company had rented a house for one of its managers to live in. The wife of the manager was injured when a bracket in a toilet fell on her head because of the vibrations of machinery on the defendant's property. The Court of Appeal decided that the wife could not make a claim of nuisance because she had no interest in the property.

Khorasandjian v Bush (1993)
The daughter of a property owner brought a claim to obtain an injunction against a man who was harassing her, including making nuisance telephone calls. The county court granted an injunction preventing the defendant from 'harassing pestering or communicating' with the claimant. It was argued by the defence that the injunction could prevent the defendant from assaulting or threatening to assault the claimant because that was covered by the tort of trespass to the person. However, it was argued by the defence that the current wording of the injunction did not reflect any known tort. The Court of Appeal held that the wording of the injunction should remain unaltered. As part of its reasoning it argued that the telephone harassment was covered by the tort of private nuisance because it was an actionable interference with the woman's ordinary and reasonable use and enjoyment of property where she is lawfully present.

The Court of Appeal was particularly concerned that, at the time of *Khorasandjian v Bush (1993)*, there was no alternative action available for the woman to take. The woman could now obtain protection under the **Protection From Harassment Act 1997**.

In *Hunter and Others v Canary Wharf Ltd (1997)* and *Hunter and Others v London Docklands Corporation (1997)* the claimants included not only property owners and tenants but members of their families and lodgers. Both cases were heard by the House of Lords at the same time. *Hunter and Others v London Docklands Corporation (1997)* concerned damage caused by dust created during the construction of a road. Both cases included actions for nuisance.

The House of Lords had to decide which persons could bring an action in private nuisance. They decided that only householders with a right to land could commence an action in private nuisance. In doing this, the House of Lords rejected the decision in *Khorasandjian v Bush (1993)* but upheld the decision in *Malone v Laskey (1907)*.

2. There must be unreasonable use of the land which is the source of the nuisance

The use of the land which is the source of the nuisance must be unreasonable for a claim of private nuisance to succeed. In deciding whether the use of land is unreasonable, the courts will consider several factors:

- **The sensitivity of the claimant**: The standard of tolerance is that of the reasonable person and ordinary land use. Abnormally sensitive claimants or using land for an unusual purpose that makes it sensitive to disruption are unlikely to succeed in a claim for private nuisance.

Robinson v Kilvert (1888)

The defendant let a floor of his property to a tenant to be used as a paper warehouse, retaining the cellar immediately below. The tenant brought an action to prevent his landlord from heating the cellar, on the grounds that the rising heat dried his special brown paper, making it less valuable. Ordinary paper would not have been damaged. There was no private nuisance. Lopes LJ at the Court of Appeal argued that a:

'man who carries on an exceptionally delicate trade cannot complain because it is injured by his neighbour doing something lawful on his property, if it is something which would not injure anything but an exceptionally delicate trade.'

- **The duration and time of the nuisance** can determine whether a private nuisance has been created. In *Halsey v Esso Petroleum Co Ltd (1961)* the High Court held that a private nuisance was created by noise at night from boilers and road tankers. Generally, the courts require a private nuisance to be a continuing state of affairs. However, there are exceptions to this requirement. For example, in *Crown River Cruises Ltd v Kimbolton Fireworks Ltd (1996)*, a firework display that set fire to some moored barges was held to be a private nuisance.

- **The character of the area** in which the alleged nuisance occurred is relevant in deciding whether there is a private nuisance.

St Helen's Smelting Co v Tipping (1865)

Damage caused by vapours from a factory was held to be a private nuisance even though there were many other factories in the neighbourhood that also emitted vapours. It was held that, although the character of the area is important, it did not prevent a successful action in private nuisance for damage to property.

Wheeler v Saunders Ltd (1994)

The claimant owned a house next to a farm. He claimed that a private nuisance had been created by the granting of planning permission for two new pig houses because the smell of the pigs and their excrement was interfering with his use and enjoyment of his house.

The defendants argued that the granting of planning permission changed the character of the area so that what would have once been a private nuisance was no longer one. The Court of Appeal decided that the granting of planning permission for a pair of pig houses did not alter the character of the area and therefore what was once a private nuisance is still a private nuisance. The granting of planning permission does not authorise the creation of a private nuisance.

The defendants were liable for private nuisance.

- **The reasonable foreseeability of the type of damage**: To succeed in an action for private nuisance, it does not need to be shown that the defendant has taken reasonable care to avoid causing a nuisance (i.e. harm, damage or inconvenience). However, it does need to be shown that the type of nuisance was reasonably foreseeable. This type of foreseeability was established in *Wagon Mound (No 1) (1961)*.

- **Any act of malice on the part of the defendant** can lead to a successful action for private nuisance even though the defendant might be abnormally sensitive or if the act would not usually amount to an unreasonable use of land.

Hollywood Silver Fox Farm Ltd v Emmett (1936)

The claimant company was a fox fur farm. The defendant, an adjoining landowner, maliciously caused his son to discharge a shotgun on his own land as near as possible to the fox pens to interfere with the female foxes during the breeding season. The court held the claimant was entitled to an injunction and damages for the private nuisance. Although it was not unreasonable for a farmer to use a shotgun on his own land, and the keeping of a fox fur farm might not be an ordinary use of land, the defendant had acted maliciously. It was also irrelevant in this case that the female foxes were unusually sensitive to noise during the breeding session.

3. The claimant must suffer some harm

Private nuisance is not actionable per se. There must be some damage, harm, injury or inconvenience.

Liability for private nuisance: Occupier

An occupier is liable in private nuisance if they bear some personal responsibility for it. This means that if the private nuisance was created by an act of:

- a stranger
- nature
- the previous occupier

the current occupier is liable if they know or ought to know about it.

Liability for private nuisance: Landlord

A landlord is liable in private nuisance if:

- the landlord authorises the tenant to commit a private nuisance
- at the date of letting, the landlord knows or ought to know of the private nuisance
- the private nuisance is created during the tenancy and there is no agreement between the landlord and tenant making the tenant responsible for such repairs needed to remove the nuisance.

Defences to private nuisance

There are two main defences to a private nuisance.

1. Statutory authority

It is a defence to private nuisance if the claimant can show that their conduct was authorised by law. For example, **s76 Civil Aviation Act 1982** states:

'No action shall lie in respect of trespass or in respect of nuisance, by reason only of the flight of an aircraft over any property at a height above the ground which, having regard to wind, weather and all the circumstances of the case is reasonable, or the ordinary incidents of such flight, so long as the provisions of any Air Navigation Order ... have been duly complied with.'

2. Prescription

The defence of prescription is a claim by the defendant that they have acquired the right to act in a particular way because they have done so for 20 years. It is sometimes referred to as an 'easement by prescription'. However, this defence is based on property law and can be difficult to use in practice.

Sturges v Bridgman (1879)

Prescription could not be used as a defence because, although the defendant had used noisy equipment for more than 20 years, it only became a nuisance the moment the claimant doctor built his consulting room nearby. In other words, the 20 years is not based on how long the act has been going on but rather on how long the act has been a nuisance.

Remedies for private nuisance

The main remedies for a private nuisance are **damages** and **injunctions**.

The overlap between private nuisance and negligence

There is an overlap between nuisance and negligence. In many cases, claimants bring an action for both private nuisance and negligence. Both require injury or harm to the claimant and require foreseeability of the type of damage. There are, however, differences between the two. A private nuisance does not need to involve a negligent act. The remedies for a private nuisance are usually damages and an injunction to stop the nuisance. The remedy for negligence is damages.

In *Miller v Jackson (1977)* Denning MR stated:

'The tort of nuisance in many cases overlaps the tort of negligence ... But there is at any rate one important distinction between them. It lies in the nature of the remedy sought. Is it damages? Or an injunction? If the plaintiff seeks a remedy in damages for injury done to him or his property, he can lay his claim either in negligence or nuisance. But, if he seeks an injunction ... I think he must make his claim in nuisance. The books are full of cases where an injunction has been granted to restrain the continuance of a nuisance. But there is no case, so far as I know, where it has been granted so as to stop a man being negligent.'

Hunter and Others v Canary Wharf Ltd (1997) and Hunter and Others v London Docklands Corporation (1997) quoted the statement from Wagon Mound (No 1) (1961):

'Nuisance is a term used to cover a wide variety of tortious acts or omissions and, in many, negligence in the narrow sense is not essential. An occupier may incur liability for the emission of noxious fumes or noise although he has used the utmost care in building and using his premises … On the other hand, the emission of fumes or noise or the obstruction of the adjoining highway may often be the result of pure negligence on his part: there are many cases … where precisely the same facts will establish liability both in nuisance and in negligence.'

Rylands v Fletcher (1868)

Blackburn J in the Court of Exchequer quoted by Lord Cairns in Rylands v Fletcher (1868):

'The person whose grass or corn is eaten down by the escaping cattle of his neighbour, or whose mine is flooded by the water from his neighbour's reservoir, or whose cellar is invaded by the filth of his neighbour's privy, or whose habitation is made unhealthy by the fumes and noisome vapours of his neighbour's alkali works, is damnified without any fault of his own; and it seems but reasonable and just that the neighbour who has brought something on his own property (which was not naturally there), harmless to others so long as it is confined to his own property, but which he knows will be mischievous if it gets on his neighbour's, should be obliged to make good the damage which ensues if he does not succeed in confining it to his own property.'

The rule from Rylands v Fletcher (1868)

The essential parts of the rule are as follows, though some of these essential parts have been modified, refined and added to by precedent over the years:

1. Something must have been **collected and kept** on the land.

2. The use of the land must be **non-natural**. Lord Cairns in *Rylands v Fletcher (1868)* suggested that if water had naturally accumulated on or below the surface of the land then liability would not have arisen.

3. The thing brought onto the land must be **likely to do mischief** if it escaped.

4. The thing brought onto land must have **escaped and caused damage**.

The development of the rule

Although the main principles of the rule have remained, precedent has adapted the rule in several ways. In particular, the courts have examined the following questions:

1. Does the thing collected and kept have to escape?

2. What is the meaning of non-natural use of land?

3. To what extent must the thing be likely to cause mischief?

4. Is foreseeability of harm needed?

The thing collected and kept

The thing collected and kept on land need not be the thing that escapes. Something collected and kept on land that causes something else to escape can lead to liability.

Miles v Forest Granite Co (Leicestershire) Ltd (1918)

Explosives kept on land were detonated to break up some rocks. Some of the rocks were forced into the air, escaped the defendant's property and injured the claimant. The explosives caused the rocks to escape the property. The defendant was held to be liable.

Non-natural use of the land
Rickards v Lothian (1913)

Water had escaped from an overflow pipe connected to a washbasin where the tap had been left running and the washbasin's waste pipe had been blocked by an unknown person. The Judicial Committee of the Privy Council held that the water from the overflow pipe did not involve the non-natural use of land. It was also accepted that damage was caused by a third party (i.e. the person who deliberately turned the tap on and blocked the wastepipe).

Non-natural use and likelihood of mischief
Transco PLC v Stockport Metropolitan Borough Council (2004)

A water pipe took water to a block of flats owned by the council. Unknown to anyone, the pipe had failed and water was escaping, eventually causing an embankment to collapse and leave a gas main exposed and unsupported. The gas company took the council to court to recover the cost of repairing the gas main. It was accepted by the House of Lords that the council had not been negligent. The case was decided using the rule in **Rylands v Fletcher (1868)**. *The House of Lords decided in favour of the council because the supply of water through the pipes was normal and did not create any special hazard.*

Non-natural use and foreseeability of harm

Cambridge Water Co Ltd v Eastern Counties Leather plc (1994)

The Cambridge Water Company provided water to Cambridge. In 1976, it purchased a borehole. In 1980, a European Directive was issued which controlled the presence of PCE (a chemical) in water. The borehole was found to be contaminated with PCE that had come from a tannery owned by Eastern Counties Leather. The contamination was caused by occasional small spillages which eventually soaked through a concrete floor until eventually entering an underground water supply. The House of Lords accepted that the storage of PCE by the defendants was a non-natural use of the land. The House of Lords decided that the claimants needed to show that the defendant should have foreseen the potential contamination of the water supply. It was held that they could not have foreseen it because, at the time of the spillages, the reasonable factory supervisor would have expected any spillage to evaporate rapidly in the air and would not have been expected it to seep through the floor of the building into the soil below. This type of foreseeability was established in Wagon Mound (No 1) (1961).

Read v J Lyons & Co Ltd (1947)

Some explosives detonated in a munitions factory, killing one person and injuring others. There was no evidence of negligence and the case was decided using the rule in Rylands v Fletcher (1868). It was held by the House of Lords that no liability arose because the persons injured were on the premises and there was no escape from the factory.

Defences: Rylands v Fletcher (1868)

Possible defences that can be used in *Rylands v Fletcher (1868)* include:

- consent
- *vis major* or an act of God
- act of a stranger
- statutory authority
- contributory negligence.

A review of the rule in Rylands v Fletcher (1868)

- The rule was decided at a time when there was growing public concern over bursting reservoir dams damaging property.
- Australia no longer follows the rule: *Burnie Port Authority v General Jones Pty Limited (1994)*.
- The rule is not followed in Scotland: *RHM Bakeries (Scotland) Ltd v Strathclyde Regional Council (1985)*.
- In English and Welsh law it is increasingly seen as part of the tort of nuisance rather than a separate tort itself.

> ### Exam Skills
>
> Torts connected to land could feature on the Eduqas A Level components 2 and 3 exams. Ensure you are able to **analyse** and **evaluate** all of the torts connected to land, and that you are also able to **apply** the legal rules and principles of the various torts connected to land to given scenarios.

STRETCH AND CHALLENGE

To fully understand the rule in *Rylands v Fletcher (1868)* read the House of Lords judgement in *Transco PLC v Stockport Metropolitan Borough Council (2004)* at www.publications.parliament.uk/pa/ld200203/ldjudgmt/jd031119/trans-1.htm. Five law lords explored the development of the rule and their reasoning and insights can help you prepare for your examination.

KEY TERMINOLOGY

vis major: Latin for 'a superior force'. Used in civil cases to denote an act of God or loss resulting from natural causes, such as a hurricane, tornado or earthquake, and without the intervention of human beings.

GRADE BOOST

For possible defences, research the following cases or statute law.

- Defence of consent: *Peters v Prince of Wales Theatre (1943)*.
- Defence of vis major or an act of God: *Nichols v Marsland (1876)*.
- Defence of act of a stranger: *Perry v Kendrick's Transport Ltd (1956)*.
- Defence of statutory authority: *Charing Cross Electric Supply Co v Hydraulic Power Co (1914)*.
- Defence of contributory negligence: *s1(1) Law Reform (Contributory Negligence) Act 1945*.

Summary: Torts connected to land

Trespass to land

▶ Four essential **elements**:

- Direct interference with the land
- Interference must be voluntary
- No need for defendant to be aware they are trespassing
- No need for claimant to experience harm or loss

▶ Three main **defences**:

- Legal authority (justification by law) • Consent • Necessity

▶ **Remedies**:

- Damages and injunctions
- Orders for possession
- Self-help ('abatement')

▶ Trespass in **criminal law**:

- Main offences • Aggravated trespass • Squatting

Public nuisance

▶ A criminal nuisance which materially affects the reasonable comfort and convenience of life of a class of Her Majesty's subjects

▶ Affects a representative cross-section of a class of society in a neighbourhood

▶ No requirement of intention or recklessness in the offence of public nuisance – the fault element is foreseeability of the risk of the type of nuisance

▶ Defendant liable if they knew or ought to have known of the risk of the type or kind of nuisance: *Wagon Mound (No 1)*

▶ Civil actions can be brought by:

- a realtor action
- a local authority under *Local Government Act 1972*
- an action for tort by a private citizen who can show that they suffered special damage beyond that experienced by other Her Majesty's subjects

Private nuisance

▶ An interference with a person's enjoyment and use of their land

▶ A civil action

▶ Nuisance is by:

- encroachment on a neighbour's land
- direct physical injury to a neighbour's land
- interference with a neighbour's quiet enjoyment of their land

▶ Key elements:

- claimant must have an interest in the land
- must be unreasonable use of the land which is the source of the nuisance
- claimant must suffer some harm or inconvenience

▶ Main defences to a private nuisance are statutory authority and prescription

▶ Main remedies are damages and injunctions

▶ Key case and defences: *Rylands v Fletcher (1868)*: Essential parts and development of the rule

Vicarious liability

Spec reference	Key content	Assessment Objectives	Where does this topic feature on each specification/exam?
Eduqas A Level 2.2.5: Vicarious liability	• Nature and purpose of vicarious liability • Liability for employees: Tests for status of employment; scope of employment; frolic of his own • Liability for independent contractors: Distinguished from employees; choice of, and supervision in relation to, unusually hazardous activities.	**AO1** Demonstrate knowledge and understanding of legal rules and principles **AO2** Apply legal rules and principles to given scenarios in order to present a legal argument using appropriate legal terminology **AO3** Analyse and evaluate legal rules, principles, concepts and issues	**Eduqas A Level:** Component 2; Section B. Component 3; Section B

KEY TERMINOLOGY

strict liability: crimes where the prosecution does not have to prove mens rea against the defendant.
vicarious liability: a third party (e.g. an employer) is held responsible for a tort committed by another (e.g. an employee).

STRETCH AND CHALLENGE

Strict liability has the potential to be unfair but there are justifications for the imposition of such liability, for example, improving safety standards. Research some other justifications for the imposition of strict liability.

What is vicarious liability?

Vicarious liability is the term used to explain the liability of one person for the torts committed by another. There must be a legal relationship between the two parties and the tort should be connected to that relationship. It mostly arises in employment when an employer might be liable for the torts of their employee. Vicarious liability is a form of **strict liability**.

Vicarious Liability

Does vicarious liability apply?

Vicarious liability is sometimes justified by the idea that, if someone over whom an employer has a degree of authority makes a mistake, then the employer bears some responsibility for this. Vicarious liability has become a practical tool to help compensate victims, as employers are often insured against such losses. Vicarious liability is, therefore, a form of **joint liability**. This means that both the person who committed the tort and their employer can be sued (though in practice it is usually only the employer that is sued, because they are most likely to have insurance).

There are two questions to determine if vicarious liability applies to an employer:

1. Is the person who committed the tort an **employee**?

2. Was the tort committed **in the course of that person's employment**?

Of course, primarily there has to be a tort committed by the employee and, therefore, the claimant must prove the elements of whichever tort is alleged. For example, if the claimant is suing for negligence, they need to establish duty, breach and resulting damage.

1. Who is an employee?

To establish vicarious liability against an employer, a claimant must show, first, that the employee has '**employee status**'. An employer is not generally responsible for the actions of an independent contractor. This seems like an obvious answer, as an employee is someone who performs services in return for payment, but it is not such a straightforward question when considering the complexities of modern working arrangements. The courts have, therefore, had to distinguish between employees and independent contractors along with other employee/ employer relationships, such as agency workers, casual workers, freelancers and those working on commission. In such cases, the courts have had to determine the 'employment status' of the worker and have developed several tests to do so.

The control test

This is the test traditionally used to determine if someone is an employee or an independent contractor. Dating back to the Victorian era and *Yewens v Noakes (1880)*, it uses the concept of the master-servant relationship.

A person would be considered an 'employee' if the employer had control over the work, and was in a position to lay down how and when tasks should be done.

A person would be considered an independent contractor if they were engaged by the employer to do a particular task, but allowed discretion as to how and when to do it (*Walker v Crystal Palace Football Club (1909)*).

However, as many types of work became increasingly skilled and specialised, the test became less useful. The control test is still used, but it has faults when dealing with highly skilled or professional workers. The level of control is now, therefore, only one of the circumstances considered by the courts when determining employee status.

The organisation (or 'integration') test

This test looks at how closely the worker is involved with the core business of the employer. Lord Denning introduced the 'integration' or 'organisation test' in *Stevenson, Jordan and Harrison v MacDonald and Evans (1952)*, where it was held the more the worker is integrated into the organisation, the more likely they are to be employed.

The multiple test

The modern test is the **multiple test**, which involves the court considering all the facts of the case and the overall impression of whether the worker is an employee or an independent contractor. It can be uncertain, as each case will involve varying factors. This test was established in *Ready Mixed Concrete Ltd v Minister of Pensions (1968)* and, though each case will be decided on its own facts, three conditions have emerged:

1. Employee agrees to provide skill in return for a wage.
2. Employer exercises a degree of control.
3. Nothing in the terms of work is inconsistent with employment (for example, the worker cannot delegate their job to someone else).

There has been a recent decision on the nature of the relationship between an organisation and an individual. In *Cox v Ministry of Justice (2016)*, the Supreme Court had to decide whether the prison service was liable for an injury to a catering supervisor caused by a prisoner working in the kitchen. The prison service was held to be liable even though it did not technically 'employ' the prisoner, as the relationship between the prisoner and the prison service was sufficiently close to an employment relationship. Engaging prisoners to work in the kitchen was a key part of the prison service activities, creating a risk that the claimant (the catering supervisor) could be injured.

2. Was the tort committed in the course of employment?

For an employer to be liable for torts committed by their employees, the employee must be acting in the course of their employment. This also applies where the employee is carrying out their duties in an unauthorised or undesired manner.

Century Insurance v Northern Ireland Road Transport (1942)

The worker, the driver of a petrol tanker, was unloading petrol from his tanker in the claimant's garage when he lit a cigarette and discarded the match onto the ground. This caused a fire and explosion, damaging the claimant's property. The defendants (the driver's employers) were found to be vicariously liable for the driver's negligence, on the basis that what he was doing at the time was part of his authorised duties, even if he was doing it in a negligent way. It was, therefore, within the course of his employment.

'A frolic of his own'

An employer is not liable for the torts committed by an employee who is on '**a frolic of his own**'. This means that they will not be liable if an employee does something unauthorised and separate from their duties if a tort is committed during the 'frolic'. This can be seen in *Storey v Ashton (1869)*.

Storey v Ashton (1869)

The defendant employer sent two employees to deliver some wine but, on their way back, they went on a diversion to do some business of their own. While doing this, the employees ran over the claimant, owing to the negligence of the employee driving the horse and cart. It was held that the defendant was not liable for the negligence of his employee because he was on a 'frolic of his own'.

Doing authorised work in a forbidden manner

An employer may still be vicariously liable for torts committed by employees even if the act is unauthorised and the employee has been expressly forbidden to carry out the act, if the prohibition relates to the way the job is done rather than the scope of the job itself. This can be seen in *Limpus v London General Omnibus (1863)*.

Limpus v London General Omnibus (1863)
A bus driver had been expressly prohibited to race with or obstruct other buses. He disobeyed and caused a collision with the claimant's bus while racing another bus. It was held that he was doing an act which he was authorised to do (driving a bus,) which meant that he was within the course of his employment, even though the way he was doing the job was improper and had been prohibited. The defendants were held to be vicariously liable.

Travelling to work

Commuting to and from work is not normally considered to be 'in the course of employment' and so an employer will not be liable for any torts committed by employees during these journeys. However, if the employee who is travelling, for example, between sites during working hours, detours from a route or gives a lift to an unauthorised person then the employer may be liable. Cases that demonstrate these principles are: *Conway v Wimpey (1951)*, *Hilton v Thomas Burton (Rhodes) Ltd (1961)* and *Rose v Plenty (1975)*.

Independent contractors

An employer is not generally responsible for the torts of independent contractors, only for those of employees. There are exceptions to this rule which make the employer jointly liable along with the independent contractor. The tests above (control, organisation and multiple) help determine if a worker is an employee or independent contractor.

Reasons for imposing vicarious liability

It is also important to be able to evaluate the law in this area. Here are some of the main justifications for vicarious liability.

- Employers are in a stronger financial position to pay compensation than the employee as they will usually be insured.

- Employers are in control of the conduct of employees and so should be responsible for their actions. Problems with this argument arise when considering more modern and flexible working arrangements.

- Employers profit from the work done by their employees so arguably should be liable for their torts and losses.

- Employers have control over who they employ and are in control of who is dismissed. They should be deterred from employing those known to create a 'risk'.

- Employers are encouraged to take care to prevent resulting accidents and to provide a safer working environment and better health and safety practices.

Exam Skills

This topic is frequently examined as a problem scenario. You will need to be able to **explain** and/or **apply** the liability of the parties involved.

You might also be required to **analyse** and **evaluate** the effectiveness of the law in this area and **consider** proposals for reform.

Summary: Vicarious liability

▶ Liability of one person for torts committed by another:

- Requirement of legal relationship between the two parties and a connected tort
- Form of strict liability and joint liability

▶ Two questions to determine if vicarious liability applies.

▶ **1. Is the tortfeasor an employee?** Employees v independent contractors:

- Control test: *Yewens v Noakes (1880)*
- Organisation (or 'integration') test: *Stevenson, Jordan and Harrison v MacDonald and Evans (1952)*
- Multiple test: *Ready Mixed Concrete Ltd v Minister of Pensions (1968)*

▶ **2. Was the tort committed in the course of employment** or on 'a frolic of his own'?

- Part of authorised duties: *Century Insurance v Northern Ireland Road Transport (1942)*
- Frolic: *Storey v Ashton (1869)*
- Doing authorised work in a forbidden manner: *Limpus v London General Omnibus (1863)*
- Travelling to work: *Conway v Wimpey (1951)*, *Hilton v Thomas Burton (Rhodes) Ltd (1961)* and *Rose v Plenty (1975)*

▶ **Reasons for imposing vicarious liability**: Employers:

- have adequate insurance/finances
- can control conduct of employees
- profit from work of employees
- should take care when recruiting
- may be encouraged to provide a safe work environment and policies

Defences: Tort

EDUQAS A LEVEL

Spec reference	Key content	Assessment Objectives	Where does this topic feature on each specification/exam?
Eduqas A Level 2.2.6: Defences: Tort	• *Volenti non fit injuria*: Must be voluntary; effect of Road Traffic Act 1988; position of rescuers • Contributory negligence: Nature and effect; Law Reform (Contributory) Negligence Act 1945	**AO1** Demonstrate knowledge and understanding of legal rules and principles **AO2** Apply legal rules and principles to given scenarios in order to present a legal argument using appropriate legal terminology **AO3** Analyse and evaluate legal rules, principles, concepts and issues	**Eduqas A Level:** Component 2; Section B. Component 3; Section B

Once all elements of a tort have been proved, the defendant may escape liability by relying on a defence. The specification requires knowledge of three defences: consent (volenti non fit injuria), contributory negligence and the defences specific to claims connected to nuisance and *Rylands v Fletcher (1868*, see page 40).

Consent: *Volenti non fit injuria*

The Latin term *volenti non fit injuria* translates as: 'there can be no injury to one who consents', although it is often said to mean 'voluntary assumption of risk'. The principle behind this defence is that, if the claimant consented to behaviour that carries a risk of harm, then the defendant is not liable in tort. Successfully claiming this defence means that the defendant is not liable for any of the claimant's losses. It is a complete defence, therefore, and the claimant receives no damages.

The use of this defence can be seen in *Morris v Murray (1991)*.

Morris v Murray (1991)
The claimant agreed to go for a drunken joyride in his friend's (the defendant's) aircraft. The aircraft crashed and the defendant was killed. An autopsy revealed a huge amount of alcohol in his system. The claimant was seriously injured and brought an action for damages against the defendant's estate. On appeal, the defence successfully argued that, as the claimant was aware of the risk he was taking and consented to it, there was no liability in negligence.

To argue this defence, it must first be shown that the defendant has committed a tort. Once this is proved, the defendant must prove that the claimant knew of the risk involved (nature and extent of risk) and that they voluntarily accepted that risk (it was claimant's free choice).

Passengers in vehicles

The courts have been reluctant to allow the *volenti* defence in cases of negligent driving even if a passenger accepts a lift with an obviously drunk driver.

Section 149(3) Road Traffic Act 1988 states:

'The fact that a person so carried has willingly accepted as his, the risk of negligence on the part of the user shall not be treated as negativing any such liability of the user.'

There may, instead, be a defence of contributory negligence.

Sporting activities

Individuals who voluntarily participate in a sporting activity by implication consent to the risks of that particular sport. The 'risk' will vary with different sporting activities, for example, rugby tackles, impact of cricket balls, boxing injuries, etc. The general principle is that, provided the activity is within the rules of the game, then an injured player cannot sue (see ***Smoldon v Whitworth and Nolan (1997)***).

Some sports carry risks for spectators, such as being hit by a rugby ball while watching a match. The approach by the courts seems to be that an error of judgement or lapse of skill does not give rise to liability, as the spectator has accepted the risks of going to watch the live activity.

Attending a high-speed car race is an example of accepting the risks of being a spectator

Contributory negligence

Unlike *volenti,* which is a complete defence, the defence of contributory negligence allows a court to apportion blame (and therefore damages) between the two parties. It means that the claimant and defendant are both partly to blame for the damage, for example, when a negligent driver hits someone who had stepped into the road without looking.

Section 1(1) Law Reform (Contributory Negligence) Act 1945 states:

'Where any person suffers damage as the result partly of his own fault and partly of the fault of any other person or persons, a claim in respect of that damage shall not be defeated by reason of the fault of the person suffering the damage, but the damages recoverable in respect thereof shall be reduced to such extent as the court thinks just and equitable having regard to the claimant's share in the responsibility for the damage.'

This means that the claimant can still make a claim against the defendant but any damages awarded will be reduced by the amount the claimant was to blame. This can be seen in ***Sayers v Harlow UDC (1957).***

Sayers v Harlow UDC (1957)

Sayers got locked in a public toilet which was owned by Harlow Urban District Council. She stood on the toilet roll holder to try to climb out but was injured in the process of doing so. She won damages after the defendants were found liable for negligence but her damages were reduced by 25% for her own 'blameworthiness' for standing on the toilet roll holder.

For a defence of contributory negligence to succeed, it must be proved that:

- the claimant failed to take care of their own safety in a way that at least partially caused their injuries, **and**
- the claimant failed to recognise that they were risking their own safety even though 'the reasonable person' would.

Summary: Defences: Tort

Consent

▶ *Volenti non fit injuria*: voluntary assumption of risk: ***Morris v Murray (1991)***

▶ Complete defence

▶ Requirements:

- Tort

- Knowledge of extent and nature of risk

- Voluntary acceptance of risk

▶ Passengers in vehicles: courts reluctance to allow volenti: ***s149(3) Road Traffic Act 1988***

▶ Sporting activities / spectators:

- Rules of the game: ***Smoldon v Whitworth and Nolan (1997)***

Contributory negligence

▶ Apportionment of blame and damages: ***s1(1) Law Reform (Contributory Negligence) Act 1945*** and ***Sayers v Harlow UDC (1957)***

CRIMINAL LAW
Fatal offences against the person

Spec reference	Key Content	Assessment Objectives	Where does this topic feature on each specification/exam?
WJEC AS/A Level 3.14: Offences against the person **Eduqas AS Level 2.3.3:** Offences against the person (non-fatal)	• Fatal offence of murder: elements and application of law • Fatal offence of involuntary manslaughter. Elements and application of law, including constructive manslaughter, gross negligence manslaughter • Fatal offence of voluntary manslaughter: elements and application of law, defences of loss of control and diminished responsibility	**AO1** Demonstrate knowledge and understanding of legal rules and principles **AO2** Apply legal rules and principles to given scenarios in order to present a legal argument using appropriate legal terminology **AO3** Analyse and evaluate legal rules, principles, concepts and issues	**WJEC AS/A Level:** Unit 3 **Eduqas AS Level:** Component 2 **Eduqas A Level:** Component 2; Component 3

Exam Skills

At A Level, the topic of 'Offences again the person' is split into fatal offences and non-fatal offences. These aspects of the topic are likely to feature separately on the exam. **The Eduqas AS specification only requires students to know about non-fatal offences. However, both WJEC and Eduqas A Level specifications require students to know about both non-fatal and fatal (homicide) offences.** Fatal offences are covered in Book 2 and non-fatal offences are covered in this book.

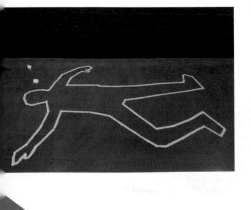

Murder

This is the most serious of all the offences of **homicide**. The definition of murder is not contained in statute; indeed, it is a common law offence, the definition of which was outlined by **Lord Justice Coke** in the seventeenth century: 'the unlawful killing of a reasonable person in being and under the King's (or Queen's) Peace and with malice aforethought, express or implied'.

Causation is an essential element that needs to be proved in murder cases, because it is a **result** crime. It has to be proved that the defendant **caused** the death of the victim **in fact** and **in law**. The table summarises this idea.

KEY TERMINOLOGY

homicide: the killing of one person by another, deliberately or not.

Actus reus	Mens rea
1. A human being is dead.	**1.** Intention to kill or cause grievous bodily harm.
2. The defendant caused the death IN FACT.	**2.** Intention can be direct or indirect.
3. The defendant caused the death IN LAW.	

52

Actus reus

1. A human being is dead

A person is a human being when it can exist independent of its mother (*AG's reference No 3 of 1994*). Therefore, a person who kills an unborn child may be criminally liable under the law, but it will not be for a homicide offence. There is much controversy over what constitutes 'dead', but it would seem that the courts favour the definition of 'brain-dead' and this was confirmed in the case of *R v Malcherek and Steel (1981)*.

2. The defendant caused the death in fact (factual causation)

1. The 'but for' test

This test asks 'but for' the conduct of the defendant, would the victim have died as and when they did? If the answer is no then the defendant will be liable for the death. The example case is *R v White (1910)*.

2. The de minimis rule

De minimis means insignificant, minute or trifling. This test requires that the original injury caused by the defendant's action must be more than a minimal cause of death. The example case is *R v Pagett (1983)*.

3. The defendant caused the death in law (legal causation)

1. The injury must be the operating and substantial cause of death

This test considers whether the original injury inflicted by the defendant is, at the time of death, still the operating and substantial cause of death; that the chain of causation has not been broken by another event. An example case is *R v Smith (1959)*, contrasted with *R v Jordan (1956)*.

2. The 'thin skull' test

A defendant has to take their victim as they find them. If the victim dies from some unusual or unexpected physical or other condition, the defendant is still responsible for the death. For example, if during a fight the defendant hits the victim with a punch that would not normally cause anything more than soreness and bruising but, because the victim has an unusually thin skull, they die, the defendant is still liable for the death. An example case is *R v Blaue (1975)*.

3. Foreseeable intervening act

If the intervening act is foreseeable, courts have concluded that it will not be enough to break the chain of causation. However, if the intervening act is so extraordinary as to **not** be foreseeable, it can break the chain of causation.

R v Roberts (1971)

When a woman was injured after jumping from a moving car after panicking that the driver was going to sexually assault her, the court held that that reaction was foreseeable and was therefore not enough to break the chain of causation.

Mens rea

The mens rea for murder is defined as **'malice aforethought'**, which has come to mean either an intention to kill or an intention to cause grievous bodily harm. The term malice aforethought causes confusion as there is neither a requirement for the defendant's actions to be malicious, nor for there to be any premeditation.

> **STRETCH AND CHALLENGE**
>
> Look up the case of *R v Cheshire (1991)*. This case also involved the question of whether substandard medical treatment was enough to break the chain of causation. Did the court agree with *R v Smith (1959)* or *R v Jordan (1956)*?

Direct and indirect intention of murder or grievous bodily harm

> **INTENTION TO KILL**
> or
> **INTENTION TO CAUSE GRIEVOUS BODILY HARM**
> **DPP v Smith (1961)**
> • The word 'grievous' means 'serious'.
> • The test of intention is subjective: it is what the defendant intended, not what the 'reasonable man' intended.

> **Direct intention**
> The defendant wants the victim to die and does what is necessary to achieve it.

> **Indirect intention (oblique intention)**
> The defendant foresees the consequences but does not want the consequences to happen.
> **R v Moloney (1985)**
> The defendant and his stepfather were messing around with a shotgun. Moloney pulled the trigger as a dare and killed his stepfather.

In relation to intention, the courts have been reluctant to devise a definitive rule but a series of cases has indicated that the more foreseeable the result, the more likely it is that the defendant would have intended the outcome.

Year	Case	Outcome
1975	*Hyam v DPP*	Where there is foresight there will always be intention.
1986	*R v Hancock and Shankland*	The greater the probability of a consequence, the more likely the consequence was foreseen, and therefore also intended.
1986	*R v Nedrick*	The judge directed that a jury can infer intention where death or grievous bodily harm is a virtual certainty of the defendant's actions and the defendant appreciates this to be the case.
1998	*R v Woollin*	The wording was changed so that a jury is entitled to find intention where death or grievous bodily harm is a virtual certainty of the defendant's actions. It is a question of evidence, not law.
2003	*R v Matthews and Alleyne*	It followed the direction taken in *Woollin (1998)* and it now seems to be the standard approach to take.

KEY CASES

R v Hancock and Shankland (1986)
The defendants were striking miners who threw a concrete block from a bridge to block the road below. It killed a passing taxi driver. The defendants were convicted of murder, which was later quashed on appeal when the court concluded that the greater the probability of a consequence, the more likely the consequence was foreseen, and therefore also intended.

R v Nedrick (1986)
The defendant was convicted of murder after throwing paraffin through the letterbox of a woman against whom he had a grudge. The woman's 12-year-old son died in the attack. An appeal was allowed and Nedrick was then convicted of manslaughter. The court held that the jury should consider how probable the consequence was and whether it was foreseen by the defendant. The jury may then **infer** intention if they are confident that the defendant realised the consequence was a **virtual certainty** and the defendant appreciated this to be the case.

R v Woollin (1998)
The defendant was a father who lost his temper with his three year old son when he choked on his food. He insisted he had not wanted the child to die, but the court held that it was a reasonably foreseeable consequence of his actions.

R v Matthews and Alleyne (2003)
This case concerned an 18-year-old who had been robbed and thrown over a bridge by two youths. The boy had told the youths that he could not swim before they pushed him. He drowned, and the court found that was a reasonably foreseeable consequence of the defendants' actions.

Criticisms of the law on murder

1. The mandatory life sentence.

2. No precise definition of when 'death' occurs.

3. Intention includes an intention to cause GBH but the conviction is the same (murder).

4. No clear definition of intention. Problems with oblique intent.

5. Cases of euthanasia.

Reform proposals for the law on murder

The Law Commission published a consultation paper in 2005, entitled 'A New Homicide Act for England and Wales?' to review the law on murder. Its proposals (described below) are currently being considered by the Home Office.

1. There would be three tiers of homicide.

First-degree murder	Second-degree murder	Manslaughter
• Intention to kill. • Intention to cause serious injury. • Defendant is aware that their conduct involves a risk of causing death.	• Intention to cause serious harm. • Intention to cause some injury, with an awareness of the risk of death. • Intention to kill with a partial defence of provocation, diminished responsibility or duress.	• Mens rea of gross negligence. • Criminal act, where the defendant only intended harm, not serious harm. • Defendant appreciated the risk involved and foresaw a serious risk of causing injury.
Mandatory life sentence	Discretionary life sentence	

2. The common law approach to **intention** is replaced with a statutory definition. This would change the law slightly from **R v Woollin (1998)** because the jury will be able to use intention as part of the substantive law, and not just part of the evidence.

A statutory definition would read:

> **A person acts intentionally with respect to a result when he or she acts either:**
> **in order to bring it about; or**
> **knowing that it will be virtually certain to occur; or**
> **knowing that it would be virtually certain to occur if he or she were to succeed in his or her purpose of causing some other result.**

We can conclude that, under the proposals, virtual certainty is intention, whereas lesser foresight is recklessness.

3. The mandatory life sentence would be abolished in order to deal with cases where the defences were being too leniently applied in order to give the judge discretion when sentencing the defendant. The government is reluctant to abolish the mandatory life sentence and this reform is unlikely to be implemented.

Voluntary manslaughter

Voluntary manslaughter is the where a defendant has committed murder but is relying on a **special defence** contained in the **Homicide Act 1957** and the **Coroners and Justice Act 2009**. If the special defence is proved, the charge of murder will be reduced to manslaughter, and the judge will have discretion in terms of sentencing the defendant. The **burden of proof** is on the **defence** to prove that the defence applies to them.

Such a defence may be:

- loss of control
- diminished responsibility
- suicide pact.

KEY TERMINOLOGY

special defence: the use of a defence which has the effect not of completely acquitting the defendant but allowing a reduction in the sentence given to the defendant.

Loss of control

It is important to compare this newer defence from the **Coroners and Justice Act 2009** with the old defence of provocation which was in the **Homicide Act 1957**.

	Provocation: *s3 Homicide Act 1957*	Loss of control: *s54 and s55 Coroners and Justice Act 2009*
Critique	It was thought that this defence was harsh to victims of continued domestic violence.	Under the newer defence, a fear of violence can justify killing, and can be used by victims of continued domestic violence.
	It has been proved that women react more slowly to an attack than men; therefore this defence was easier for men to rely on, because of the requirement of 'sudden' loss of control.	The omission of the word 'sudden' in the defence makes it easier for women to rely on the defence where they have reacted slightly slower than a man would have done.

	Provocation: *s3 Homicide Act 1957*	Loss of control: *s54 and s55 Coroners and Justice Act 2009*
Elements of the defence	**1. 'Sudden and temporary loss of control'.** • The loss of control equated with a loss of temper: *R v Cocker (1989)*. • 'Sudden and temporary' suggests no allowance of a 'cooling off' period: *R v Duffy (1949)* and *R v Ibrams (1982)*. • The court was lenient in allowing a time lapse between the provocation and the killing in *R v Thornton (1992)*, but stopped short of allowing acts of revenge in *R v Baille (1995)*.	**1. 'Loss of control'** • Defendant must have lost their self-control at the time of the actus reus. • The loss of control here need not be sudden, which means that women with a 'slow-burn' reaction will not be treated less fairly. • Cumulative loss of self-control may be possible: *R v Dawes, Hatter and Bowyer (2013)*.
	2. 'By things done or things said' • The persistent crying of a baby was held to amount to provocation in the case of *R v Doughty (1986)*. • A father who had subjected the defendant's brother to years of abuse was killed by the defendant in *R v Pearson (1992)*, which shows that the provocation need not be directed at the defendant. • *R v Brown (1972)* showed that a mistake was made by the defendant that he was being attacked by a gang member.	**1. 'By a qualifying trigger'** • *s55(i) Coroners and Justice Act 2009* suggests that this can be from a fear of serious violence from the victim. • This is a new concept which protects women who have been subjected to continuous domestic violence by their abusive partners, or a homeowner who protected their property by killing a burglar. • The test is **subjective,** which means it is how the **defendant** fears, not how the 'reasonable man' or someone else in their position would fear the serious violence. It has been suggested, however, that the victim has to be the source of violence, and the defendant has to fear that the violence is directed towards them. • *s55(ii) Coroners and Justice Act 2009*: Things are said or done of an extremely grave character, causing the defendant a justifiable sense of being seriously wronged. • This is a narrow approach because, although the sense of being wronged is subjective, it has to be justified, which is an objective test and one which can only be determined by the jury. The Court of Appeal observed in *R v Clinton, Parker and Evans (2012)* that this requires an objective evaluation.
	3. Would a reasonable person have been provoked in the same way? • *DPP v Camplin (1978)* held that the only characteristics relevant to compare to the reasonable person are age and sex. • In *R v Smith (Morgan) (2000)*, the House of Lords held that the jury can take into account 'abnormal characteristics' of the defendant, such as depression, where those characteristics affect the standard of their control. • *A-G for Jersey v Holley (2005)* provides a contrast because the court refused to take into account alcoholism as an 'abnormal characteristic'. The guidance given was that the reasonable person must exercise the power of self-control expected of an ordinary person of like sex and age.	**3. Would a reasonable person have acted in the same way?** This objective test asks whether a person of the defendant's sex and age, with an ordinary level of tolerance and self-restraint, and in similar circumstances, might have acted in the same or a similar way to the defendant *(s54(1)(c))*. The new defence seems to have followed *A-G for Jersey v Holley (2005)*. It is thought that where abnormal characteristics are present, it is more likely that the defendant will rely on the defence of diminished responsibility.
Burden of proof	The judge left the interpretation of the defence to the jury.	The prosecution must disprove the defence of loss of control beyond reasonable doubt.

There is limited case law on the 'loss of control' defence. *R v Clinton, Parker and Evans* reached the Court of Appeal in 2012, where the court stated that the 'common law heritage is irrelevant'; therefore, the old case law on provocation is now only of limited legal significance.

Other significant cases are:

- *R v Jewell (2014)*
- *R v Workman (2014)* and *R v Barnsdale-Quean (2014)*
- *R v Dawes, Hatter and Bowyer (2013)*.

The use of this defence has implications of discrimination against women. The so-called **battered woman's syndrome** was brought to light in the cases of *Thornton* and *Ahluwalia* which both involved women who killed their husbands after they had endured years of abuse. In both cases there seemed to be a 'cooling off period', which means the element of 'sudden' loss of control was not satisfied. It was raised in these cases that a sudden loss of control is a male reaction, and takes no account of the fact that women react to provocation in different ways. Helena Kennedy QC described the female reaction as 'a snapping in slow motion, the final surrender of frayed elastic'. Because of this criticism, the courts seemed to become more lenient and, in the case of *Ahluwalia*, an appeal was allowed and the defence of diminished responsibility accepted instead. More encouraging was the judge's approach in *Thornton*'s appeal, where the concept of 'battered woman's syndrome' was accepted and could be taken into account when considering whether there had been a sudden and temporary loss of control. Under the new defence, this is still relevant because, although the loss of control need not be sudden, a time delay is relevant in deciding whether there had been a loss of control.

STRETCH AND CHALLENGE

Consider the cases of *R v Doughty (1986)*, *R v Pearson (1992)* and *R v Brown (1972)* in the table above, which were decided under the old defence of provocation. How do you think they would have been decided under the new defence?

- *R v Doughty (1986)*: under the new defence, persistent crying of a baby does not equate to circumstances of an extremely grave character for trigger (ii).
- *R v Pearson (1992)*: acts of third parties would be irrelevant for trigger (i), but may be relevant for trigger (ii).
- *R v Brown (1972)*: the new Act is not clear about the situation where a mistake has been made, but this will be resolved by the courts in due course.

STRETCH AND CHALLENGE

Look up some of the criticisms of the law on loss of control. These will be required for an essay question which requires you to analyse and evaluate the law.

GRADE BOOST

Make sure you show an awareness of the *Coroners and Justice Act 2009* throughout. You will lose marks if you only refer to the *Homicide Act 1957*.

Diminished responsibility

	Diminished responsibility: *s2 Homicide Act 1957*	Diminished responsibility: *s52 Coroners and Justice Act 2009*
Critique	The **old** defence used the phrase 'abnormality of mind'.	The new definition includes the phrasing 'abnormality of mental functioning'. The purpose of this was to clarify the law but no changes were made to the applicability of the defence. The **new** definition of the defence means that one of the essential elements of the defence is a recognised medical condition. The old case law is expected to still be helpful in determining what may count as an 'abnormality of mental functioning'.
Elements of the defence	**1a. The defendant suffered from an abnormality of the mind.** This could be depression, 'mercy killing', premenstrual syndrome or, in *R v Hobson (1997)*, 'battered woman's syndrome'. **1b. The abnormality:** **arose from a condition of arrested or retarded development; or** **any inherent causes; or** **induced by disease or injury.**	**1. The defendant is suffering from an abnormality of mental functioning which arose from a recognised medical condition.** This is a narrow definition but is a more modern approach which takes into account an understanding of mental health issues. It is thought that some abnormalities of the mind under previous law may not succeed under the new defence because they are not recognised medical conditions. *R v Martin (Anthony)(2001)* would probably have succeeded under this defence because the defendant was suffering from a paranoid personality disorder when he killed an intruder in his home.
	2. The abnormality was a substantial cause of the defendant's act of killing. Here, the defendant's abnormality needs to have been a substantial cause of the killing but not necessarily the only cause. *R v Dietschmann (2003)* illustrates this, as it was held that his depression was a substantial cause.	**2. The abnormality of mental functioning must be a significant contributory factor to the killing.** This means that the abnormality must cause, or at least be a significant contributory factor to, the killing. If *R v Dietschmann (2003)* were to be decided under the new defence, it is unclear whether the case would have got past the first hurdle of depression being recognised as a medical condition. However, it does seem that it does not matter if drink or drugs are involved; the key question is whether the medical condition overrides that and is a significant contributor to the killing.
	3. The abnormality substantially impaired the defendant's mental responsibility for their acts.	**3. The abnormality of mental functioning must have substantially impaired the defendant's ability to:** **understand the nature of their conduct; or** **form a rational judgement; or** **exercise self-control.** This is a much more specific element of the crime and it makes clear what aspects of the mental functioning must be affected. The word 'substantial' was considered in the case of *R v Golds (2014)*.
Burden of proof	The defence must prove that the defendant was suffering from diminished responsibility at the time of the offence on the balance of probabilities. Expert evidence is required from at least two witnesses.	

R v Dietschmann (2003)
The defendant was suffering from depression, but was also drunk when he killed his victim. Even though the abnormality was the depression, the court accepted diminished responsibility because, even though he may not have killed had he been sober, the depression was a substantial cause.

Involuntary manslaughter

Involuntary manslaughter is where a defendant has committed the actus reus of murder but does not have the mens rea. There are two forms of involuntary manslaughter:

1. manslaughter by an unlawful and dangerous act (**constructive manslaughter**)

2. **gross negligence manslaughter**.

Unlawful and dangerous act manslaughter (constructive manslaughter)

All common elements of murder are present.

Actus reus

It has to be an **unlawful** act, not an omission.

R v Lowe (1973)
This involved the commission of the offence of child neglect, and the neglect caused the child's death.

The act has to be **criminal**, not civil. This was held in the case of *R v Franklin (1883)*.

R v D (2006)
The victim, having suffered years of domestic abuse from her husband, committed suicide. Prior to the suicide, her husband had cut her forehead when he struck her with his bracelet. This was held to be enough of an unlawful criminal act because it constituted an offence under s20 Offences Against the Person Act 1861.

It also has to be a **dangerous** act. The test is whether a reasonable person would foresee that the act would cause harm.

R v Church (1966)
The court held that the test has to be whether a 'sober and reasonable person would realise the risk' of their act.

It does not matter what form that harm takes, as long as some harm is foreseeable, as in *R v JM and SM (2012)*. The defendant must have the same knowledge as the sober and reasonable person.

R v Dawson (1985)
The victim was a 60-year-old with a serious heart condition. The defendants were not to know about this condition and neither was a sober and reasonable person; therefore, the act could not be dangerous.

R v Watson (1989)
The victim was an 87-year-old man. The court held that the defendants should be reasonably expected to know that the man would be frail and easily scared; therefore the act was dangerous.

Causation

It must be established that the unlawful and dangerous act was the cause of the death.

R v Johnstone (2007)
The victim was subjected to a series of taunts which involved spitting and shouting (not deemed to be a dangerous act) and stones and wood being thrown (deemed to be a dangerous act). The victim suffered a heart attack brought on by stress. The defendants could not be convicted of constructive manslaughter because it was not clear whether it was the dangerous act that brought on the heart attack, and thus caused the death of the victim.

If the victim intervenes in the chain of causation with a voluntary act, this will be sufficient to break the chain of causation.

Consider the case of *R v Lamb (1967)*, where the defendant pointed a gun at his friend as a joke. The defendant had no intention of hurting the victim but one of the bullets slipped out and killed his friend. Can you identify a) the unlawful act and b) the mens rea of that act? Based on this, is the defendant guilty of constructive manslaughter?

Look up some of the criticisms of the law on constructive manslaughter. These will be required for an essay question where you are asked to analyse and evaluate the law.

R v Adomako (1994)
The defendant was a doctor who had inserted a ventilator tube into a patient's mouth, but the patient died from lack of oxygen when the tube became detached from the machine. Adomako had not realised quickly enough that his patient was dying, and he appealed to the House of Lords against his conviction of gross negligence manslaughter. Lord Mackay in the House of Lords held that there were several elements that had to be satisfied to uphold the conviction:
• duty of care
• gross negligent breach of that duty
• risk of death.

R v Kennedy (No 2) (2007)
The court held that a drug dealer can never be held responsible for the death of a drug user.

But contrast this case with *R v Cato (1976)* which shows an exception to the rule laid down in the case above.

R v Cato (1976)
The drug dealer injected heroin into the victim so, in this case, the defendant would have been liable for the manslaughter of the victim.

Mens rea
This is the mens rea of the unlawful act. For example, if the unlawful act was *s18 Offences Against the Person Act 1861*, then the mens rea would be intention.

Gross negligence manslaughter

Negligence is usually covered under the civil law but there is some negligent behaviour (leading to death) which is so severe as to require punishment under the criminal law.

The test was laid down in the case of *R v Adomako (1994)*.

As with constructive manslaughter, all common elements of murder are present.

Duty of care
A duty of care is established under the 'neighbourhood principle' contained in *Donoghue v Stevenson (1932)*. Whether or not a duty of care is owed is a matter for the jury to decide using the 'neighbourhood principle'.

A few key exceptions arose in *R v Willoughby (2004)*, where it was held that there will almost always be a duty of care between doctor and patient.

Gross negligent breach of that duty
Whether or not the breach of the duty amounts to gross negligence is a matter for the jury to decide, though in the case of *R v Bateman (1925)*, Lord Hewart CJ suggested that it 'showed such disregard for life and safety of others as to amount to a crime against the state and conduct deserving punishment'.

Risk of death
As well as being expressed in *R v Adomako (1994)*, this provision was further confirmed in *R v Misra and Srivastava (2005)* where doctors failed to diagnose a post-operation infection which led to the death of the patient. The lack of diagnosis, and the subsequent lack of treatment, was held to constitute a risk of death.

Summary: Fatal offences against the person

Murder
▶ 'The unlawful killing of a reasonable person in being and under the King's (or Queen's) Peace and with malice aforethought, express or implied.' LJ Coke
▶ Actus reus elements:
  • Human being: independent of mother: *AG's Reference No 3 of 1994*
  • Death: *R v Malcherek and Steel (1981)*
  • Causation in fact: 'but for test' *R v White (1910)*; de minimis rule: *Pagett (1983)*
  • Legal causation:
    ◦ injury as the operative and substantial cause of death: *R v Smith (1959)*, *R v Jordan (1956)*
    ◦ 'thin skull test': *R v Blaue (1975)*
    ◦ foreseeable intervening act: *R v Roberts (1971)*

▶ Mens rea elements: malice aforethought: Intention to kill OR intention to cause GBH: *DPP v Smith (1961)*

- Direct intention
- Oblique intention: *R v Woollin (1998)*: virtual certainty test

Voluntary manslaughter

▶ Murder elements + Special defence: *Homicide Act 1957* and *Coroners and Justice Act 2009*

▶ Partial defence:

- Loss of control
- Suicide pact
- Diminished responsibility

▶ Loss of control: *s54 Coroners and Justice Act 2009*:

- Loss of control
- Reasonable person
- Qualifying trigger
- Prosecution to disprove

▶ Diminished responsibility: *s52 Coroners and Justice Act 2009*:

- Abnormality of mental functioning
- Arising from a recognised medical condition
- Abnormality of mental functioning must be a significant contributory factor to the killing
- The abnormality of mental functioning must have substantially impaired the defendant's ability to:
  - understand the nature of their conduct; or
  - form a rational judgement; or
  - exercise self-control
- Defence to prove on the balance of probabilities, using expert evidence

Involuntary manslaughter

▶ Actus reus of murder + either unlawful and dangerous act OR gross negligence

▶ Unlawful and dangerous act manslaughter

- Elements of actus reus of murder
- Unlawful act: act not omission; criminal act not civil
- Dangerous act: reasonable person
- Causation
- Mens rea is the mens rea of the unlawful act

Gross negligence manslaughter

▶ *Adomako (1994)*

- Elements of actus reus of murder
- Duty of care
- Grossly negligent breach of that duty of care
- Risk of death

Property offences

Spec reference	Key content	Assessment Objectives	Where does this topic feature on each specification/exam?
WJEC A Level 3.15: Property offences **Eduqas A Level 2.3.4:** Property offences	• Theft and robbery: Actus reus (appropriation, property, belonging to another), mens rea (dishonesty, intention to permanently deprive), (s1 Theft Act 1968) • Robbery: Theft with use or threat of force (s8 Theft Act 1968) • Burglary: Elements of s9(1)(a) and s9(1)(b) Theft Act 1968, burglary in dwellings and other buildings	**AO1** Demonstrate knowledge and understanding of legal rules and principles **AO2** Apply legal rules and principles to given scenarios in order to present a legal argument using appropriate legal terminology **AO3** Analyse and evaluate legal rules, principles, concepts and issues	**WJEC A Level:** Unit 3; Section C. Unit 4; Section C **Eduqas A Level:** Component 2; Section C. Component 3; Section C

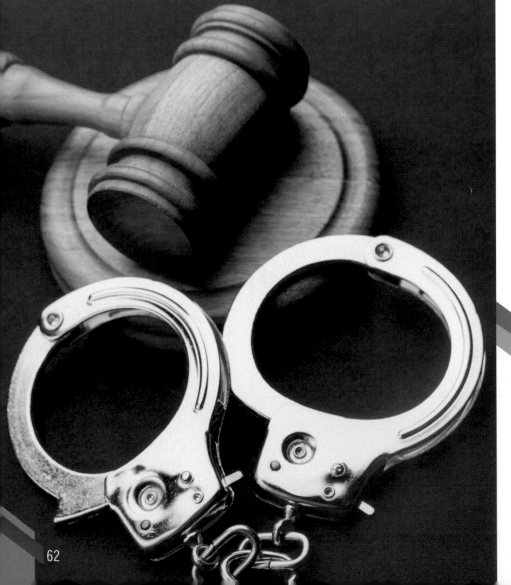

At A Level, the topic of **property offences** covers three separate offences:

• Theft.

• Robbery.

• Burglary.

Prior to the *Theft Act 1968*, this area of law was covered by **common law** and was complex. The *Theft Act 1968* effectively codified the law of some property offences. It has, however, continued to evolve through the interpretation of various parts of the Act by judges deciding certain cases. Since the original 1968 Act, there have been two further statutory updates: the *Theft Act 1978* and the *Theft (Amendment) Act 1996*, which amends the 1968 and 1978 Acts.

KEY TERMINOLOGY

common law (also case law or precedent): law developed by judges through decisions in court.

Theft

This is defined in **s1 Theft Act 1968**:

'A person is guilty of theft if he dishonestly appropriates property belonging to another with the intention of permanently depriving the other of it.'

The **actus reus** elements of theft are:

1. appropriation *(s3)*

2. property *(s4)*

3. belonging to another *(s5)*.

The **mens rea elements of theft** are:

1. intention to permanently deprive *(s6)*

2. dishonesty (*s2* and *Ghosh* test; see page 66).

The maximum sentence for theft is seven years' imprisonment.

Each element will be considered in turn.

Actus reus of theft

1. Appropriation

This element is defined in **s3(1) Theft Act 1968**:

'Any assumption by a person of the rights of an owner amounts to an appropriation, and this includes where he has come by the property (innocently or not) without stealing it, any later assumption of a right to it by keeping or dealing with it as owner.'

This means that the defendant has physically taken an object from its owner (e.g. a handbag or tablet computer). The defendant is **assuming some or all their rights**. This aspect has been interpreted widely and includes assuming any rights of the owner (e.g., moving, touching, destroying, selling, etc.). They are doing something with the property that the owner has a right to do (**'bundle of rights'**) and that no one else has the right to do without the permission of the owner. One right is sufficient, as seen in *R v Morris (1923)*, when the defendant switched the price on an item in a shop, intending to pay the lower price. Even though he did not make it to the checkout, the price switch and the placement of the goods in his trolley was considered to be an 'appropriation', as owners have the right to price their own goods.

Section 3(1) also covers situations where someone does not steal property (e.g. they are lent a bracelet by a friend) but then assumes the rights of the owner by refusing to return it. The 'appropriation' takes place once the person decides to keep it.

An appropriation can still take place even if the victim consents to the property being taken, as in *Lawrence v MPC (1972)*.

Viscount Dilhorne said: 'Parliament by the omission of these words (consent) has relieved the prosecution establishing that the taking was done without the owner's consent.'

Keith LJ said: 'An act may be an appropriation notwithstanding that it is done with the consent of the owner.' This principle was followed in *R v Gomez (2000)*.

In *R v Hinks (2000)*, the defendant's charge of theft was upheld regardless of it being a gift, as the defendant had 'appropriated' the money. This has the advantage of protecting vulnerable people.

Property

This element is defined in *s4 Theft Act 1968*:

'Property includes money and all other property, real or personal, including things in action and other intangible property.'

Property may seem easy to define at first but there are some issues that need to be considered in further detail.

Things that can be stolen (so count as property) include:

- money (physical existence rather than its value)
- personal property
- **real property**
- **intangible property**
- **things in action**.

Real property includes land and buildings, although *s4(2)* provides that land, and things forming part of the land and severed from it (e.g. flowers, picked crops), cannot normally be stolen, except in the circumstances laid down in that section.

Intangible property means property that does not exist in a physical sense, such as copyright or patents.

A **'thing in action'** (or a **'chose in action'**) is a technical term describing property that does not exist in a physical sense but which provides the owner with legally enforceable rights. Examples include a bank account in credit where the bank refuses the customer their money, investments, shares and intellectual property such as patents. People have legal rights over these things but they can't physically hold them.

The courts have, however, decided that some things are not 'property' within the definition. In *Oxford v Moss (1979)*, it was held that seeing unopened exam questions was not theft as they were not 'property' but 'information'.

Electricity is treated separately under the Act. It is considered intangible property that cannot be stolen but if a person *(s11)* 'dishonestly uses electricity without authority or dishonesty causes it to be wasted or diverted' then they may be liable for an offence.

Things that cannot be stolen are set out in *s4(3)* and *s4(4)* of the Act and cover situations where a person picks mushrooms, flowers fruit or foliage growing wild on land. This is not to be treated as theft unless it is done for reward, sale or other commercial purpose (*s4(3)*). *Section 4(4)* relates to tamed or untamed wild animals.

A human body cannot normally be stolen. However, *R v Kelly and Lindsay (1998)* held that, although a dead body is not normally property, the body parts in this case could be as their 'essential character and value has changed'.

Belonging to another:

'Property shall be regarded as belonging to any person having possession or control of it, or having in it any proprietary right or interest.'

It includes where a person owns the property but also where they have **possession or control** over it or a **proprietary right or interest** over it. It includes property belonging to someone under civil law and covers mere possession without rights of ownership. For example, a hired wedding suit is not owned by the person hiring it but they are in control of it at the time they are in possession of it. If someone takes the hired suit from the hiree (person who hired it), they can be said to have appropriated property belonging to the hiree, even though the hiree does not actually own the suit.

A person can, therefore, be **liable for stealing their own property** (*R v Turner No 2 (1971)*). In this case, Turner had taken his car to a garage to be repaired. After the repairs had been completed, he drove the car away from outside the garage, without paying. The garage was 'in possession' of his car at the time he took it, consequently making him liable for stealing his own car.

Even if property is legally obtained, there is still an **obligation to use it in a particular way**. *Section 5(3)* states:

'Where a person receives property from, or on account of another, and is under an obligation to the other to retain and deal with that property or its proceeds in a particular way, the property shall be regarded (as against him) as belonging to the other.'

If you gave your teacher a deposit for a class trip but the teacher spent that money on a set of textbooks for the class, the teacher has not 'used the money in the right way' so has committed theft. This section also covers things like charity collections. In *R v Hall (1972)*, the Court of Appeal said that each case depended on its facts. In this case, there was no obligation to use the deposit money in a particular way as it was paid into a general account.

What about situations where property is passed to the defendant **by mistake**, for example, the overpayment of wages? *Section 5(4)* provides that property which is passed to the defendant by mistake is to be treated as 'belonging to' the original owner and, therefore, once the defendant realises the mistake and refuses to return the property, a theft takes place. The failure to return the property, on realising the mistake must be deliberate, was defined in *Attorney General's Reference (No 1 of 1983) (1985)*.

Mens rea of theft

The mens rea of theft comprises two elements: **intention to permanently deprive** and **dishonesty.**

Intention to permanently deprive

The defendant must intend to permanently deprive the other of the property, regardless of whether the other is actually deprived of the property. This is covered in *s6 Theft Act 1968*.

'A person ... is regarded as having the intention of permanently depriving ... if his intention is to treat the thing as his own to dispose of regardless of the other's rights ... (B)orrowing or lending ... may amount to so treating it if, but only if, the borrowing or lending is for a period and in circumstances making it equivalent to an outright taking or disposal.'

Borrowing without permission (e.g. joyriding a car) without the intention to permanently deprive is not theft. There are other offences for dealing with situations like this, for example, the offence of 'taking without consent' (TWOC).

Section 6 (1) covers situations where the property is 'borrowed' temporarily. This is not normally theft because there is no intention to permanently deprive. But, in *R v Lloyd (1985)*, the court held that borrowing could fall within the remit of *s6* if the property was borrowed 'until the goodness, the virtue, the practical value ... has gone out of the article'. In this case, the defendant, who worked in a cinema, removed films to make pirate copies. He returned the films a few hours later, after the copying process had taken place. The 'temporary deprivation' of the films, in this case, was not sufficient for a conviction of theft.

> **GRADE BOOST**
>
> Research *R v Marshall (1998)* on this issue.

However, in *R v Velumyl (1989)*, the defendant was convicted after he, without lawful authority, took cash from his employer's safe and lent it to his friend, intending for the cash to be repaid the following Monday. However, a spot-check took place before the money was returned, and it was discovered missing. He was convicted of theft on the basis that he intended to permanently deprive the owner of the exact notes and coins despite intending to return items of the same value.

Dishonesty

Section 2 Theft Act 1968 does not define dishonesty but gives examples of what is not dishonest. It says:

'A person's appropriation of property belonging to another is not to be regarded as dishonest:

(a) *if he appropriates the property in the belief that he has in law the right to deprive the other of it, on behalf of himself or of a third person; or*

(b) *if he appropriates the property in the belief that he would have the other's consent if the other knew of the appropriation and the circumstances of it; or*

(c) *(except where the property came to him as trustee or personal representative) if he appropriates the property in the belief that the person to whom the property belongs cannot be discovered by taking reasonable steps.'*

Section 2(2): *'A person's appropriation of property belonging to another may be dishonest notwithstanding that he is willing to pay for the property.'*

All the tests above are **subjective**: they are decided on the basis of what the defendant believes, rather than what the reasonable person should know or believe (**objective**).

If none of the tests above apply, the test for dishonesty outlined in the key case *R v Ghosh (1982)* should be used. This provides the test for the jury on what is to be regarded as dishonesty.

1. Has the defendant been dishonest by the standards of the ordinary, honest and reasonable person?

2. If the answer is 'yes', did the defendant realise that they were dishonest by those standards?

If the answer is 'yes' to both questions, the defendant can be legally dishonest. If the answer to either question is 'no', the defendant is not dishonest.

In *R v Ghosh (1982)*, Lord Lane said:

'In determining whether the prosecution has proved that the defendant was acting dishonestly, a jury must first of all decide whether, according to the ordinary standards of reasonable and honest people, what was done was dishonest. If it was not dishonest by those standards, that is the end of the matter and the prosecution fails. If it was dishonest by those standards, then the jury must consider whether the defendant himself must have realised that what he was doing was by those standards dishonest.'

The first part of the test is objective and the second part asks whether the defendant realised that they had been dishonest by those standards (even if the defendant did not consider themselves to be dishonest). Under common law, a person is dishonest if they behave dishonestly by the standards of reasonable people and the defendant realised this.

Robbery

This offence is similar to theft but involves the use of force to facilitate the theft. Burglary (see page 69) involves intrusion into property in order to steal. It is important to understand these key differences between the three property offences.

Robbery is defined in *s8(1) Theft Act 1968*:

'A person is guilty of robbery if he steals, and immediately before or at the time of doing so, and in order to do so, he uses force on any person or puts or seeks to put any person in fear of being then and there subjected to force.'

It is an **indictable** offence so is triable on indictment in the **Crown Court**. It is a more serious offence than theft and can carry a maximum sentence on conviction of **life imprisonment**.

Some have called it **aggravated theft** as it involves the offence of theft **plus** force or the threat of force.

The **actus reus** elements of robbery are:

1. actus reus of theft

2. uses force or there is a threat of force in order to steal

3. immediately before or at the same time as stealing

4. on any person.

The **mens rea** elements of robbery are:

1. mens rea of theft

2. intention to use force in order to thieve.

KEY TERMINOLOGY

indictable: the most serious offences, triable only in the Crown Court.

Actus reus of robbery

1. Theft

All the elements of theft must be present for there to have been a robbery. If one element is missing there is no robbery. This was confirmed in *R v Robinson (1977)*. To recap, the elements of theft defined in *s1 Theft Act 1968* are:

• dishonestly

• appropriates

• property

• belonging to another

• with the intention to permanently deprive the other of it.

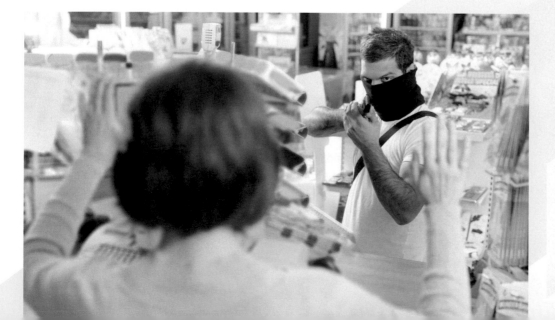

2. Intentional force

This element distinguishes robbery from theft. Examples of 'force' could be shoving someone in order to take their handbag or punching someone to take their mobile phone. A **threat of force** is also sufficient, for example, waving a knife at someone and demanding they hand over their wallet. However, the force must be used **in order to steal** AND **be immediately before or at the time of the theft**. Once the theft is **complete**, there is a robbery. This was confirmed in *Corcoran v Anderton (1980)* where the theft had not been completed (the woman kept hold of her bag and did not let the attackers take it) so there was only an **attempted robbery**.

Force (or threat of) used in order to steal

Whether there is sufficient force (or threat of it) to steal is a question for the jury to decide. It can include a small amount of force, as confirmed in *Dawson and James (1976)* and *R v Clouden (1987)*.

Force can be indirectly applied to the victim, for example, if applied via property. In *R v Clouden (1987)*, the defendant had wrenched a shopping bag from the victim's hand. This conduct was sufficient to amount to force for the purposes of the offence of robbery.

However, it may not be considered to be 'force' as required for robbery if, for example, a mobile phone fell out of a person's hand or if the defendant grabbed a laptop from a person's lap. In *P v DPP (2012)*, it was held that snatching a cigarette held by the victim would not amount to force.

It is not a requirement that the force be applied; mere fear of force through a threat or gesture is sufficient. For example, saying 'I have a knife which I will stab you with unless you give me your wallet' would be sufficient for fear of force.

It is important to remember that the force (or threat of it) must be used **in order to steal**. For example, a defendant pushes a woman to the ground intending to rape her and she offers him her designer watch if he stops. If he takes the watch, there is both force and theft but it would not amount to robbery. This is because the force used was intended to rape her and not to steal.

Force used immediately before or at the time of the theft

The question of how 'immediate' is immediate has been debated in the courts. The courts confirmed in *R v Hale (1979)* that if the act of theft **continues** when the force is used then it can be a robbery.

R v Hale (1979)

Two defendants forced their way past a woman into her house. One put his hand over her mouth while the other went upstairs and took a jewellery box. Before they left the house, they tied up the woman. The Court of Appeal held that there was force (the defendant putting his hand over the victim's mouth) immediately before the theft (the taking of the jewellery box). They also considered that, as a continuing act, tying up the woman before leaving the house with the jewellery box could also constitute force for the purposes of robbery. The 'appropriation' was ongoing. This rationale was followed in R v Lockley (1995).

On any person

The theft does not have to happen to the person being threatened. For example, in an armed bank robbery, a random customer in the bank that is being held up would be in fear of force being used against them but the money stolen would be the bank's property. This would still be a robbery.

Mens rea of robbery

The mens rea of robbery is mens rea of theft (dishonesty and intention to permanently deprive the other of the property) **plus** the intention to use force to steal.

Burglary

The offence of burglary is generally considered to be someone breaking into a private residence and stealing property from it. *Section 9 Theft Act 1968* makes it clear that it goes further than this. *Section 9 Theft Act 1968* defines the offence:

'*(1) A person is guilty of burglary if—*

(a) he enters any building or part of a building as a trespasser and with intent to commit any such offence as is mentioned in subsection (2) below; or

(b) having entered any building or part of a building as a trespasser he steals or attempts to steal anything in the building or that part of it or inflicts or attempts to inflict on any person therein any grievous bodily harm.

(2) The offences referred to in subsection (1)(a) above are offences of stealing anything in the building or part of a building in question, of inflicting on any person therein any grievous bodily harm, and of doing unlawful damage to the building or anything therein.'

There are in fact **two** offences of burglary under *s9(1)(a)* and *s9(1)(b)*. There is also an offence under *s10 Theft Act 1968* of **aggravated burglary**.

The maximum sentence on conviction for burglary is 14 years if the burglar has entered a **dwelling** or maximum of 10 years if the burglar has entered any other building. Aggravated burglary carries a maximum of life imprisonment.

According to *R v Flack (2013)*, the word 'dwelling' is to be interpreted by the jury without guidance from the judge.

Burglary under s9(1)(a)

A person is guilty of burglary under *s9(1)(a)* if they enter a building, or any part of a building, as a trespasser, with intent to commit theft, inflict grievous bodily harm (GBH) on any person in the building or commit criminal damage.

The actus reus has three elements:

- entry
- into a building or part of a building
- as a trespasser.

The mens rea has two elements:

- intention or recklessness as to trespass
- ulterior intent (the intention to commit theft, GBH or damage the building or its contents).

Burglary under s9(1)(b)

A person is guilty of burglary under **s9(1)(b)** if, having entered a building or part of a building as a trespasser, they steal or attempt to steal anything in the building, or inflict or attempt to inflict GBH on any person inside it.

The actus reus has four elements:

- entry
- into a building or part of a building
- as a trespasser
- actus reus of theft or GBH, or at attempt theft or GBH inside it.

The mens rea has two elements:

- intention or recklessness as to trespass
- mens rea for theft or GBH, or attempt at theft or GBH inside it.

The main difference between the two offences of burglary is that under **s9(1)(a)** the intention must be formed by the defendant at the time of entry, whereas under **s9(1)(b)** the intent to commit the ulterior offence can come later, as what the defendant intends on entry is not relevant. Also, **s9(1)(a)** covers unlawful damage whereas **s9(1)(b)** does not.

Actus reus of burglary

The elements that make up the actus reus of the offence of burglary are common to both **s9(1)(a)** and **s9(1)(b)**. They are:

1. entry

2. into a building or part of a building

3. as a trespasser.

These common elements will now be explored in turn.

1. Entry

This element has been defined by the courts in case law. It is not defined in statute.

R v Collins (1973) held there had to be an 'effective and substantial entry'. The next case on the matter was *R v Brown (1985)*, where the definition was changed to just require an 'effective entry', removing the requirement for a 'substantial entry'. In this case, there was a partial entry as the defendant only put his head and shoulders through an open window to steal property from inside and this was considered to be an 'effective' entry. In *R v Ryan (1996)*, the requirement of an 'effective' entry was not followed.

R v Ryan (1996)

The defendant had attempted to enter a house through a window but was found trapped half-inside the house by the home-owner. His head and one arm were inside the house but he was unable to reach any property to steal. His conviction for burglary was upheld even though it was not an 'effective' entry. There is no requirement for the theft to have been completed to be a conviction under s9(1)(a).

What if a defendant does not physically enter the building but uses some other means to access the inside of the building? Using an instrument such as a fishing rod through an open window in order to steal something from inside may amount to 'entry' for the purposes of burglary.

2. A building or part of a building

The defendant must enter a building or part of a building as a trespasser. A 'building' is not defined in the Act but has been given a wide definition. It includes traditional structures such as flats, factories, shops and houses, but sheds and outbuildings are also considered to be 'buildings'. **Section 9(3) Theft Act 1968** says that a 'building' includes 'inhabited vehicles or vessels' covering things like caravans and houseboats. Tents, being temporary structures, are not included; therefore, stealing something from a tent is theft and not burglary.

What about more temporary structures that have been used for storage or work, such as a container or a portacabin? There have been some cases on the issue. *B and S v Leathley (1979)* held that an outdoor freezer connected to an electric supply was a building.

However, in *Norfolk Constabulary v Seekings and Gould (1986)*, a lorry trailer with wheels, connected to the electric supply, was not considered to be a building.

A burglary can also take place from **part of a building.** This covers situations where a defendant is in a part of a building that they do not have permission to be in. They would therefore be a trespasser in that part. For example, customers in a supermarket have the right to be in the shop but become trespassers if they enter a part of the building (e.g. a storeroom or staff room) where they are not permitted to be. It would, therefore, be theft of an item from a supermarket shelf but burglary from the storeroom.

R v Walkington (1979)

The defendant entered a shop as a customer but then went behind the partitioned counter to access the till. He became a trespasser at that point and was charged with burglary. He was permitted to be in the shop but not in the counter area, where he was a trespasser. He had the intention to steal from the till and so this was burglary.

3. As a trespasser

Trespassing is a civil law concept. A trespasser is a person who does not have permission to be in a building or part of the building (as in *R v Walkington (1979)*, above).

If a defendant has permission to enter the building or part of the building then they are not a trespasser, as seen in *R v Collins (1972)*. It must be shown that the defendant was aware they were trespassing or that they were **subjectively** reckless in doing so.

It might be that a person has permission to enter but goes beyond that permission, as in *R v Smith and Jones (1976)*. This covers a range of situations where a person stays beyond their permission (e.g. they have a ticket to enter an art show but stay after closing and steal a sculpture).

Mens rea of burglary

The mens rea under *s9(1)(a)* is different to that under *s9(1)(b)*.

Mens rea under s9(1)(a)

First, it needs to be proved that the defendant had intention or subjective recklessness to trespass and, secondly, that the defendant, **at the time of entry**, intended to commit one of the offences listed in *s9(2)*. Known as **ulterior offences**, these are theft, inflicting GBH or unlawful damage to the building or anything in it. The intention must exist at the time of entry. If the intent is not present upon entry, subsequent formation of ulterior intent will not amount to burglary. Provided the defendant enters with the relevant intention, the full offence of burglary is committed at the point of entry; the defendant need not actually go on to commit the ulterior offence.

Mens rea under s9(1)(b)

This section is different and easier to prove. As with *s9(1)(a)*, it needs to be proved that the defendant had intention or subjective recklessness to trespass. There is no need to prove any mens rea on entering the building. However, it must be proved that, once inside, there was actual or attempted offending of the ulterior offence.

Exam Skills

This topic is frequently examined as a problem scenario. You will need to be able to **explain** and/or **apply** the criminal liability of the parties involved. You will need to determine if the offence of theft, robbery and/or burglary has been committed. More than one property offence may feature so be careful with identifying the correct burglary offence under *s9(1)(a) or (b)*.

You might also be required to **analyse** and **evaluate** the effectiveness of the law in this area and **consider** proposals for reform.

Summary: Property offences

Theft: *s1 Theft Act 1968*

- Maximum sentence seven years' imprisonment
- Triable either way offence
- **Actus reus** has three elements:
  - Appropriation (*s3*): Bundle of rights: *R v Morris (1923)*, *Lawrence v MPC (1972)*, *R v Gomez (2000)*, *R v Hinks (2000)*
  - Property (*s4*): Real property, intangible property, things in action, *Oxford v Moss (1979)*, things that cannot be stolen
  - Belonging to another (*s5*): Possession or control, proprietary right or interest, own property: *R v Turner No 2 (1971)*, obligation to use in a particular way, mistake

▶ **Mens rea**:
- Dishonesty: *s2* and *Ghosh* test
- Intention to permanently deprive (*s6*): *Lloyd (1985)*, *Velumyl (1989)*

Robbery: *s8 Theft Act 1968*

▶ Maximum sentence life imprisonment

▶ Indictable offence

▶ Actus reus:
- Actus reus of theft: *s1 Theft Act 1968*
- Uses force or there is a threat of force in order to steal: *Corcoran v Anderton (1980)*, *Dawson and James (1976)*, *Clouden (1987)*
- Immediately before or at the same time as stealing: *Hale (1979)*
- On any person

▶ Mens rea of robbery:
- Mens rea of theft
- Intention to use force in order to thieve

Burglary: *s9(1)(a)* and *s9(1)(b) Theft Act 1968*

▶ Maximum sentence 14 years' imprisonment

▶ Triable either way offence

▶ **Burglary under *s9(1)(a)***: A person is guilty if they enter a building, or any part of a building, as a trespasser, with intent to commit theft, inflict GBH on any person in the building or commit criminal damage

▶ **Actus reus** of burglary under *s9(1)(a)* has three elements:
- **Entry**: *R v Collins (1973)*, *R v Brown (1985)*, *Ryan (1996)*
- (Into a) **building**: *B and S v Leathley (1979)*, or **part of a building**: *Walkington (1979)*
- as a **trespasser**: *Walkington (1979)*. Permission to enter: *Collins (1972)*, *Smith and Jones (1976)*

▶ **Mens rea** of burglary under *s9(1)(a)* has two elements:
- **Intention** or **recklessness** as to trespass
- **Ulterior intent**: intention to commit theft, GBH or damage to the building or its contents

▶ **Burglary under *s9(1)(b)***: Guilty if, having entered a building or part of a building as a trespasser, someone steals, attempts to steal or inflicts or attempts to inflict GBH on any person inside.

▶ **Actus reus** of burglary under *s9(1)(b)* has four elements:
- **Entry**: *R v Collins (1973)*, *R v Brown (1985)*, *Ryan (1996)*
- (Into a) **building**: *B and S v Leathley (1979)*, or part of a building: *R v Walkington (1979)*
- As a **trespasser**: *R v Walkington (1979)*, permission to enter: *R v Collins (1972)*, *R v Smith and Jones (1976)*
- **Actus reus of theft/GBH**, or attempted theft/GBH inside

▶ **Mens rea** of burglary under *s9(1)(b)* has two elements:
- **Intention** or **recklessness** as to trespass
- Mens rea for theft/GBH or attempt theft/GBH inside

Capacity defences

Spec reference	Key content	Assessment Objectives	Where does this topic feature on each specification/exam?
WJEC A Level 3.16: Defences **Eduqas A Level 2.3.5**: Capacity defences of insanity and intoxication **2.3.6** Necessity defences of self-defence, duress and duress of circumstances	• Capacity defences of insanity and intoxication • Intoxication by alcohol • Intoxication by drugs • Insanity • Automatism: insane and non-insane automatism • Necessity defences of self-defence, duress and duress of circumstances • Mistake • Self-defence • Duress by threat • Duress of circumstances • Necessity • Consent	**A01** Demonstrate knowledge and understanding of legal rules and principles **A02** Apply legal rules and principles to given scenarios in order to present a legal argument using appropriate legal terminology **A03** Analyse and evaluate legal rules, principles, concepts and issues	**WJEC A Level:** Unit 3; Section C; Unit 4; Section C **Eduqas A Level:** Component 2; Section C Component 3; Section C

KEY CASE

M'Naghten (1843)
Daniel M'Naghten had become so obsessed with the Prime Minister, Robert Peel, that he decided to shoot him, but he missed and shot and killed the Prime Minister's secretary, Edward Drummond, instead. He was found to be suffering from extreme paranoia, and was found not guilty by reason of insanity.

Criminal law defences: Capacity defence of insanity

The M'Naghten Rules were devised by the House of Lords following the ***M'Naghten*** case due to public outcry.

The defendant should be presumed sane unless, at the time of the offence, they can prove they were:

1. labouring under such a defect of reason
2. caused by a disease of the mind
3. that they did not know either the nature and quality of the act or, if they did know it, that they didn't know what they were doing was wrong.

1. Defect of reason

The courts have stated that there needs to be a complete absence of the power to reason. Absentmindedness or confusion is not sufficient. In ***Clarke (1972)***, a woman was accused of theft from a supermarket, but it was said that she was acting absentmindedly due to depression and diabetes. The court said the rules on insanity do not apply to those who retain the power to reason but don't use it in moments of confusion or absentmindedness.

2. Disease of the mind

This can be either a mental or physical disease which affects the mind. It is a legal term and not a medical one. Medical conditions such as schizophrenia are covered but so are many other conditions which would not be defined as being diseases of the mind in any medical sense; however, it must be caused by an **internal factor**.

In **R v Quick (1973)**, the condition was caused by an **external factor**, the drug insulin. Therefore, the defendant could rely on the defence of automatism and **not** insanity.

Voluntary intoxication

Where the defendant voluntarily takes an intoxicating substance which causes a temporary psychotic episode, the defence of **insanity cannot be used**. This is because the intoxicating substance is an **external factor**. The key cases of **R v Coley (2013)** and **R v Harris (2013)** illustrate this point well.

KEY CASE

R v Coley (2013)

The defendant, who was a regular cannabis user, attacked his neighbour and her partner with a knife. On arrest, he said he had blacked out and had no memory of what had happened. A psychiatric report suggested that he could have suffered a brief psychotic episode brought on by the taking of cannabis. The judge refused to accept the defence of insanity and Coley was convicted of attempted murder. The Court of Appeal upheld his conviction as the situation was one of voluntary intoxication and the abnormality was caused by an external act.

STRETCH AND CHALLENGE

To prepare for a discussion of the other conditions that can amount to a disease of the mind, research the key cases of **R v Kemp (1956)**, **Sullivan (1984)**, **Hennessy (1989)** and **Burgess (1991)**. Ensure you know the facts of these key cases and how the defence of insanity worked in each of them.

3. Nature and quality of the act

This refers to the physical character of the act. There are two ways in which the defendant would not know the physical character of the act:

1. they are in a state of unconsciousness or impaired consciousness; or

2. they are conscious but do not understand or know what they are doing, due to their mental condition.

If the defendant can show that either of these applied at the time of the act then this part of the M'Naghten rules is satisfied. Both defendants in **Kemp (1956)** and **Burgess (1991)** were in a state of lost consciousness, and the more recent case of **Oye (2013)** indicates a defendant not knowing the nature and quality of their act.

R v Oye (2013)

Oye was behaving strangely at a café and the police were called. On their arrival, Oye began throwing plates at the police, so he was arrested and taken to a police station. He continued to behave strangely, including drinking water out of a toilet cistern. When he was moved to the custody suite, he became angry and punched an officer in the face, breaking her jaw. Oye was charged with assault occasioning actual bodily harm and two accounts of affray.

Oye argued in his defence that he had believed the police were demons and agents of evil spirits. At his trial, medical evidence stated that Oye had had a psychotic episode and that he had not known what he was doing and/or that what he was doing was wrong. Despite this evidence and the judge directing the jury on the defence of insanity, Oye was found guilty. The Court of Appeal substituted a verdict of not guilty by reason of insanity.

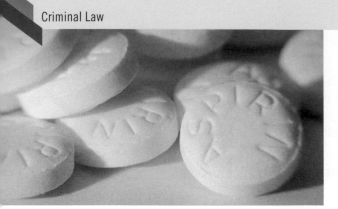

The defendants must prove they did not know what they were doing was legally wrong. If the defendant knows the nature and quality of the act and that it is legally wrong, they cannot use the defence of insanity, even if they are suffering from a mental illness, as in *R v Windle (1952)*.

R v Windle (1952)

The defendant gave his wife an overdose of aspirin. When the police arrived he said, 'I suppose they'll hang me for this!' This last statement was evidence that he knew what he was doing was wrong and he was hanged.

Windle was shown to know what he was doing was wrong and knew the punishment in law for his actions. The same logic was followed in *R v Johnson (2007)*.

R v Johnson (2007)

*The defendant forced his way into his neighbour's flat and stabbed him. He was charged with wounding with intent to do grievous bodily harm under the **Offences Against the Person Act 1861**. During his trial, two psychiatrists gave evidence that he was suffering from paranoid schizophrenia and hallucinations; however, both psychiatrists agreed that, despite these conditions, Johnson did know the nature and quality of his acts, and knew that what he had done was legally wrong. Johnson was convicted of wounding with intent. At the Court of Appeal, his conviction was upheld. The defence of insanity was not available in this case as Johnson knew the nature and quality of his acts and that they were legally wrong (that is, he knew that the act was contrary to law).*

The verdict

When a defendant successfully proves the defence of insanity, the jury must return a verdict of 'not guilty by reason of insanity'. Prior to 1991, the only punishment was a hospital order, which was not appropriate for those suffering with conditions such as diabetes and epilepsy.

The Criminal Procedure (Insanity and Unfitness to Plead) Act 1991 introduced new orders available to extend the options available to a judge. A judge can now impose a:

- hospital order without time limit (mandatory for murder)
- hospital order with time limit
- guardianship order
- supervision and treatment order
- absolute discharge.

Problems with the defence of insanity

- One of the main issues with the defence of insanity is that the definition of insanity was set in *M'Naghten*, a case dating back to 1843. At this time, medical knowledge was limited and, with advances in medical knowledge of mental disorders, a more modern definition should now be used.
- Another issue is that the definition of insanity is legal definition and not a medical one. Some defendants who should be regarded as insane are not (e.g. *R v Byrne (1960)*).
- On the other hand, defendants suffering with physical diseases like diabetes or even those who sleepwalk are considered insane (e.g. *R v Hennessy (1989)* and *R v Burgess (1991)*).
- Furthermore, the defendant has to prove insanity, which may breach *Article 6 European Convention on Human Rights* (the defendant is innocent until proven guilty).
- There is also a stigma to being labelled insane, yet it is the only defence available to many defendants.
- It is the jury's job to decide whether the defendant is insane and they are not really qualified to do this.

Reforming the defence of insanity

There have been several attempts at reforming the defence of insanity.

- **1953**: The Royal Commission on Capital Punishment suggested those with irresistible impulses would have been covered, but it never became law. Instead, the government introduced the defence of diminished responsibility but this is only available for murder charges.

- **1975**: The Butler Committee suggested it should be replaced by verdict of 'not guilty on evidence of mental disorder' but this never became law.

- **1989**: *Draft Criminal Code* suggested a defendant should be not guilty on evidence of severe mental disorder or handicap but it never became law.

- *The Criminal Procedure (Insanity and Unfitness to Plead) Act 1991*: This gave judges more discretion on disposals where the defendant uses the defence of insanity.

- **2012**: The Law Commission's paper on insanity and automatism offers alternatives but does not make any definite proposals.

Links with automatism

Insanity is also known as insane automatism; automatism is also known as non-insane automatism.

Insanity is caused by an internal factor; automatism is caused by an external factor.

The verdict for insanity is 'not guilty by reason of insanity' and will usually result in some form of treatment order. A successful plea of automatism will lead to a complete acquittal.

Criminal law defences: Automatism

For automatism to work as a defence, the actions of the defendant must be completely involuntary. In *Bratty v Attorney General for Northern Ireland (1963)*, it was defined as:

'an act done by the muscles without any control by the mind, such as a spasm, a reflex action or a convulsion; or an act done by a person who is not conscious of what he is doing such as an act done whilst suffering from concussion or whilst sleepwalking.'

Sleepwalking can be defined as automatism

There are two types of automatism:

1. **Insane automatism** is where the case of automatism is a disease of the mind within the M'Naghten rules. In such cases, the defence is insanity and the verdict is not guilty by reason of insanity.

2. **Non-insane automatism** is where the cause is **external** and where the defence succeeds it is a complete defence and the defendant is not guilty.

Non-insane automatism

This is a defence because the actus reus is not voluntary and the defendant does not have the required mens rea for the offence. For automatism to work as a defence, it must be caused by an **external factor** which makes the defendant totally lose control over their actions. Examples of external causes include a blow to the head, being attacked by bees or a prolonged sneezing fit.

In *Hill v Baxter (1958)*, the issue of no fault when the defendant was in an automatic state through an external cause was approved. The court approved the earlier decision in *Kay v Butterworth (1945)* that a person should not be convicted if, through no fault of their own, they lose control due to an external cause. In this case, the judge said:

'A person should not be made liable at the criminal law who, through no fault of his own, becomes unconscious when driving, as, for example, a person who has been struck by a stone or overcome by a sudden illness, or when the car has been put temporarily out of his control owing to his being attacked by a swarm of bees.'

In *T (1990)*, it was accepted that exceptional stress can be an external factor which may cause automatism, although the defence was not successful in this case.

In *Attorney General's Reference (No 2 of 1992) (1993)* reduced or partial control of one's actions is not sufficient to constitute non-insane automatism.

Attorney General's Reference (No 2 of 1992) (1993)

The defendant was a lorry driver who had been driving for several hours when he began to drive along the hard shoulder of the motorway. He drove along it for approximately half a mile, whereupon he hit a broken-down car and killed two people. He pleaded the defence of non-insane automatism, arguing that he was suffering from a condition called 'driving without awareness' which puts a driver in a trance-like condition. He was found not guilty by the jury. On a referral by the Attorney General to the Court of Appeal, on a point of law, the court ruled that, because his condition only caused partial loss of control, the defence of automatism could not be used.

External factors: Automatism and diabetes

In *R v Quick (1973)*, hypoglycemia was caused by an external factor as the defendant had taken his insulin but not eaten and then drunk alcohol. He was able to use automatism as a defence.

In *R v Hennessy (1989)*, hyperglycemia was caused by an internal factor (his diabetes), as he had not taken his insulin. He had to rely on the defence of insanity.

Self-induced automatism

The defence is unlikely to be available if the accused caused the automatism themselves.

R v Bailey (1983)

The defendant was in a hypoglycemic state as he had taken his insulin but not eaten. He then attacked his ex-girlfriend's new boyfriend with an iron bar. He knew the risks, as he had been feeling unwell, so his actions were regarded as reckless, and there was insufficient evidence to successfully raise the defence of automatism.

In *R v Hardie (1984*, see page 80), the defendant had taken Valium, which would normally have a calming effect but instead it made him very agitated, and he set his ex-girlfriend's flat on fire. He was allowed to use the defence of automatism as he had thought that the Valium would calm him down, which is its normal effect, so therefore he had not been reckless.

If the automatism is caused by drink or drugs, the defence will not be available.

STRETCH AND CHALLENGE

Compare *T (1990)* with *Burgess (1991)*. What are the differences in these cases?

Proposals for reform

One of the main problems with the defence of automatism is that in each case it has to be decided whether the situation is one of insane or non-insane automatism.

In July 2012, the Law Commission published a paper on the defences of insanity and automatism. The paper pointed out that the two defences are closely related and that if the defence of insanity is reformed then the defence of automatism must be reformed at the same time.

Exam Skills

The defence of insanity and automatism could feature on the WJEC A Level units 3 and 4 exams and Eduqas A Level components 2 and 3 exams.

Ensure you are able to **analyse** and **evaluate** the defence of insanity and automatism and that you are also able to **apply** the legal rules and principles of the defence of insanity and automatism to given scenarios.

Criminal law defences: Intoxication

This defence covers intoxication by alcohol, drugs or other substances (e.g. glue-sniffing).

As a general rule, if a person is voluntarily intoxicated and commits a crime, there is no defence.

Intoxication is relevant as to whether or not the defendant has the required mens rea for the offence. If the defendant does not have the required mens rea because of their intoxicated state, they may not be guilty; however, this depends on whether the intoxication was voluntary or involuntary and whether the offence charged is one of specific or basic intent.

Voluntary intoxication and specific intent offences

These are crimes where intention is required in addition to the basic offence. For example, *s18 Offences Against the Person Act 1861* is grievous bodily harm (GBH) or malicious wounding with intention to cause GBH.

Voluntary intoxication can negate the mens rea for a specific intent offence. If the defendant is so intoxicated that the mens rea for the offence is not formed, they are not guilty.

DPP v Beard (1920)

The defendant had been charged with murder. He argued in his defence that he was too intoxicated to have formed the mens rea for the murder. He was convicted but, on appeal, Lord Birkenhead stated the rule that still applies today:

'If he was so drunk that he was incapable of forming the intent required, he could not be convicted of a crime which was committed only if the intent was proved.'

R v Sheehan and Moore (1975) is a good example of where it was held that the defendants were so drunk that they did not have the mens rea for murder:

The defendants had thrown petrol over a tramp and set fire to him. They were too drunk to have formed any intent to kill or cause GBH; therefore, as they did not have the mens rea for murder, they were able to use intoxication as a defence. However, they were found guilty of manslaughter as that is a basic intent offence.

This usually means the charge is reduced rather than escaping liability. For example, in ***R v Lipman (1970***, see page 81**)**, where he killed his girlfriend while hallucinating on the drug LSD, he was convicted of manslaughter instead of murder.

Also bear in mind ***AG for Northern Ireland v Gallagher (1963)***, where it was held that drunken intent is still intent. The defendant bought a knife to kill his wife and drank a large amount of whisky to give him the courage to do it. He was convicted of murder.

Voluntary intoxication and basic intent offences

Where the offence is one of basic intent, intoxication is **not** a defence. This is because, as said in the key case of ***DPP v Majewski (1977)***, voluntarily becoming intoxicated is considered a reckless course of conduct, and recklessness is enough to constitute the necessary mens rea.

Fotheringham (1989)

The defendant had been out drinking. On his return home, he climbed into bed with the 14-year-old babysitter who was sleeping in his bed. He started to have sexual intercourse with her in the mistaken belief that it was his wife. On appeal, his conviction for rape was upheld. Rape is a crime of basic intent and therefore his drunken mistake could not be relied on in his defence.

Involuntary intoxication

This covers situations where the defendant did not know they were taking an intoxicating substance, for example spiked drinks. It also covers situations where prescribed drugs have the unexpected effect of making the defendant intoxicated

It was said in ***R v Pearson (1835)*** that 'If a party be made drunk by stratagem, or the fraud of another, he is not responsible.' Therefore, there may be defence for basic and specific intent crimes.

R v Hardie (1985)

The defendant set light to a wardrobe after consuming some Valium tablets which had been prescribed to his girlfriend. He took the Valium because he was feeling stressed that his partner had asked him to leave their home. He was charged with arson.

At his trial, he stated that he remembered nothing about starting the fire due to his intoxicated state, but accepted that he must have started it as he was the only one in the room when it started. The trial judge directed the jury that, as the defendant had voluntarily consumed the Valium, his intoxication could be no defence to the crime.

KEY CASE

DPP v Majewski (1977)
The defendant had taken large amounts of drugs and alcohol before attacking the landlord of the pub where he was drinking, and then police officers who came after receiving a call from the landlord. The House of Lords held that getting drunk is a reckless course of conduct and recklessness is sufficient to constitute the necessary mens rea for assault.

Hardie successfully appealed that he had not been reckless. It was held that the actions in this case did not necessarily amount to voluntary intoxication. Parker LJ said:

'Valium is wholly different in kind from drugs which are liable to cause unpredictability or aggressiveness ... if the effect of a drug is merely soporific or sedative the taking of it, even in some excessive quantity, cannot in the ordinary way raise a conclusive presumption against the admission of proof of intoxication for the purpose of disproving mens rea ...The jury should have been directed that if they came to the conclusion that, as a result of the Valium, the appellant was, at the time, unable to appreciate the risks to property and persons from his actions, they should then consider whether the taking of the Valium was itself reckless.'

Compare *R v Hardie (1985)* with *R v Allen (1988)*.

R v Allen (1988)

Allen had consumed some homemade wine, which had a much greater effect on him than he anticipated. He committed several sexual assaults and claimed he was so drunk he did not know what he was doing. He argued that he had not voluntarily placed himself in that condition, as the wine was much stronger than he realised. The court held that the intoxication was still voluntary even though he had not realised the strength of it. The crime of sexual assault is one of basic intent and therefore the appellant was unable to rely on his intoxicated state to negate the mens rea.

The test, therefore, is: 'Did the defendant have the necessary mens rea when they committed the offence?' If the answer is 'yes', then the defendant will be guilty.

R v Kingston (1994)

The defendant's coffee was drugged by a couple who were in dispute with him over business matters and wanted to blackmail him. The defendant was invited to abuse a 15-year-old boy who had been set up by the blackmailers. The defendant abused the boy and was photographed doing so by the blackmailers. The House of Lords upheld his conviction for sexual assault, saying:

'There is no principle of English law which allows a defence based on involuntary intoxication where the defendant is found to have the necessary mens rea for the crime. The prosecution had established the defendant had the necessary intent for the crime – a drunken intent is still intent.'

Intoxicated mistake

If the defendant makes a mistake due to intoxication, it will depend what the mistake was as to whether the defence is available. Where the mistake means the defendant did not have the necessary mens rea for the offence, they have a defence when the offence is one of specific intent. However, where the offence is one of basic intent, there is no defence, as seen in *Lipman (1970)*.

R v Lipman (1970)

The appellant had taken some LSD. He was hallucinating and believed he was being attacked by snakes and descending to the centre of the earth. While in this state, he killed his girlfriend by cramming bed sheets into her mouth. The court held that his intoxication could be used to demonstrate that he lacked the mens rea for murder, as murder is a crime of specific intent. His intoxication, however, **could not** be a defence to manslaughter, as that is a crime of basic intent.

R v O'Grady (1987)

O'Grady was an alcoholic and had spent the day drinking large quantities of alcohol with two friends. The friends then went to O'Grady's house to sleep. O'Grady claimed he was woken by one of the friends hitting him on the head. He said that he picked up some broken glass and started hitting his friend in order to defend himself. He said he only recalled hitting him a few times. O'Grady then said the fight ended and he cooked them both some food before going back to sleep. In the morning, he found his friend dead. The death was caused by loss of blood: he had 20 wounds to his face in addition to injuries to his hands and a fractured rib. There was also severe bruising to his head, brain, neck and chest.

*O'Grady was convicted of manslaughter. His appeal was dismissed and the conviction upheld because a defendant is not entitled to rely, as far as self-defence is concerned, upon a **mistake of fact which has been induced by voluntary intoxication**. The judge said:*

'There are two competing interests. On the one hand, the interest of the defendant who has only acted according to what he believed to be necessary to protect himself, and on the other hand, that of the public in general and the victim in particular who, probably through no fault of his own, has been injured or perhaps killed because of the defendant's drunken mistake. Reason recoils from the conclusion that in such circumstances a defendant is entitled to leave the court without a stain on his character.'

The ruling in ***O'Grady*** was confirmed in ***R v Hatton (2005)***.

R v Hatton (2005)

The defendant had drunk over 20 pints of beer. He and the victim went back to Hatton's flat. In the morning, Hatton found the victim dead with injuries caused by being hit with a sledgehammer. Hatton said he couldn't remember what had happened but thought that the victim had tried to attack him and that he was defending himself. Hatton was convicted of murder. The Court of Appeal upheld his conviction and stated that the decision in O'Grady was not limited to basic intent crimes but also applied to specific intent crimes. A defendant's drunken mistake cannot be relied on for the purposes of self-defence.

Problems with the defence of intoxication

The decision in ***DPP v Majewski (1977)*** is that a person is reckless and therefore guilty if they get drunk, but this does not comply with the principle that the actus reus and mens rea of a crime must coincide.

- Usually, if recklessness is sufficient for the mens rea, the defendant needs to be aware of the risk, but this is not the case with intoxication.
- Where there is a lesser offence, the charge will be reduced to a basic intent crime, but where there is no lesser offence the defendant escapes liability.

Exam Skills

The defence of intoxication could feature on the WJEC A Level units 3 and 4 exams and Eduqas A Level components 2 and 3 exams

Ensure you are able to **analyse** and **evaluate** the defence of intoxication and that you are also able to **apply** the legal rules and principles of the defence of intoxication to given scenarios.

Criminal defences: Necessity defences of duress and duress of circumstances

This defence exists where the defendant is put under considerable pressure to commit a crime or face death or serious injury to them or another for whom they feel responsible, and the defendant is faced with a terrible dilemma. The problem is that the defendant commits the actus reus with the mens rea, so the defence takes the circumstances into account.

Duress can be used as a defence to all crimes **except** murder, manslaughter and perhaps treason.

The defence takes two different forms:

1. **Duress by threats**: This consists of direct threats to the defendant to commit a crime or face death or serious personal injury to themselves or another.

2. **Duress of circumstances**: This consists of external circumstances that the defendant believes constitute a serious threat.

There are some similarities to the defence of necessity (see page 88).

KEY CASES

DPP for Northern Ireland v Lynch (1975)
It was originally held in this case that the defence of duress was available to a secondary party on a charge of murder. The defendant was ordered by Meehan, a member of the terrorist group the IRA, to drive a car. The defendant did not know Meehan personally but knew of his reputation and knew that he would be shot if he did not comply. Three armed men in got into the car and the defendant drove them as directed. The three men then shot and killed a policeman. The defendant was convicted of murder, the trial judge having ruled that the defence of duress was not available in the circumstances. The Court of Appeal dismissed the appeal and the defendant appealed to the House of Lords, where his appeal was allowed, ruling that the defence of duress is available to a participant to murder who does not personally do the act of killing.

R v Howe and others (1986)
However, in this case the House of Lords ruled that the defence in *DPP for Northern Ireland v Lynch (1975)* was not available to anyone charged with murder, even if they were only a secondary party and had not done the killing themselves.
Howe and Bailey, aged 19, and Bannister, aged 20, were acting under orders of Murray, aged 35. The charges related to two murders. The first murder related to 17-year-old Elgar, who was being tortured. Howe and Bannister kicked and punched Elgar and were told they would receive similar treatment if they did not do as Murray ordered. Elgar might have died of his injuries if Bailey hadn't then strangled him. The second killing took place the following night at the same location, when Murray ordered Howe and Bannister to strangle a 19-year-old man and they complied. The House of Lords, upholding their convictions for murder, said that the defence of duress is not available for murder, for either the principal or secondary offender.

R v Gotts (1982)
A 16-year-old boy was ordered by his father to kill his mother, otherwise his father would shoot him. He stabbed his mother, causing serious injuries, but she survived. He was charged with attempted murder and the trial judge ruled that the defence of duress was not available to him. He pleaded guilty and then appealed the judge's ruling. His appeal was dismissed and his conviction upheld. The House of Lords held that the defence of duress was not available for attempted murder. Lord Griffiths said:
'We face a rising tide of violence and terrorism against which the law must stand firm, recognising that its highest duty is to protect the freedom and lives of those that live under it. Attempted murder requires proof of an intent to kill, whereas in murder it is sufficient to prove an intent to cause really serious injury. It cannot be right to allow the defence to one who may be more intent upon taking a life than the murderer.'

1. Duress by threats

The courts have to consider the seriousness of the harm that the accused has been threatened with and the criminal behaviour they commit.

In deciding if the defence should succeed, the jury must consider a **two-stage test** laid down in *R v Graham (1982)* and approved of in *R v Howe (1987)*:

- **Subjective test**: Did the defendant feel they had to act the way they did because they reasonably believed they would face death or serious personal injury?
- **Objective test**: Would a sober person of reasonable firmness with the same characteristics as the defendant respond in the same way as the defendant?

R v Graham (1982)

The defendant lived in a flat with his wife, Mrs Graham (the victim), and his gay lover, King. The defendant suffered from anxiety attacks for which he was prescribed Valium. King was of a violent disposition and both the defendant and his wife were frightened of him and had experienced violence from him. On one occasion, King attacked Mrs Graham with a knife and the defendant intervened, sustaining cuts to his hands. As a result of the attack, Mrs Graham went to stay with the defendant's mother. King and the defendant began drinking heavily and the defendant also took a large quantity of Valium. King then told the defendant it was time to get rid of Mrs Graham for good. Together, they devised a plan. The defendant phoned up Mrs Graham and told her that he had cut his wrists and to come round straight away. When she arrived, King strangled her with a wire. The defendant helped by holding onto the wire. He then helped King to dispose of the body. King pleaded guilty to murder and was sentenced. The defendant raised the defences of duress and intoxication. In relation to duress, the defendant raised an argument which was supported by medical evidence that his anxiety and intake of Valium would have made him more susceptible to threats. He was still found guilty. On appeal, his conviction was upheld on the grounds that the fact that a defendant's will to resist has been eroded by the voluntary consumption of drink or drugs or both should not be taken into account.

The threat must be of death or serious personal injury. The cumulative effect of threats can be considered by the court, as in *R v Valderrama-Vega (1985)*.

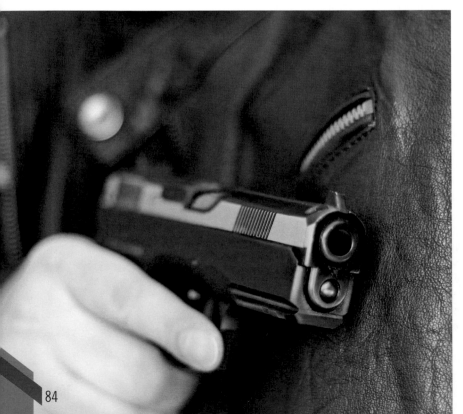

R v Valderrama-Vega (1985)

The defendant had been convicted of importing drugs. He had done so because he had received threats of serious violence against him and his family if he did not comply. There were also threats to reveal his homosexual activities to his wife. He also received financial rewards for his action. The trial judge refused to allow the defence of duress to be put before the jury. He appealed his conviction. The appeal was allowed. Threats to reveal his homosexuality alone would be insufficient to support the defence of duress but could be taken into account when coupled with threats of serious personal violence, as was the case here.

The threat must be unavoidable

- In *R v Gill (1963)*, the defendant had the opportunity to inform the police between the threats and carrying out the crime, so could not use the defence.

- In *R v Hudson and Taylor (1971)*, the defence was allowed because the threat was still operating when the defendants were giving evidence in the court, as they believed it could be carried out immediately.

- *R v Hasan (2005)* stated the current law, which takes a stricter approach, as in *Gill*. Here the defendant joined a criminal gang so was unable to use the defence when he was threatened because he should have realised that could happen.

The threat must be operative at the time of committing the crime

R v Abdul-Hussain (1999)

The defendants were Shi'ite Muslims who had fled from Iraq to Sudan because of the risk of punishment and execution because of their religion. They feared they would be sent back to Iraq so they hijacked a plane, which landed in the UK. The defendants were charged with hijacking and pleaded the defence of duress. The trial judge ruled that the defence could not be used as they were not in sufficiently close and immediate danger, so they were convicted. The Court of Appeal quashed their convictions, holding that the threat need not be immediate, but it had to be imminent in the sense that it was 'hanging over them'.

2. Duress of circumstances

This defence was first recognised in *R v Willer (1986)* and confirmed in *R v Conway (1988)*.

R v Willer (1986)

The defendant's car was surrounded by a gang of youths, who threatened him. He drove along the pavement as his only route of escape but was convicted of reckless driving. The Appeal Court allowed duress of circumstances.

R v Conway (1988)

Two men ran towards the defendant's car. The defendant's passenger had been shot at a few weeks earlier so he considered the two men to be a threat. He drove off and was charged with reckless driving. His appeal was successful and duress of circumstances was allowed as a defence.

In *R v Martin (1989)*, the court stated that the two-stage test in *R v Graham (1982)* for duress by threats also applies to duress of circumstances.

R v Martin (1989)

The defendant had driven while disqualified from driving. He claimed he did so because his wife threatened to commit suicide if he did not drive their son to work. His wife had previously attempted suicide and the son was late for work and she feared he would lose his job if her husband did not get him to work. Martin pleaded guilty to driving while disqualified following a ruling by the trial judge that the defence of duress of circumstances was not available to him. On appeal, his conviction was quashed as the defence of duress should have been available to him. It did not matter that the threat of death arose through suicide rather than murder.

In *R v Pommell (1995)*, the court ruled that the defence was available to all offences except murder, manslaughter and treason. In *R v Cairns (1999)*, the defendant had been driving a car. It was surrounded by a group of youths, one of whom threw himself on the bonnet. The defendant, feeling threatened, drove off and the man on the bonnet was injured. The court said, when establishing the defence of duress of circumstance, the defendant needed only to show a reasonable and genuine perception of a threat of serious physical injury, not necessarily that the threat was genuine.

Problems with duress

- The defence is not available for murder but there are situations where it might be necessary and unjust to not allow it.
- *R v Hasan (2005)* has narrowed the circumstances in which the defence can be available which may mean it is not available to those who need it.
- A defendant's low IQ is not considered by the court following *R v Bowen (1996)*.
- *R v Hudson and Taylor (1971)* shows that, even where the defendant is surrounded by police protection, they may not consider this more powerful than the threat.

Criminal defences: Self-defence

This defence not only covers the actions needed to defend oneself from an attack, but also actions taken to defend another person. The defences of self-defence and defence of another are common law defences; in addition, there is also a statutory defence.

Section 3 Criminal Law Act 1967: Statutory defence

'*A person may use such force as is reasonable in the circumstances in the prevention of crime or in assisting in the lawful arrest of offenders or suspected offenders, or of persons unlawfully at large.*'

The amount of force that can be used in self-defence, defence of another or in the prevention of crime is set out in *s76 Criminal Justice and Immigration Act 2008*.

Factors taken into account when deciding whether the force used was reasonable in the circumstances include:

- a person acting for a legitimate purpose may not be able to weigh to a nicety the exact measure of necessary action; and
- evidence of someone having only done what they honestly and instinctively thought was necessary for a legitimate purpose constitutes strong evidence that only reasonable action was taken by that person for that purpose.

Section 76 allows that a person facing an attack is under stress and cannot be expected to work out the exact amount of force needed in the circumstances. If there is evidence that the person 'honestly and instinctively' thought the level of force was reasonable to protect themselves or another, or to prevent a crime, this is strong evidence that the action was reasonable in the circumstances.

However, if the force is used after all danger is over (e.g. for revenge or retaliation), this defence is not available.

Hussain and another (2010)

The defendant's house was broken into and he and his family were threatened by armed men. The defendant and one of his sons managed to escape and chased the armed men as they ran from the house. They caught one of the men and beat him up. It was held that they could not use the defence of self-defence as all danger to them from the original attack was over.

Householder cases

Section 43 Crime and Courts Act 2013 has amended **s76 Criminal Justice and Immigration Act 2008** to allow for a wider defence to householders where an intruder enters their property. In such cases, the degree of force will **only** be regarded as unreasonable where its use was 'grossly disproportionate'.

To be a householder case, the:

- force must be used by the defendant while in, or partly in, a building that is a dwelling
- defendant must not be a trespasser
- defendant must have believed the victim to be a trespasser.

Self-defence and excessive force

The amount of force used to defend oneself or another must be reasonable. If the force is excessive the defence will fail.

R v Clegg (1995)

Clegg was a soldier on duty in Northern Ireland. A car, with its headlights on full beam, sped towards him at the checkpoint he was manning. One of the soldiers with Clegg shouted for the car to stop, but it did not. Clegg fired three shots at the car and a further shot as the car passed him. The final shot hit and killed a passenger in the back of the car. Clegg could not use self-defence as a defence because evidence showed that the car had gone past him by the time he fired the last shot so there was no danger when he fired the shot. The force was regarded as excessive and his murder conviction was upheld. In 1999, Clegg's case was sent back to the Court of Appeal by the Criminal Cases Review Commission and his conviction was quashed as new evidence cast doubt on whether Clegg actually fired the fatal shot.

R v Martin (Anthony) (2002)

Martin shot two burglars who had broken into his remote farmhouse, killing one of them. Evidence showed that the burglars were leaving when Martin shot them, and that the one who died had been shot in the back. Martin was found guilty of murder. He appealed, arguing he should have been allowed to use the defence of self-defence as he was suffering from a paranoid personality disorder which made him think he was in a very dangerous situation. His appeal was rejected by the Court of Appeal, which held that personality disorders could not be taken into account when considering the defence of self-defence. His conviction was, however, subsequently reduced to manslaughter on the grounds of diminished responsibility.

Relevance of the defendant's characteristics

As seen in *R v Martin (2002)*, his appeal was rejected by the Court of Appeal, which held that personality disorders could not be taken into account when considering the defence of self-defence.

This decision was followed in *R v Cairns (2005)*, where the court held that, when deciding whether the defendant had used reasonable force in self-defence, it was not appropriate to take into account whether the defendant was suffering from a psychiatric condition.

The law in *R v Martin (2002)* and *R v Cairns (2005)* was upheld in *R v Oye (2013*, see page 75).

Mistaken use of force in self-defence

In *R v Williams (Gladstone) (1987)*, the defendant had to have a 'genuine' mistaken belief which may or may not be reasonable.

R v Williams (Gladstone) (1987)

The defendant witnessed what he thought was a fight and intervened, saying he was a police officer and trying to make an arrest. In fact, one of the people involved had just mugged a woman and the other was trying to arrest him. The defendant was prosecuted for assaulting the victim but the jury was told he could only use the defence of mistaken force in self-defence if it was reasonable. On appeal, the court said that the jury should have been told that, if they believed it was a genuine mistake, they should decide the case on this basis, and Williams was able to use the defence of protection of others.

GRADE BOOST

Visit the Crown Prosecution Service (CPS) website (www.cps.gov.uk) and read the CPS paper 'Self-defence and the Prevention of Crime' (2011). What were the findings in this paper?

KEY CASE

R v Dudley and Stephens (1884)
Four people were shipwrecked miles from land. Three weeks later, the two defendants, being the stronger men, killed and ate the cabin boy in order to survive. They were rescued four days later and were charged with murder on their return to England. They used necessity as a defence. Although that defence was not allowed, the usual sentence of death was lowered to six months imprisonment in recognition that they were faced with a terrible dilemma.

Criminal defences: Necessity

This is a very limited defence, as the courts have generally not been prepared to accept it.

Defendants are placed in a position where they believe they have to commit an offence to prevent a worse evil from happening. The original case where necessity was raised is the key case of *R v Dudley and Stephens (1884)*.

Although there is not much move to recognise this as a defence in criminal cases, there has been more recognition of its availability in civil cases.

Re F (Mental Patient: Sterilisation) (1990)

F was a 36-year-old woman. She had a serious mental disability caused by an infection when she was a baby. She had been a voluntary in-patient at a mental hospital since the age of 14. She had the verbal capacity of a child of two and the mental capacity of a child of four. When she developed a sexual relationship with a fellow patient, her mother and medical staff at the hospital were concerned that she would not cope with pregnancy and childbirth and would not be able to raise a child herself. Methods of contraception other than sterilisation were not practical for her so they sought a declaration that it would be lawful for her to be sterilised. F was incapable of giving valid consent since she did not appreciate the implications of the operation.

The declaration was granted. It would be lawful for the doctors to operate without her consent.

Re A (Conjoined Twins) (2000)

Mary and Jodie were conjoined twins, joined at the pelvis. Jodie was the stronger of the two and capable of living independently. However, Mary was weaker and was completely dependent on Jodie for her survival. According to medical evidence, if the twins were left as they were, Mary would eventually be too much of a strain on Jodie and they would both die. If they operated to separate them, this would inevitably lead Mary's death, but Jodie would have a strong chance of living an independent life. The parents refused consent for the operation to separate them. The doctors applied to the court for a declaration that it would be lawful and in the best interests of the children to operate. The High Court granted the declaration on the grounds that the operation would be the same as a withdrawal of support, that is, an omission rather than a positive act and also that the death of Mary, although inevitable, was not the primary purpose of the operation. The parents appealed to the Court of Appeal but the appeal was dismissed. The operation could be lawfully carried out by the doctors.

Four circumstances were developed where necessity would be permissible:

1. Where an act was done only to avoid consequences which could not otherwise be avoided.

2. The consequences would have inflicted inevitable and irreparable evil.

3. No more was done than was reasonably necessary for the purpose.

4. The evil inflicted was not disproportionate to the evil avoided.

The defence of necessity was also considered in *R v Shayler (2001)* where a further criterion for the defence to be available was added to those in *Re A (2000)*:

- The evil must be directed towards the defendant or to someone for whom they had responsibility.

R v Shayler (2001)

The defendant was a member of MI5 who had disclosed official secrets. He argued it was out of necessity to improve the efficiency of MI5, but he did not fulfil the criteria for necessity, so therefore he could not use the defence.

Following *Southwark London Borough Council v Williams (1971)*, Lord Denning stated that allowing the defence of necessity would 'open a door that no man could shut' and would give an excuse for all types of behaviour.

Although there are questions about this defence, the Law Commission in the *Draft Criminal Code* states: 'We are not prepared to suggest that necessity should in every case be a justification; we are equally unprepared to suggest that necessity should in no case be a defence.'

Criminal defences: Mistake

To use mistake as a defence, the defendant must have made a mistake in the facts and not a mistake in the law: 'Ignorance of the law is no excuse', as stated in *R v Reid (1973)*.

There are several points to note here for the defence to work:

- The mens rea of the offence must be made negative by the mistake.
- The defence can be used where the defendant's actions can be excused or justified in some way.
- A statute may also specifically provide for instances where the defendant has a 'lawful excuse'.

The mistake must be reasonable, as shown in the following cases, along with *R v Williams (Gladstone) (1987*, see page 88).

R v Tolson (1889)
The defendant thought her husband was dead and married someone else. Her husband returned and she was prosecuted for bigamy. She appealed and her conviction was quashed as her actions were considered to be natural and legitimate by the court and in no way immoral. The court allowed the defence of mistake but did stress that the mistake had to be both reasonable and honest.

DPP v Morgan (1976)
The defendant was a senior officer in the RAF and told three of his junior officers to go to his house and have sex with his wife. He assured them that it would be fine, despite their concerns. They followed his orders despite the woman's severe protests, resulting in their prosecution. At their trial, the judge told the jury that their belief in the wife's consent had to be reasonable. On appeal, the court said that the judge's direction was incorrect and that the belief only had to be genuine and not necessarily reasonable. Their convictions were still upheld.

Mistake and intoxication

Mistake cannot be used as a defence where the defendant is voluntarily intoxicated. In *R v O'Grady (1987*, see page 82), the court held that an intoxicated mistake regarding how much force could be used in self-defence did not provide a defence. *R v Fotheringham (1989*, page 80) is another example.

Criminal defences: Consent

Consent is often used as a defence to non-fatal offences against the person. It can never be a defence to murder or serious injury.

R v Donovan (1934)
The defendant caned a 17-year-old girl for sexual gratification, causing bruising. He was convicted of indecent assault and common assault. On appeal, his conviction was quashed as the victim had consented to the act.

R v Slingsby (1995)
The defendant was charged with involuntary manslaughter. The defendant and victim had taken part in 'vigorous sexual activity', which the victim had consented to. During the activity a ring worn by the defendant caused small cuts to the victim which led to blood poisoning, from which she later died. The victim's consent meant there was no battery or assault, so the defendant was not guilty of manslaughter as there was no unlawful act.

There must be **true consent**. In **R v Tabassum (2000)**, the defendant had persuaded women to allow him to measure their breasts for the purpose of compiling a database for sale to doctors. While the women were aware of the act, they had only consented because they thought that the defendant had a medical qualification or training.

A victim submitting through fear does not mean that consent is real. In **R v Olugboja (1982)**, the victim and her friend had been raped by the defendant's friend. When the defendant tried to have sex with her, she submitted. The defendant claimed that this was consent but the Court of Appeal held there was a difference between real consent and mere submission.

In **R v Dica (2004)**, consent was given to sexual intercourse without knowledge of the fact that the defendant was HIV positive. The Court of Appeal held that there was no consent to the risk of the infection.

Implied consent

The courts will consider that some injuries are impliedly consented to by everyone in society. In **R v Wilson v Pringle (1987)**, the court held that ordinary 'jostlings' of everyday life were not battery. Sports injuries, during properly conducted games and sports, also fall into this category.

R v Barnes (2004)
*The defendant made a tackle on the victim during an amateur football game. The victim suffered a serious leg injury. The defendant's conviction under **s20 Offences Against the Person Act 1861** was quashed on appeal. The Court of Appeal said that, where an injury is caused during a match, a criminal prosecution should be kept for those situations where the conduct was sufficiently bad to be properly categorised as criminal.*

GRADE BOOST

See also **R v Konzani (2005)** for more about consent and HIV.

Exceptions

The question is whether it is in the public interest to allow an exception or not.

In *Attorney General's Reference (No 6 of 1980) (1981)*, where two men had agreed to fight in the street to settle their differences following an argument, the Court of Appeal held that consent could not be a defence to such an action as it was not in the public interest.

It is now accepted that consent is not a defence to a *s47 Offences Against the Person Act 1861* offence unless it falls within one of the exceptions listed in *Attorney General's Reference (No 6 of 1980) (1981)*:

- Properly conducted games and sports.
- Lawful chastisement or correction.
- Reasonable surgical interference.
- Dangerous exhibitions.

The list is not exhaustive and the courts have also recognised tattooing, rough horseplay, ear-piercing and male circumcision as valid exceptions.

Consent to minor injuries

The question is whether it is in the public interest to allow such an exception or not.

In *R v Brown (1993)*, the House of Lords held that consent was **not** a defence to gay sadomasochistic acts, even though they were all adults and the injuries inflicted were minor and transitory.

Compare this with *R v Wilson (1997)*, where the Court of Appeal held that, where a defendant had branded his initials on his wife's bottom with a hot knife at her request, this was not an unlawful act, even though she had to have medical treatment for the burns caused. The court held it was not in the public interest that such consensual behaviour should be criminalised.

Mistaken belief in consent

Provided the defendant genuinely believes the victim has consented, there is a defence to an assault even if they are mistaken in this belief.

R v Jones (1986)

Two boys aged 14 and 15 were tossed into the air by older boys. One suffered a broken arm and the other ruptured his spleen. The defendants argued that they believed that the two boys had consented to the activity. On appeal, their convictions for offences under s20 Offences Against the Person Act 1861 were quashed. The court decided that a genuine mistaken belief in consent could be a defence and that this fell into the recognised exception of rough horseplay.

The courts have proposed a case-by-case approach, which could make the law very uncertain.

Consent and euthanasia

No one can consent to their own death. This means that, if a terminally ill person wants to die, they must take their own life. If anyone kills them, it is murder. Even if someone helps them to take their own life, that person is guilty of the offence of assisting suicide. This was decided in *R (on the application of Pretty) v DPP (2001)*.

Exam Skills

These defences could feature on the WJEC A Level units 3 and 4 exams and Eduqas A Level components 2 and 3 exams.

Ensure you are able to **analyse** and **evaluate** the all the criminal law defences and that you are also able to **apply** the legal rules and principles of the various defences to given scenarios.

Summary: Capacity defences

Insanity and automatism

▶ **Definition**: *M'Naghten (1843)*:
  - defect of reason
  - disease of the mind
  - not knowing nature and quality of act or they are doing wrong

▶ Insanity and automatism overlap

▶ For **insanity**, defence must prove, on the balance of probabilities, defendant has a defect of reason due to disease of the mind
  - Verdict not guilty by reason of insanity
  - Judge can make one of four orders

▶ For **automatism**, defendant must raise the defence and the prosecution must disprove it:
  - Must be caused by an external factor
  - If not guilty, defendant is free (unlike insanity)

Intoxication

▶ Specific intent crimes: **Voluntary intoxication**:
  - If defendant has mens rea, they are guilty: *R v Gallagher (1963)*
  - If defendant has no mens rea, they are not guilty

▶ Specific intent crimes: **Involuntary intoxication**:
  - If defendant has mens rea, they are guilty: *R v Kingston (1994)*
  - If defendant has no mens rea, they are not guilty: *R v Hardie (1984)*

▶ Specific intent crimes: **Drunken mistake**:
  - If the mistake negates mens rea, the defendant is not guilty.
  - If the mistake is about the need to defend oneself, it is not a defence and the defendant will be guilty, in both specific and basic intent offences: *R v O'Grady (1987)*, *R v Hatton (2005)*

▶ Basic intent crimes: **Voluntary intoxication**:
  - Defendant is guilty as becoming intoxicated is a reckless course of conduct: *R v Majewski (1977)*

▶ Basic intent crimes: **Involuntary intoxication**:
  - Defendant is not guilty as they have not been reckless: *Hardie (1984)*

▶ Basic intent crimes: **Drunken mistake**:
  - Defendant is guilty as it is a reckless course of conduct

Duress

▶ Can be by threats or circumstances

▶ Available for all offences except murder (*R v Howe (1987)*) and attempted murder (*R v Gotts (1992)*)

▶ Threat must be serious (death or serious injury), but can consider cumulative effect of other threats with threat of injury: *R v Valderrama-Vega (1985)*

▶ Two tests: **objective** and **subjective**: *R v Graham (1982)*

▶ Threat does not need to be immediate but it must be **imminent**

▶ Duress not available where:

- defendant joins a criminal gang they know is violent: *R v Sharp (1987)*, *R v Hasan (2005)*

- defendant puts themselves in a position where they foresaw, or should have foreseen, the risk of being subject to compulsion

Consent

▶ Not a defence for murder or *s18 Offences Against the Person Act 1861*

▶ Generally not a defence to the offences in *s20* and *s47 Offences Against the Person Act 1861*, but there are exceptions (e.g. properly conducted sports, surgery, tattoos)

▶ Allowed as a defence for battery

▶ There must be true consent: *R v Tabassum (2000)*

▶ Can be implied to the everyday 'jostlings' of life: *R v Wilson and Pringle (1987)*

Necessity and self-defence

▶ **Definition** of necessity: circumstances force a person to act to prevent a worse evil

▶ Doubts whether necessity is a defence in its own right, but **forms basis of other defences**

▶ Must be **reasonable force** to defend oneself or another. If the force is excessive, the defence will fail

▶ Defence of necessity is only recognised as duress of circumstances in **criminal law**: *Dudley v Stephens (1884)*

▶ Civil cases recognise defence of necessity: *Re A (Conjoined twins) (2000)*

Preliminary offences of attempt

Spec reference	Key content	Assessment Objectives	Where does this topic feature on each specification/exam?
WJEC A Level **3.17:** Preliminary offences of attempt **Eduqas A Level** **2.3.7:** Preliminary offences of attempt	• Statutory definition; mens rea and actus reus; meaning of 'more than merely preparatory' • Attempts to do the impossible	**AO1** Demonstrate knowledge and understanding of legal rules and principles **AO2** Apply legal rules and principles to given scenarios in order to present a legal argument using appropriate legal terminology **AO3** Analyse and evaluate legal rules, principles, concepts and issues	**WJEC A Level:** Unit 3; Section C. Unit 4; Section C **Eduqas A Level:** Component 2; Section C. Component 3; Section C

Preliminary offences of attempt

An **attempt** is where a person tries to commit an offence but for some reason fails to complete it. Attempt is defined in **s1 Criminal Attempts Act 1981**:

'if, with intent to commit an offence to which this section applies, a person does an act which is more than merely preparatory to the commission of the offence, he is guilty of attempting to commit the offence.'

The **actus reus** of the offence is: a person does an act which is more than merely preparatory to the commission of an offence.

The **mens rea** is: with intent to commit that offence.

Actus reus of attempt

Before the definition in the **Criminal Attempts Act 1981**, two main tests came from the courts:

- **Last act test**: Had the defendant done the last act they could do before committing the crime?

- **Proximity test**: Were the defendant's acts ' so immediately connected' to the actus reus of the offence as to justify liability for attempt?

The courts have now held these common law tests to be irrelevant. The important point is whether the defendant has done an act which is 'more than merely preparatory'.

More than merely preparatory
The act has to be more than merely preparation for the main crime. There have been many cases on the meaning of 'merely preparatory' but there is no single clear principle that comes from them.

Attorney General's Reference (No 1 of 1992) (1993)
The defendant dragged a girl to a shed with the intent of raping her. He lowered his trousers and assaulted the girl but did not rape her. His conviction for attempted rape was upheld. It was held that the defendant need not have performed the last act before the crime proper, nor need he have reached the 'point of no return'.

R v Gullefer (1987)

The defendant jumped onto a greyhound racetrack to try to stop a race so it could be declared void and he could claim back the money he had bet. His conviction for attempting to steal was quashed because his action was merely preparatory to committing the offence and he had not 'embarked on the crime proper'.

R v Geddes (1996)

The defendant was found in the boys' toilets in a school in possession of a large knife, some rope and masking tape. He had no right to be in the school. He had not spoken to or contacted any pupils.

The Court of Appeal asked two questions:

1. Had the accused moved from planning or preparation to execution or implementation?

2. Had the accused done an act showing that he was actually trying to commit the full offence, or had he only got as far as getting ready, or putting himself in a position, or equipping himself to do so?

Geddes' conviction for attempted false imprisonment was quashed on appeal.

R v Campbell (1990)

The defendant was outside a post office with an imitation gun, wearing sunglasses and with a threatening note in his pocket. His conviction for attempted robbery was quashed on appeal.

Going beyond more than merely preparatory

The following cases show where a defendant has gone beyond more than merely preparatory.

R v Boyle and Boyle (1987)

The defendants were found standing next to a door with a broken lock and hinge. Their conviction for attempted burglary was upheld. Trying to gain entry was an attempt, and they were embarking on the crime proper.

R v Tosti (1987)

The defendant, intending to burgle premises, took metal-cutting equipment with him and hid it behind a nearby hedge. He then examined the padlock on the door but did not damage the padlock. He was found guilty of attempted burglary.

R v Jones (1990)

The defendant's partner told him she wanted to end their relationship because she was seeing someone else (the victim). The defendant bought a gun, got into the victim's car wearing a crash helmet, obscuring his face, and pointed the gun at the victim. The victim grabbed the gun and threw it out of the window. The defendant's conviction for attempted murder was upheld.

Mens rea of attempt

Normally, the defendant must have the same intention as would be required for the full offence. If the prosecution cannot prove that intention then the defendant is not guilty of attempt.

R v Easom (1971)

The defendant picked up a bag in a cinema, looked through it and put it back without taking anything. There was no evidence that the defendant had intended to permanently deprive and therefore could not be guilty of attempted theft.

R v Husseyn (1977)

The defendant and another man were seen hanging around the back of a van. When approached by the police they ran off. The defendant was convicted of attempting to steal equipment that was in the van. The Court of Appeal quashed his conviction.

However, see **Attorney General's Reference (Nos 1 and 2 of 1979)**, where the Court of Appeal decided that, if a defendant had a conditional intent (they intended stealing if there was anything worth stealing), they could be charged with an attempt to steal.

Mens rea of attempted murder

For attempted murder, the prosecution must prove an intention to kill (to cause GBH is not enough for attempted murder, it must be to kill). This is shown in **R v Whybrow (1951)**, where the defendant wired up his wife's bath and caused her to have an electric shock. He was convicted of attempted murder.

Is recklessness enough to satisfy the mens rea of attempt?

R v Millard and Vernon (1987)

The defendants pushed many times against a fence on a stand at a football ground. The prosecution said they were trying to break it and they were convicted of criminal damage but the Court of Appeal quashed their convictions. It was held that recklessness is not enough for the mens rea for attempted criminal damage.

Attorney General's Reference (No 3 of 1992) (1994)

*The defendant threw a petrol bomb towards a car with four men inside. The bomb missed and harmlessly hit a wall. He was acquitted at first because the judge said that it had to be proved that the defendant intended to damage property **and** to endanger life. On appeal, the Court of Appeal said that the trial judge was wrong. While it was necessary to prove he intended to damage property, it was only necessary to prove that he was reckless as to whether life would be endangered. He was therefore convicted of attempting to commit arson with intent to endanger life.*

Attempting the impossible

Section 1(2) Criminal Attempts Act 1981 says:

'A person may be guilty of attempting to commit an offence ... even though the facts are such that the commission of the offence is impossible.'

STRETCH AND CHALLENGE

Research the House of Lords decision on impossibility in **Anderton v Ryan (1985)**, overruled a year later in **R v Shivpuri (1986)**. Do you think the House of Lords was correct to overrule its previous decision in **Anderton v Ryan**?

Problems with the law on attempt

It is not always clear in deciding the dividing line between what is merely preparatory and what is an attempt. Due to the wording in the **Criminal Attempts Act 1981**, which states that the defendant must do an act, that attempt cannot be committed by an omission (a failure to act). Should a defendant be guilty where it is impossible for them to commit the full offence?

Exam Skills

This topic could feature on the WJEC A Level units 3 and 4 exams and Eduqas A Level components 2 and 3 exams.

Ensure you are able to **analyse** and **evaluate** the preliminary offences of attempt and that you are also able to **apply** the legal rules and principles of the preliminary offences of attempt to given scenarios.

Summary: Preliminary offences

▶ An attempt is where a person tries to commit an offence but fails to complete it: defined in *s1 Criminal Attempts Act 1981*

▶ **Actus reus**: a person does an act which is more than merely preparatory to the commission of an offence

▶ **Mens rea**: person has intent to commit that offence

▶ Problems with the law on attempt:

  • Not always clear what is merely preparatory and what is an attempt

  • Should a defendant be guilty where it is impossible for them to commit the full offence?

Exam practice and techniques

There is a degree of overlap between the assessments in Eduqas AS, Eduqas A Level and WJEC Law, with similar questions but variations in the wording, weighting of Assessment Objectives and timings. The Assessment Objectives (AOs) are the same on both the Eduqas and WJEC specifications.

- **AO1:** You must **demonstrate knowledge and understanding** of legal rules and principles.
- **AO2:** You must **apply** legal rules and principles to given scenarios in order to present a legal argument using appropriate legal terminology.
- **AO3:** You must **analyse and evaluate** legal rules, principles, concepts and issues.

How exam questions are set

The WJEC and Eduqas specifications in Law aim to encourage students to:

- develop and sustain their enjoyment of, and interest in, law
- develop knowledge and understanding of selected areas of law and the legal system in England and Wales
- develop an understanding of legal method and reasoning
- develop the techniques of logical thinking, and the skills necessary to analyse and solve problems by applying legal rules
- develop the ability to communicate legal arguments and conclusions with reference to appropriate legal authority
- develop a critical awareness of the changing nature of law in society
- gain a sound basis for further study
- develop knowledge of the rights and responsibilities of individuals as citizens including, where appropriate, an understanding of moral, spiritual and cultural issues
- develop, where appropriate, skills in communication, application of number and information technology
- improve, where appropriate, their own learning and performance, to facilitate work with others and solve problems in the context of their study of law.

Examination questions are written by the principal examiner responsible for the unit well in advance of the examination. A committee of experienced examiners discusses the quality of every question and changes are made to the questions until the committee agrees that they are appropriate. The questions are written to reflect the substantive content and success criteria outlined in the specification.

Exam answers are marked in relation to three AOs. The sample assessment questions for each paper on AS Eduqas Law, A Level Eduqas Law and WJEC Law explain the marks available under each AO.

Improving your exam performance

There are a few important things to remember, and common errors made by law students.

Read the instructions

There is a mixture of compulsory questions and questions where you can choose which question to answer. It is important to answer the correct number of questions and to choose your questions wisely. Rubric errors will get you no marks.

AO1: You must demonstrate knowledge and understanding of legal rules and principles

Questions where AO1 marks are available are generally testing your knowledge and understanding of a topic, and command words such as **explain**, **describe** and **outline** are all indicative of this.

AO2: You must apply legal rules and principles to given scenarios in order to present a legal argument using appropriate legal terminology

Questions where AO2 marks are available are generally testing your ability to apply your knowledge and understanding of a topic to a given scenario in order to reach a conclusion. They use the command words **apply** or **advise**. Use legal authority to support your answers.

AO3: You must analyse and evaluate legal rules, principles, concepts and issues

Questions where AO3 marks are available generally require you to provide a **balanced** argument. There will always be an opportunity to look at two sides of an argument, and you should make sure that you explore both sides thoroughly. The command words **analyse** and **evaluate** are indicative of this requirement. The examiner is looking for a reasoned, balanced argument, supported with relevant legal authority, and a rounded conclusion.

Take time over your introduction

For an extended essay answer, it is good practice to write a strong introduction because it shows the examiner that you understand the topic from the start. Do not fall into the trap of writing a 'waffly' introduction; spend a couple of minutes thinking and planning before you begin to write.

Begin with a definition of the key terms contained in the question. Some examples are highlighted below:

To what extent does the Misrepresentation Act 1967 protect buyers against negligent statements made by sellers? Analyse and evaluate whether the law on murder should be reformed.

"The courts in recent years have developed a completely clear set of principles for deciding whether an offence should be one of strict liability." Discuss.

Analyse and evaluate the burden that the law on vicarious liability imposes on employers.

Use cases to add legal authority

Use as much **legal authority** as you can remember. This is especially important when you are being tested on your skills of application (AO2) and analysis and evaluation (AO3). You also need to make sure you explain the relevance of the case.

Example: *R v Young (1995)*

Answer A

Another disadvantage of juries is that you do not know how the jury arrived at their verdict. This was seen in the case of *R v Young (1995)*.

Answer B

Another disadvantage of juries is that you do not know how the jury arrived at their verdict. This was seen in the case of *R v Young (1995)*, where the jury used a Ouija board to contact the dead victim.

The highlighted section of Answer B shows that the candidate knows and understands the relevance of the case, whereas the candidate in Answer A has just used the case to support their point and not actually progressed to showing **how**.

Where possible, try to cite the legal authority in full. An attempt at citation will be credited, but obviously it is more appropriate to learn the cases and relevant legal authority.

Answer A

Another disadvantage of the jury system is that you do not know how the jury reached their verdict as was seen in the case where the jury used a Ouija board.

Answer B

Another disadvantage of juries is that you do not know how the jury arrived at their verdict. This was seen in the case of *R v Young (1995)*, where the jury used a Ouija board to contact the dead victim.

It is quite clear that the candidate who wrote Answer A knows the case, but the candidate who wrote Answer B has actually cited it in full, making it clear to the examiner that there is an **excellent** or **good** knowledge, rather than just a **basic** knowledge.

Show you are aware of recent developments

Be aware of recent reforms, criticisms and current affairs in the area. Your lecturer may have made you aware of some such reports and news, but it is always good practice to keep abreast of recent developments.

Only answer the question that has been asked

Make sure you answer the question. Many candidates will have learned essays by heart and then merely repeat this answer in the examination, only to find that it does not actually answer the question at all. Read and reread the question to ensure that your planned answer is actually what is required.

Expect topics to be combined

When you are revising, be careful if you decide to omit certain topics. It is possible that a question may be asked which combines topics, and you may find that you can answer **part a** but have not done enough revision to answer **part b** as competently. Look back over past papers and see what combination of topics have been asked.

Use stimulus material with care

Where there is stimulus material, you are required to use it as a source to support what you are saying but, ultimately, you are being examined on **your** knowledge. Rewriting a table in your own words, or quoting copious amounts from the source is not going to get you any marks.

Use terminology correctly

You will be marked on your appropriate use of legal terminology and your understanding of core legal principles, yet candidates often make very simple errors. Do you know the difference between:

- CJEU and ECHR?
- CPS and CPR?
- Guilty and liable?
- Magistrates and juries?

As obvious as these errors may seem, they are very common, so make sure you have a good grasp of definitions. It is also important to check your spelling, especially of commonly misspelt words like:

- defendant
- sentence
- precedent
- trial.

The format of the exam

If you are studying Law in Wales then you are probably entered for WJEC papers. In England, you will almost certainly be studying for the Eduqas qualification. Check with your teachers which examination you are entered for because there are differences in the papers and the expectations for each vary a great deal.

The separate examinations are known as **components** (Eduqas) or **units** (WJEC).

WJEC papers in Law

If you are studying for a WJEC paper then your AS paper is a building block for A2. Your marks for AS will contribute to your overall examination grade. The AS papers offer slightly less challenge than A2 papers so the skills you display at A2 will be at a higher level. There may be reference to Welsh examples on examination papers and you are encouraged to use Welsh-based examples where applicable.

Below is a summary of the different papers for WJEC A Level.

WJEC units for A Level Law
A Level Law with WJEC builds upon the skills developed at AS. It consists of a further two papers, Unit 3 and Unit 4, and is worth 60% of the overall A Level.

UNIT 3: The Practice of Substantive Law
- Written examination: 1 hour 45 minutes.
- 30% of qualification.
- 100 marks available.

This unit requires you to learn about **two areas** of substantive law. You will need to ensure you answer the questions only on the areas you have studied. The options are:

- human rights law (Section A)
- the law of contract (Section B)
- criminal law (Section C).

The Unit 3 exam will test your knowledge and understanding of legal rules and principles in relation to the two areas of substantive law you have studied. Unit 3 examines your ability to explain the law (AO1 skills) and apply that law to a given hypothetical scenario (AO2 skills).

- The examination offers a choice of two questions per section. You therefore need to answer a total of two questions, one per section, based on the areas of law you have studied. For example, you could answer one question from Section A (human rights law) and one question from Section C (criminal law).
- Each question is worth 50 marks and you should spend approximately 52½ minutes on each question.
- Each question examines your knowledge and understanding (AO1 skills) and your ability to apply the law (AO2 skills).

UNIT 4: Substantive Law Perspectives

- Written examination: 2 hours.
- 30% of qualification.
- 100 marks available.

This unit requires you to learn about **the same two areas** of substantive law as you did for Unit 3. You will need to ensure you answer only the questions about the areas you have studied. The options are:

- human rights law (Section A)
- the law of contract (Section B)
- criminal law (Section C).

The Unit 4 exam will test your knowledge and understanding of legal rules and principles in relation to the two areas of substantive law you have studied. Unit 4 examines your ability to explain the law (AO1 skills) and analyse and evaluate the law (AO3 skills).

- The examination offers a choice of two questions per section. You therefore need to answer a total of two questions, one per section, based on the areas of law you have studied. For example, you could answer one question from Section A (human rights law) and one question from Section C (criminal law).
- Each question is worth 50 marks and you should spend approximately one hour on each question.
- Each question examines your knowledge and understanding (AO1 skills) and your ability to analyse and evaluate the law (AO3 skills).

WJEC assessment weightings for AS and A Level

Assessment objective weightings are shown below as a percentage of the full A Level, with AS weightings in brackets.

	AO1	AO2	AO3	Total
AS Unit 1	10% (25%)	7.5% (18.75%)	7.5% (18.75%)	25% (62.5%)
AS Unit 2	6% (15%)	4.5% (11.25%)	4.5% (11.25%)	15% (37.5%)
A Level Unit 3	12%	18%	–	30%
A Level Unit 4	12%	–	18%	30%
Overall weighting	**40%**	**30%**	**30%**	**100%**

Eduqas components for A Level Law

The separate examinations are known as components. For the full A Level, there are three components.

Below is a summary of the different papers for Eduqas A Level.

Eduqas A Level Law
COMPONENT 1: The Nature of Law and the English Legal System

- Written examination: 1 hour 30 minutes.
- 25% of the A Level law qualification.
- 60 marks available.

This component focuses on the structure of the English legal system, including its relationship with the European Union. You will also learn about the different sources of primary and secondary law in the English legal system and will consider how those laws are used by judges to make decisions. You will also develop a knowledge and understanding of the criminal justice system, civil justice system (including relevant legal personnel) and legal funding.

This component also includes a study of the nature of law: the distinction between enforceable legal rules and principles and other rules and norms of behaviour; criminal and civil law; and the different sources of law (including custom, statutory law and common law). The nature of law is widespread throughout this component and reference should be made to it, where appropriate, in your examination responses. The nature of law includes law and society, law and morality, and law and justice.

The examination for Unit 1 is broken down into two sections.

Section A focuses on the nature of law and the various methods of law making in the English legal system, including its relationship with the European Union.

- You should spend approximately 45 minutes on this section of the exam.
- You are required to answer two compulsory questions, each worth 5 marks, and one question from a choice of two, worth 15 marks.
- You should spend approximately 9 minutes on each of the two compulsory questions (questions 1 and 2) and 27 minutes on **either** question 3 **or** 4.
- **Questions 1** and **2** examine your knowledge and understanding (AO1 skills).
- **Questions 3** and **4** examine application of legal principles of and rules to a given scenario (AO2 skills).

Section B focuses on key features of the criminal and civil justice systems within the English legal system, including legal personnel and legal funding. It also includes the nature of law.

- You should spend approximately 45 minutes on this section of the exam.
- You are required to answer one question consisting of a **part a** and a **part b** from a choice of two. The question totals 25 marks, with 10 marks for part a and 15 marks for **part b**.
- You should spend approximately 18 minutes on **part a** and approximately 27 minutes on **part b** of your chosen question.
- **Part a** examines your knowledge and understanding (AO1 skills).
- **Part b** examines your analysis and evaluation of legal rule, principles, concepts and issues, and the nature of law (AO3 skills).

COMPONENT 2: Substantive Law in Practice

- Written examination: 2 hours 15 minutes.
- 37.5% of the A Level Law qualification.
- 75 marks available.

This component requires you to study **three areas of substantive law (including at least one public law area and at least one private law area)**. There are four sections and you need to answer three questions in total, each from a different section. They are all scenario-style questions.

It is important that you only answer questions on the areas of private or public law that you have studied and that you answer questions on the same areas in the exams for both Component 2 and Component 3. The options are:

- **Section A:** Law of contract (private law)
- **Section B:** Law of tort (private law)
- **Section C:** Criminal law (public law)
- **Section D:** Human rights law (public law).

Each of your chosen examination questions consists of one question testing both AO1 (knowledge and understanding) and AO2 skills (application of legal rules and principles to the scenario).

Each question is worth 25 marks and you should spend approximately 45 minutes on each of the three answers.

COMPONENT 3: Perspectives of Substantive Law

- Written examination: 2 hours 15 minutes.
- 37.5% of the A Level Law qualification.
- 75 marks available.

This unit requires you to study **three areas of substantive law (including at least one public law area and at least one private law area)**. There are four sections and you need to answer three questions in total, each from a different section. They are all essay-style questions.

It is important that you only answer questions on the areas of private or public law that you have studied and that you answer questions on the same areas in the exams for both Component 2 and Component 3. The options are:

- Section A: Law of contract (private law)
- Section B: Law of tort (private law)
- Section C: Criminal law (public law)
- Section D: Human rights law (public law).

Each of your chosen examination questions consists of one question testing both AO1 (knowledge and understanding) and AO3 skills (analyse and evaluate legal rules, principles, concepts and issues).

Each question is worth 25 marks and you should spend approximately 45 minutes on each of the three answers.

Eduqas assessment weightings for A Level Law

	AO1	AO2	AO3	Total
Component 1	10%	7.5%	7.5%	25%
Component 2	15%	22.5%	–	37.5%
Component 3	15%	–	22.5%	37.5%
Overall weighting	40%	30%	30%	100%

Sample practice questions and answers

This section uses sample questions from the specimen assessment materials (SAMs) published by the WJEC/Eduqas. They represent the different questions that can feature on each paper of the WJEC/Eduqas specifications. **The question numbers reflect those in the SAMs so do not follow a logical order within this book.**

Sample answers are supplied for each question: a stronger response and a weaker one. You can refer to the mark schemes in the SAMs while you work through these sample answers.

The responses are not the work of students but have been written by the authors of this book to provide a framework for the commentary. The commentary reflects the opinions of the authors alone and has not been produced by the examination board.

WJEC A2 Law: Unit 3

Unit 3 papers require you to answer two questions from two different sections, reflecting the areas of substantive law you have studied. For example, you could answer one question from Section A (human rights) and one question from Section C (criminal law). Each question is worth 50 marks and it is suggested you spend about 52½ minutes per question. The questions are problem-style and are examining **AO1 Knowledge and understanding** and **AO2 Application skills**.

WJEC A2 Law: Unit 3 Section A

Question 2

PC Smith and PC Walker were sitting in their police car when Llyr walked past wearing a hoodie and carrying a full plastic shopping bag. PC Smith said, 'Let's get him,' and shouted to Llyr, 'Stop now; thief!' PC Walker grabbed Llyr's arm roughly, took the plastic bag from him and opened it. Within the bag were several tablet computers and a few mobile phones. PC Smith said to Llyr, 'Get in the car, you're coming with us.' Llyr complied, and was driven to the police station.

On the way in the car, Llyr explained that members of the tennis club he was a member of were donating their old electronic products to raise money for the refugee crisis in Syria and that he had been helping out. When they arrived at the police station, Llyr asked to be allowed to contact his fiancée, who would be worried, and consult a solicitor. The custody officer said that he was not able to contact his fiancée and would have to wait to speak to a solicitor until the police had finished questioning him. Llyr was then detained for 52 hours, during which time he was interviewed for lengthy periods without a break and with no food or water. The police took Llyr's fingerprints and a mouth swab which they informed him would be kept indefinitely on police records. At the end of that time, the police told Llyr that he would be bailed pending further enquiries.

In light of reported case law and other sources of law, advise Llyr as to the legality of the actions of the police. [50]

The command word **advise** requires you to briefly explain a legal concept and then apply it to the scenario in order to provide advice.

Question 2 stronger response

Under **s1–3 Police and Criminal Evidence Act 1984**, PC Smith and PC Walker are allowed to stop and search Llyr if they have reasonable belief or suspicion that he is carrying stolen or prohibited articles, which he was. Under **s117** they are also permitted to use reasonable force and seize any prohibited articles as contained in Code A.

Section 24 Police and Criminal Evidence Act 1984 was amended by the **Serious Organised Crime and Police Act 2005** with the leading case being O'Hara (2002). PC Smith and PC Walker must have reasonable belief that Llyr has, is, or is about to, commit an offence and have reasonable grounds to believe that the arrest is necessary – that is to prevent the disappearance of Llyr, to prompt the swift investigation of the cases, to prevent harm to others or to prevent harm or interference to witnesses and evidence. The guidelines for this are contained in Code G. However, under **s28** of the Act, PC Smith and PC Walker must inform Llyr he is under arrest even if the reason is perfectly obvious, as in Christie v Leachinsky (1947), but it is not clear that they do this and therefore, if they don't, this is in breach of the Codes.

Upon arriving at the station, Llyr should be met by a custody officer under sections 36 and 37, who will decide whether there is enough evidence to charge him or detain him for further questioning or to grant bail under **s38**. However, it is not clear if Llyr is met by this person straight away.

Llyr asks to contact his fiancée and, under **s56 Police and Criminal Evidence Act 1984**, he is entitled to have someone informed of his arrest. However, this may be delayed for up to 36 hours if it is an indictable offence or if PC Smith and PC Walker believe it would interfere with witnesses or harm evidence. Llyr is also entitled to have access to a duty solicitor free of charge. However, this may also be delayed for up to 36 hours under **s58**, under the same circumstances as in R v Samuel (1988) and R v Alladice (1988). Under **s41 Police and Criminal Evidence Act 1984**, Llyr should only be detained for questioning for 96 hours before charging. This was briefly amended in 2011 in the Hookway case but that was held to undermine the reality of policing and was therefore reversed under the **Detention and Bail Act**, which means that, for the 96 hours, the clock would stop in between sessions. However, under the new **Policing and Crime Act 2017**, Llyr may only be held on bail for 28 days without charge. Beyond that there is an extension of three months if authorised by a senior police officer. Anything beyond three months requires authorisation of a magistrate.

At the station, Llyr should be treated according to Code C. The cell he is placed in should be adequately lit and heated with access to toilets and washing facilities. When questioned, Llyr should not be required to stand and should be given breaks every two hours during questioning, which he is not. Llyr should also be given two light meals and one main meal in a period of 24 hours and should be allowed a continuous break of eight hours, which he is not, and therefore this could affect the outcome of the case. Under **s40** of the Act, Llyr's detention should also be reviewed first at six hours and then every nine hours following this.

The candidate shows good practice by stating the law and then applying it to the situation. This is a helpful structure to use in problem-style questions and shows off AO1 (Knowledge and understanding) as well as AO2 (Application skills).

This shows really good knowledge of bail, including up-to-date and current laws relating to police bail without charge.

There should be reference to the consequences of the police breaching the requirements of the Police and Criminal Evidence Act 1984.

If Llyr's DNA had been taken under **s64**, the police are allowed to compare it to data already available to them in the DNA National Database. However, the storage of this was seen as a breach of **Article 8 ECHR** (the right to privacy) in the case of **Marper v UK (2008)**, where it was stated that only the DNA of convicted defendants could be stored indefinitely.

The police can grant bail to Llyr under **s38 Police and Criminal Evidence Act 1984** and ask him to comply with certain conditions, for example, reporting to the police station, a curfew or tagging. Any breach of the codes under **s78** must be taken very seriously and must be substantial to affect the case.

> This is a bit waffly in places and does not really make it clear what s78 stipulates and how breaching s78 would affect the admissibility of the evidence in court.

> This would achieve a high level 3 or low level 4 mark as there is mostly accurate description of the law for AO1 (Knowledge and understanding) with application to the scenario for AO2 (Application skills).

Question 2 weaker response

As Llyr was wearing a hoodie and carrying a full plastic shopping bag, PC Smith and PC Walker must have had a general suspicion about what Llyr was carrying in his bag and that he had carried out an illegal act. So far, Llyr is innocent and has not done anything wrong except walking past. However, if the police have reasonable suspicion they have a right to stop and search under Code C. By PC Smith saying 'Let's get him', there was no reason to say this. It looks like the police targeted Llyr because he was wearing a hoodie and carrying a full plastic bag. Llyr was then stopped and searched but the police did not explain to Llyr why he was being searched. PC Smith then saying 'Get in the car, you are coming with us' was wrong as there was no reason why they were arresting Llyr which most definitely should have been stated under Code G. Llyr obeyed and, once they arrived at the police station, Llyr asked to contact his fiancée and consult a solicitor. The custody officer said he would have to wait. Llyr should have been allowed to contact his fiancée, making her aware of his arrest as it is his human rights to make a phone call. Llyr should also have been allowed to contact a solicitor. Llyr was then detained for 52 hours which is legal as he can be kept for up to 96 hours if given the right to do so by the Crown Court or judges. However, Llyr was not allowed a break while being interviewed for lengthy periods as he should have been allowed a short break. Llyr had no food or water which he should have been granted if requested.

I believe the police breached a duty of care to Llyr while in police custody as he was denied the right to contact his fiancée and consult a solicitor, which he requested. Llyr was also denied food and water while being detained and was not allowed a break, therefore there was no legality to the actions of the police.

> The candidate has quoted Code C incorrectly.

> Knowledge of the Codes is commendable, but it only shows convincing knowledge when it is correct and also supported with sections from the relevant Act.

> Again, there is a lot of rehash of the facts in the question and no reference to any legal authority or supporting sections from the Police and Criminal Evidence Act 1984.

> The answer is starting to get repetitive and there is no legal authority given for detention rights in custody or reference to the taking of DNA. There is also little reference to the law relating to police bail and the requirements of s38 Police and Criminal Evidence Act 1984.

> There is no reference here to the consequences of the breach of police powers in relation to the admissibility of evidence in court.

> This answer does not include much legal authority and the description of the law is basic for AO1 (Knowledge and understanding). There is some attempt at application for AO2 (Application skills) but this is high level 1/low level 2.

WJEC A2 Law: Unit 4

Unit 4 papers require you to answer two questions from two different sections, reflecting the areas of substantive law you have studied. For example, you could answer one question from Section A (human rights) and one question from Section C (criminal law). Each question is worth 50 marks and it is suggested you spend an hour (60 minutes) per question. The questions are essay-style and are examining **AO1 Knowledge and understanding** and **AO3 Analysis and evaluation skills**.

WJEC A2 Law: Unit 4 Section C

Question 6

Analyse and evaluate the criteria used by the courts in deciding whether Parliament intends an offence to be one of strict liability.   [50]

The command words '**analyse** and **evaluate**' require you to critically evaluate legal issues by identifying different perspectives, supporting the identification of the strongest viewpoint and demonstrating your ability to counter alternative viewpoints. Legal authorities should be used to support your arguments.

Question 6 stronger response

It is presumed that all crimes must have an actus reus (guilty act) and a mens rea (guilty mind). However, it is possible for some crimes to have an actus reus only. These are called strict liability crimes. Within this group of crimes are a selection called absolute liability where not only need there not be a mens rea but also the actus reus need not even be voluntary.

In **Larsonneur (1933)**, a French National was deported from England to Ireland. However, the Irish authorities would not allow her to stay and she was immediately sent back to England, where she was arrested. She was found guilty as she was in England. How she got there (voluntarily or not) was irrelevant. Similarly, in **Winzar v Chief Constable of Kent**, Winzar was taken to hospital, where he was identified as being drunk. He was told to leave the hospital but fell asleep in a corridor. The police were called and walked him to the highway, where they arrested him for being 'drunk on the highway'. In the case of **Pharmaceutical Company of Great Britain v Storkwain**, the pharmacist dispensed drugs from a forged prescription. They did not know it was forged but were still convicted. Their appeal failed and this demonstrates the courts' role in determining whether an offence is one of strict or absolute liability.

All the above cases illustrate absolute liability, which show that the mens rea need not be present and the actus reus need not be voluntary. I will look now at strict liability cases where mens rea is not required. In **Gammon (Hong Kong) v Attorney General**, it was held that the starting point for courts is to presume that mens rea is always needed but that this presumption can be rebutted by considering four factors. The court's role is central. In this case, builders had deviated from plans and part of a building fell down. They hadn't meant to deviate or for the building to collapse but that was irrelevant – they had done it and so they had the actus reus. The problem with English statutes is that they don't always state whether a crime is strict liability or not. It is up to the judge using the questions below and statutory interpretation, such as the literal rule or mischief rule to decide. It is important to look at the wording and the intended meaning of Parliament.

A strong opening paragraph where the candidate does well to focus on strict liability and the presumption of mens rea. The candidate also brings in the additional concept of absolute liability offences.

The candidate has correctly identified and considered a range of case law here to illustrate absolute liability. They have done well to get the case titles, facts and conclusion correct, making a link to the question posed. The candidate writes concisely and to the point.

In this successful paragraph, the candidate has correctly explained how the actus reus doesn't need to be voluntary for absolute liability offences. The candidate has then correctly progressed to consider strict liability, which is the main focus of this question. The presumption of mens rea is introduced, along with the role that judges play using the Gammon guidelines. This is important as it focuses the answer back on the question. The candidate's explanation and use of key terminology is very good and is well focused on the question (though they could refer to the specific wording of the question).

This part of the answer is very good indeed, with a sophisticated evaluation of the four factors. The candidate includes correct case law and explains these cases' relevance to the concept of strict liability. The level of depth demonstrates knowledge and understanding, such as considering a range of words in factor 1 that indicate whether a crime is one of strict liability or not. This provides strong focus on the question.

In this paragraph, the candidate has considered the fairness of strict liability to enhance the analysis evaluation. The candidate has used a couple of good cases to substantiate their assertions. They make a nice point about mistake being no defence.

Here, the candidate has considered some advantages and disadvantages of strict liability which, though not strictly required for the question, enhance the answer. The candidate has done well to limit the time spent on this aspect as it is not the primary focus of the question. To focus this paragraph better on the question, lack of consistency from judges could have been considered (along with the cases of Lim Chin Aik and Smedleys v Breed).

The candidate has given a conclusion, which is an essential element of an essay question. They have summarised some of the main aspects, though it could have been a little longer. The candidate also hints at inconsistency but could have discussed some case law in relation to this earlier in their answer.

The four Gammon questions judges ask are:

1. Does the statute through the words used imply that it is strict liability? This means, do the words 'intentionally' or 'knowingly' appear in the statute or is it 'cause' or 'possession', which would mean the crime is strict liability? The case of **Alphacell v Woodward** demonstrates this, where a company caused polluted matter to enter into a river. They hadn't meant to do this and had installed a filter which became clogged with leaves but they were the ones who had caused it.

2. Is the offence regulatory or a true crime? With regulatory offences, there is generally not much stigma attached (e.g. speeding). The case of **Sweet v Parsley** held that true crimes are criminal and have a stigma attached (such as losing your job because of the conviction).

3. Is there a public or social concern aspect to the crime? This may be something like selling alcohol or lottery tickets to underage people, as in the case of **Harrow v Shah**.

4. What is the penalty for the crime? In the case of **Gammon**, there was a $HK250,000 fine or a five-year prison sentence but this was exceptional as the fines are usually small. The smaller the fine (as with speeding), the more likely a case is to be classed as strict liability.

In some ways, strict liability can seem unfair as in the case of **Callow v Tillstone**. The butcher sold bad meat but had asked his vet to check the meat to see if it was fit for human consumption. The vet said it was so he sold it. However, it was found not to be fit for human consumption and the butcher was fined. The fine was only small but the effect on his reputation must have been a lot greater. He had taken due care but had still committed the actus reus and so was guilty. Nowadays, there can be a defence of due diligence for certain offences. Mistake, however, is no defence. A case involving a mistake while selling alcohol is **Cundy v Le Coq**, where it was evident that the person was drunk and shouldn't have been sold alcohol.

There are various advantages and disadvantages to strict liability. An advantage is that it promotes care and attention but, conversely, some people are convicted even when they have taken all reasonable steps to avoid committing an offence. Larger companies sometimes continue to pay small fines as they have little impact on their finances, whereas small companies can be affected both by the fine and damage to their reputation. Once someone realises that there is no defence and courts start imposing larger fines, behaviour will change. A good example of this is wearing seatbelts in cars. Some years ago, lots of people would not wear a seatbelt but, since the law changed and there are lots of fines, most people now wear one.

To look back at the question, it is important to have a consistent approach when it comes to judges determining if a crime requires mens rea or not. Parliament is sovereign yet judges have been the ones to determine the scope of strict liability law. Absolute liability crimes seem the most unfair but, with strict liability, because it is up to judges, they can also be inconsistent and unfair, unless precedent is set and followed.

This answer displays excellent knowledge and understanding and would, therefore, achieve a mark in band 4 for AO1. For AO3, the answer does not quite achieve band 5 but would achieve a high band 4 mark as it displays a very good analysis of legal rules, principles, concepts and issues relevant to the question, very good evaluation of the debates surrounding the question, including a valid judgement, and very good use of supporting case law and legal authorities
If they had included a point about lack of consistency and some contrasting case law, the candidate might have achieved band 5 for AO3. There were also some missed opportunities to focus on the question.

Question 6 weaker response

The majority of crimes require an actus reus and mens rea. These are a guilty act and a guilty mind. For example, the actus reus for murder is unlawful killing of a human being and the mens reus for murder is malice aforethought or, for GBH, it is 'unlawful wounding recklessly or intentionally'. It is the decision of the court to see if there needs to be an actus reus and a mens rea.

Actus reus means guilty act and in English law and it is not a crime to fail to act unless under a duty to do so. There are, as a result, some crimes which require a certain result to be guilty, such as murder, where the victim has to die. There are also action crimes, where the result doesn't matter, as in perjury, where lying under oath is enough to be convicted even if the lie has no impact on the case. There are also 'duty to act' situations, where a person is under a duty to act and, if they don't and someone gets injured, they can be guilty of an offence. This is seen in the case of **Pitwood** where a train track gatekeeper left the gate open when he went on lunch and someone died. He had a duty in his contract to make sure the gate was closed. In the case of **Miller**, a squatter, who lit a cigarette, fell asleep and then woke up with his mattress on fire! He didn't call the fire brigade but moved to the next room and went back to sleep! He had made the dangerous situation and so was under a duty to get help or try to put it out. But only those under a duty to act will have to act.

There are also different types of mens rea such as intentionally, recklessly (Cunningham recklessness) or negligence. The type depends on the offence. For murder, it has to be intention but you can be reckless to commit a battery.

The judge will interpret the statute using statutory interpretation because statutes don't always state whether mens rea is needed. It would be helpful if they did! The judge must use four tests from the Gammon case to establish if mens rea but start with the test given in **B v DPP**, where they presume mens rea is always needed. Crimes that don't require mens rea are known as strict liability.

First, they ask if the crime is a true crime, as in the case of the landlady who rented her property to people using drugs. She didn't know about this but was still convicted before, on appeal, her conviction was squashed. Second, they look to see the size of the penalty. Usually small penalties mean strict liability. Third, they look to see if the crime is a social concern, as in the case **Harrow**, where lottery tickets were sold to underage children. It doesn't matter if they looked over 16. Fourth, they see if the wording of the Act tells them that it is a strict liability offence. Some words like 'cause' in the case of **Alphacell v Woodward** indicate to the judge that the crime can be strict liability.

The candidate has defined the terms actus reus and mens rea as an introduction and given examples of an actus reus and a mens rea.

This candidate has interpreted the question as requiring a discussion of the elements of crime (actus reus and mens rea). The candidate has focused on omissions and the concept of a 'duty to act'. The candidate generally does this well and shows their understanding through some relevant case law. They do not, however, focus on the specific question posed.

This is much better focused on the question but a lot of time has been spent on less relevant matters.

Finally, the candidate has moved on to correctly consider strict liability, which should have been the focus of the answer from the start. The candidate correctly touches upon the role of the judge in interpreting statutes. A lot of important information is given in this paragraph, such as the presumption of mens rea and the four Gammon case tests. These points would have benefited from further explanation. Case law was needed on each of the 4 Gammon tests.

The candidate has discussed, albeit briefly, the four Gammon factors. They have correctly identified them and attempted to use case law to illustrate them. However, the candidate doesn't adequately consider the cases or their implications. This should have been the main focus of the answer, along with an evaluation of the four factors and how the courts use this guidance to determine if a crime requires both an actus reus and mens rea.

This is a decent conclusion, where the candidate has focused on the question, perhaps realising that the question was about strict liability. Ideally, no new information should be introduced in a conclusion, as it should be a summary of the main body. However, this candidate has used it as an opportunity to give further information about strict liability and the role of judges. There are hints at the inconsistency that this approach can give but this could have been developed earlier, along with some cases such as Lim Chin Aik and Smedleys v Breed.

So it can be seen that mens rea and actus reus are very important concepts but the judge has a big role to play. The problem with this is that judges are not elected and might make the wrong decision or there can be some people convicted of the offence and some not. There are different actus reus and mens rea for different offences but with strict liability, offences are designed to regulate behaviour for example speeding regulates the flow of traffic. It makes companies more vigilant which protects lives and the general public. The courts cannot insist that all crimes require an actus reus and mens rea otherwise there would be no deterrent to companies and no safeguard to the public in regards to regulatory behaviour but this is sometimes at the expense of fairness.

Overall, this is an 'adequate' answer. The question required a discussion of strict liability but this candidate has taken too broad an approach and not demonstrated a thorough understanding of strict liability. They do fortunately move on to strict liability but, despite showing an understanding of the presumption of mens rea, four factors and some case law, do not develop the points nor show a depth of understanding. The conclusion, however, is well focused on the question and ends well.
The AO1 mark would be low band 2 and the AO3 mark high band 1 or bottom band 2.

Eduqas A Level Law: Component 2

Component 2 papers require you to answer three questions from three different sections, reflecting the areas of substantive law you have studied. For example, you could answer one question from Section A (law of contract), one question from Section B (law of tort) and one question from Section C (criminal law). Each question is worth 25 marks and it is suggested you spend about 45 minutes per question. The questions are problem-style and are examining **AO1 Knowledge and understanding** and **AO2 Application skills**.

Eduqas A Level Law: Component 2 Section C

Question 5

Jamal became very depressed after his girlfriend, Jenny, ended their relationship and married David. He wrote dozens of letters to Jenny, begging her to leave David and come back to him. Eventually, David went to see Jamal at his flat, and told him that this behaviour would have to stop. Jamal was overcome by a jealous rage and struck David on the head with a coffee pot. The blow fractured David's skull, which was abnormally thin. Jamal immediately summoned an ambulance, and David was taken to hospital. By the time the ambulance arrived at the hospital, David's heart had stopped and he was no longer breathing. David was rushed to the intensive care unit and placed on a life-support system. The doctors told Jenny that, even if David survived, he would be irreversibly brain-damaged. Jenny wanted to let David die with dignity so, while the doctors were out of the room, she disconnected the machines that were keeping him alive.

Advise both Jamal and Jenny as to whether they may be criminally liable for David's death, applying your knowledge and understanding of legal rules and principles. [25]

The command word **advise** requires you to briefly explain a legal concept and then apply it to the scenario in order to provide advice.

Question 5 stronger response

Murder is a common law offence and the most substantial crime in English law, with a maximum sentence of life in prison. To be liable for murder, Jamal must have the actus reus for murder. He must have caused the death of a human being under the Queen's peace within the realm and within a year and a day. The mens rea of the crime for Jamal would be malice aforethought and that would either be express malice, intention to kill or implied malice, or intention to cause GBH, and this is implied by law. Jamal also needs the intention of murder as defined in **Nedrick** and then **Woolin**. This would be determined by the jury in Crown Court as either direct or oblique intent. Direct intention would be intention to kill, while oblique intent would be if Jamal's actions were a 'virtually certain consequence' (barring some unforeseen intervention). On these facts, it would be likely that the jury would say Jamal has the intent.

> This is a fairly good opening paragraph, identifying and explaining the standard elements, with supporting case law.

Therefore, it would next be a question of causation, firstly factual causation and the 'but for test'. This means but for the actions of Jamal would David have died, as used in **White (1910)** and **Dalloway (1847)**. Therefore, with this causation, Jamal would probably be guilty as David wouldn't have died without Jamal's actions. The 'but for' test can be seen in operation in **Pagett (1983)**. However, the courts also look at legal causation. Here, Jamal could be guilty if his conduct was more than a minimal cause of the consequence, but Jamal's conduct need not be a substantial cause to be guilty. In **Kimsey (1996)**, the court said it was acceptable to tell the jury that the defendant's conduct must be 'more than a slight or trifling link' to the consequence, as it clearly seems to be in Jamal's case. In this scenario, Jenny's act may have contributed to

The candidate discusses causation with supporting case law, showing a real attempt to apply it to the scenario.

the death; however, Jamal can still be guilty even though his conduct was not the only cause of death. Jamal must also take his victim as he finds him. We know David had an abnormally thin skull, and here the 'thin-skull' rule would apply. This means that, if the victim has something unusual about their physical state, as David did, which makes an injury more serious, then the defendant is liable for the more serious injury. So here David had an unusually thin skull, which means that the blow to the head from Jamal gave him a serious injury, then Jamal is liable for that injury. This is the case even though the blow may have only caused bruising in a normal person. An example of this is the case of **Blaue (1975)**.

There must be a direct link between Jamal's actions and David's death. Sometimes an intervening act can break the chain of caution, and therefore the defendant is no longer liable. In this scenario, have Jenny's actions broken the chain of causation? To break the chain of causation so that Jamal is no longer responsible for David's death, the intervening act by Jenny must be sufficiently independent of Jamal's conduct and sufficiently serious. In this case, Jenny has turned off the life-support machine. A doctor switching off life-support machines when it has been decided that the victim is brain dead does not break the chain of causation, as was decided in **Malcherek (1981)**. However, while in this case the court recognised that brain death is the accepted medical criterion of death, they did not actually decide that this is the legal definition of death. Therefore, in Jenny's situation, it is possible that the courts might decide that a defendant who switches off a life-support machine, not as a medical decision but intending to kill the victim, could be guilty of murder. However, Jenny could argue that, if David is 'brain dead' as the doctors have suggested, he may no longer be a 'reasonable creature in being', which is needed to satisfy the actus reus of murder.

This is a detailed discussion and application of the chain of causation. Jenny's liability is also considered. The candidate could also have discussed the decision in Bland, where it was suggested that brain stem death is the legal test of death.

If Jamal's actions are held to be the legal cause of death, he may be guilty of murder or manslaughter, depending on his state of mind when he hit David. If he lacked intention to kill or cause grievous bodily harm, he may be convicted of involuntary manslaughter on the basis of an unlawful and dangerous act, as seen in the cases of **Franklin** and **Newbury**. The mens rea needed here is simply the intention to do the unlawful act, as seen in **Scarlett** and **Owino**.

Good recognition here of involuntary manslaughter; cases could have been discussed in a little more detail

Jamal could possibly use the partial and special defence of diminished responsibility on the basis that he suffers from depression. This defence has been consolidated into **s2 Homicide Act 1957 (via S52 CJA 2009)**. To use this defence, Jamal would have to show that he suffers from an abnormality of the mind resulting from a recognised medical condition, as seen in **Byrne (1960)**. Jamal could also plead the partial defence of loss of control, which is also found under **s54 Coroners and Justice Act 2009**. Jamal would not be convicted of murder if he can prove he lost self-control when hitting David and that this was caused by a qualifying trigger (**s55**), and that a person of his sex and age might have reacted in the same way. It appears unlikely that a qualifying trigger does apply here, as Jamal was not in fear of serious violence from David, and it is unlikely that things said or done by Jenny or David caused Jamal to have a sense of being seriously wronged. Cases where the triggers have been considered are **Dawes (2013)** and **Zebedee (2012)**.

Good discussion here of the special defences. This is a strong answer that conveys all aspects of murder and manslaughter with very good use of case law to support. It ends a little abruptly: a summarising conclusion would have rounded things off nicely.

This answer demonstrates excellent knowledge for AO1 (Knowledge and understanding) and would achieve a level 4 mark. For AO2 (Application skills) marks, there is clear and detailed application of each element to the scenario. A conclusion would have enhanced the answer but it would likely also achieve a level 4 for AO2.

Question 5 weaker response

David has died, therefore homicide will be discussed. It appears that Jamal had the mens rea for murder. Lord Coke defines murder as the unlawful killing of another human being with malice aforethought. The actus reus for murder is unlawfully causing death to another human being under the Queen's peace.

> This introduction is brief but the standard elements of homicide have been recognised.

The mens rea for murder is held to be two things. In **Moloney**, these were expressed as malice (intention to kill) and implied malice (intention to cause GBH). GBH is defined in **Saunders** as 'serious' harm. It appears that Jamal had the mens rea to cause GBH (grievous bodily harm) with direct intent.

> This introduction is brief but the standard elements of homicide have been recognised.

We need to look at causation to see if Jamal is responsible. Causation is established in fact (**White** and **Pagett**) and in law (**Kimsey**). Jamal can only be guilty if David's death would not have happened but for his actions.

> This paragraph lacks detail on mens rea with supporting cases such as Woolin and Nedrick.

If Jamal's actions are held to be the legal cause of death, he may be guilty of murder or manslaughter, depending on his state of mind when he hit David. This is called involuntary manslaughter. If Jamal lacked intention to kill or cause GBH, he may be convicted of manslaughter on the basis of an unlawful and dangerous act.

> It is good to recognise here that Jamal could be guilty of the lesser offence of manslaughter. However, the answer lacks application to the scenario and supporting case law.

Jamal may be able to plead a defence of loss of control. This is a special defence and only a partial defence, because if Jamal is successful in using this defence he would not be acquitted of murder, but it would be reduced to manslaughter. To use this defence, Jamal would have to show he was suffering from a qualifying trigger that made him lose control and hit David. In conclusion, it looks as if Jamal would be guilty of manslaughter and the judge will sentence.

> The candidate has considered a special defence but more detail is needed on loss of control. Also, diminished responsibility would have been the obvious point here, as Jamal was suffering from depression.
> This answer is typical of answers on homicide. The candidate has included the standard elements of homicide, but the application and detail are weak. The candidate has also not considered Jenny's liability.

> This answer would achieve a level 2 for AO1 (Knowledge and understanding) and a low level 2 for AO2 (Application skills).

Eduqas A Level Law: Component 3

Component 3 papers require you to answer three questions from three different sections, reflecting the areas of substantive law you have studied. For example, you could answer one question from Section A (law of contract), one question from Section B (law of tort) and one question from Section C (criminal law). Each question is worth 25 marks and it is suggested you spend about 45 minutes per question. The questions are essay-style and are examining **AO1 Knowledge and understanding** and **AO3 Analysis and evaluation skills**.

Eduqas A Level Law: Component 3 Section A

> **Question 2**
>
> Analyse and evaluate the importance of the doctrine of the privity of contract. [25]

The command words **analyse** and **evaluate** require you to critically evaluate legal issues by identifying different perspectives, supporting the identification of the strongest viewpoint and demonstrating your ability to counter alternative viewpoints. Legal authorities should be used to support your arguments.

Question 2 stronger response

A good introduction which offers a definition of privity of contract, with the support of a key case.	The rule of privity of contract means that a contract can only create obligations between the parties to the contract, and not third parties. This is illustrated in the case of **Tweddle v Atkinson**, where two fathers entered into an agreement that they would each make a payment of £200 to the son of one of the fathers. One father made his payment but the father-in-law died before he made the payment. The son sued but his claim was not allowed on the principle that the agreement was between the two fathers and, although he would have benefited from the contract, he was not privy to the contract. This obviously causes an injustice, and therein lies one of the problems with the privity of contract.
There is an immediate attempt to focus on the question here, by looking at the inherent problem with the doctrine of privity.	Another case which illustrates how this doctrine can leave people without a remedy is **Dunlop Pneumatic Tyre Co v Selfridge**, where tyres were sold by the claimants to a distributor on the basis that they would not be sold on for less than a certain price. The distributor sold the tyres to the defendant for less than the price that was agreed. The claimants' action failed because they were not a party to the contract. The contract was between the distributor and the defendant. Again, this seems to be unjust but an advantage is it ensures that people cannot come forward and claim on a contract or be sued on a contract of which they had no knowledge. It also promotes the idea that people should have the free will to enter a contract with whoever they want. However, as can be seen by these cases, it is unduly restrictive and unfair because, for example, it would stop a sub-contractor from being held liable on the basis that there is no contract with the original party who contracted for the work to be done.
There are some excellent evaluative points here which really focus on the question and provide an analysis of the doctrine of privity as required in the question.	
The candidate demonstrates an excellent consideration of exceptions here which show the other side of the argument, and ways in which the harshness of the doctrine of privity can be mitigated.	With this in mind, a number of exceptions have been developed by the courts and by statute, which enable third parties to lay a claim on a contract, even if they are not one of the original parties. The first common law exception is collateral contracts, which is a contract made between one party and two others. Here, the court will find a contract to evade the privity rule, as seen in the case of **Shanklin Pier v Detel Products Ltd**. Another exception is where someone has made a contract on behalf of someone else. This could happen where an agent is acting on behalf of his principal, as seen in the case of **Scruttons Ltd v Midland Silicones** or where there is a trust holding property on behalf of another. Also, in the case of **Jackson v Horizon Holidays**, it was ruled that the compensation was not excessive for a holiday that failed to match the description, which had been purchased not only for the claimant but also for his family.

From 2000, an Act was introduced which specifically entitles a third party who was benefiting under a contract to enforce that contract even though they were not a party. This was the **Contract (Rights of Third Parties) Act 1999** and is more useful than the common law exceptions that have already been discussed. The 1999 Act allows a third party to enforce terms of a contract when the third party is specifically mentioned in the contract or where the contract purports a benefit on them. This was seen in the case of **Nisshin Shipping v Cleaves**, where the contract conferred a benefit on a third party and therefore was entitled to an action under the contract.

> It may also be useful to discuss other statutory exceptions to the privity of contract, such as the Married Woman's Property Act 1882 and the Road Traffic Act 1988 as well as the Law of Property Act 1925.

The 1999 Act is seen to be more acceptable in mitigating the harshness of the doctrine of privity, and so therefore the theory of privity has become less important over the years.

> There is an attempt to conclude the essay here with a summative statement on the usefulness of the 1999 Act.

Question 2 weaker response

Privity of contract means that only those who have signed the contract are part of it, and that no third parties are allowed to be part of the contract. The case that illustrates this is **Tweddle v Atkinson**. This rule is really unfair because it can leave people who have benefited from a contract without a remedy.

> This is a good opening paragraph which immediately gives a definition of the key issue in the question. This is good exam practice as it should focus the rest of the answer.

Over the years the courts have developed exceptions to this rule in the **Contract (Rights of Third Parties) Act 1999**, which entitles a party who was supposed to benefit under contract, even though they were not a party, to enforce the contract. There is also an exception in the **Road Traffic Act 1988**, which entitles an individual to enforce an insurance policy despite not being an original party under the requirement that all car owners take out third-party insurance cover. Another exception is in the **Married Woman's Property Act**, which overcomes the problem of divorced women, who were unable to take an interest in the marital property.

There are also some common law exceptions, such as collateral contracts, trusts and restrictive covenants in land law. Another big exception is holiday contracts whereby a person can claim for a bad holiday on behalf of his family even though his family were not part of the original contract. This can be seen in the case of **Jackson v Horizon Holidays**. This is a good exception and shows that privity of contract is not so relevant anymore as there are lots of exceptions to the rule.

> This is very much an explanation of the exceptions, which does not go on to evaluate how these exceptions may have improved the situation of the doctrine of privity of contract.

> This looks as if it is going to be developed further, but comes to an abrupt end so, in terms of analysis and evaluation, there is not enough here to justify a high range of AO3 marks.

> Overall, this demonstrates a good AO1 (Knowledge and understanding) response as there is an explanation of privity of contract, but the lack of evaluation will mean this is no more than adequate in terms of AO3 (Application skills), severely reducing the overall mark.

Case index

Legislation index

Acknowledgements

page 8 fizkes / Shutterstock.com; page 9 (top) Alter-ego / Shutterstock.com; page 9 (bottom) Irma07 / Shutterstock.com; page 10 Joggie Botma / Shutterstock.com; page 12 William Potter / Shutterstock.com; page 13 Denphumi / Shutterstock.com; page 16 (top) igorstevanovic / Shutterstock.com; page 16 (bottom) sumire8 / Shutterstock.com; page 17 megaflopp / Shutterstock.com; page 18 Pressmaster / Shutterstock.com; page 21 create jobs 51 / Shutterstock.com; page 22 Sorbis / Shutterstock.com; page 23 (top) Jet Shopping Media / Shutterstock.com; page 23 (bottom) veryulissa / Shutterstock.com; page 24 (left) VanderWolf Images / Shutterstock.com; page 24 (right) Featureflash Photo Agency / Shutterstock.com; page 26 misastudio / Shutterstock.com; page 27 Vladimir Arndt / Shutterstock.com; page 28 (top) Thampapon / Shutterstock.com; page 28 (bottom) seeshooteatrepeat / Shutterstock.com; page 29 Claire Plumridge / Shutterstock.com; page 30 Frederico Rostagno / Shutterstock.com; page 31 Neil Roy Johnson / Shutterstock.com; page 32 vchal / Shutterstock.com; page 33 ABB Photo / Shutterstock.com; page 34 moomsabuy / Shutterstock.com; page 35 Production Perig / Shutterstock.com; page 36 (top) QQ7 / Shutterstock.com; page 36 (bottom) Darryl Sleath / Shutterstock.com; page 37 sparksy37 / Shutterstock.com; page 38 mkant / Shutterstock.com; page 40 (top) Lesterman / Shutterstock.com; page 40 (bottom) Nick Beer / Shutterstock.com; page 44 designer491 / Shutterstock.com; page 45 Jirsak / Shutterstock.com; page 46 Peryn22 / Shutterstock.com; page 47 Brian A Jackson / Shutterstock.com; page 49 sylv1rob1 / Shutterstock.com; page 50 (top) Sergey Nivens / Shutterstock.com;

page 50 (bottom) KKulikov / Shutterstock.com; page 52 (top) Liukov / Shutterstock.com; page 52 (bottom left) nasirkhan / Shutterstock.com; page 52 (bottom right) BeRad / Shutterstock.com; page 62 Billion Photos / Shutterstock.com; page 66 plantic / Shutterstock.com; page 67 Marius Pirvu / Shutterstock.com; page 68 Morakod1977 / Shutterstock.com; page 70 Lucky Business / Shutterstock.com; page 71 (top) sdecoret / Shutterstock.com; page 71 (bottom) Sunday_Studio / Shutterstock.com; page 74 anucha maneechote / Shutterstock.com; page 75 (top) Max Sky / Shutterstock.com; page 75 (bottom) The Adaptive / Shutterstock.com; page 76 / Shane Maritch Shutterstock.com; page 77 Africa Studio / Shutterstock.com; page 78 (top) eggeegg / Shutterstock.com; page 78 (bottom) sezer76 / Shutterstock.com; page 79 AlenKadr / Shutterstock.com; page 80 VonaUA / Shutterstock.com; page 81 (top) Pawel Michaelowski / Shutterstock.com; page 81 (bottom) mrjo / Shutterstock.com; page 82 VGstockstudio / Shutterstock.com; page 83 Erce / Shutterstock.com; page 84 kubicka / Shutterstock.com; page 86 John Gomez / Shutterstock.com; page 87 Christopher Slesarchik / Shutterstock.com; page 88 Melkor3D / Shutterstock.com; page 89 chrisdorney / Shutterstock.com; page 90 (top) Qualivity / Shutterstock.com; page 90 (bottom) TungCheung / Shutterstock.com; page 91 EFKS / Shutterstock.com; page 92 Koldunov / Shutterstock.com; page 96 (top) Juhku / Shutterstock.com; page 96 (bottom) Franck Boston / Shutterstock.com; page 97 tomertu / Shutterstock.com

Acknowledgements

Dear Reader

Technology puts science to work for us. You can find technology all around you – in the materials you use, in the machines you work, and in all the different products that you buy. Technology affects every part of your life, from the moment when the alarm clock wakes you up in the morning to the time when you switch off your bedside light at night.

New technologies have made this age a very exciting one to live in. This is an age of automation and atom-smashers, e-mail and endoscopes, faxes and floppy disks, hydrofoils and hovercraft, modems and multimedia, pacemakers and polymers, robots and rocket motors, CDs, CFCs, LCDs, TGVs and VDUs.

If you are not quite sure what these marvels of modern technology are, then look inside this book to find out. But this is not just a book about basic everyday technologies; it tells you about the more advanced ones too. So on your way from **abacus** to **zip fastener**, you can also find out about ball-bearings and gears, dams and bridges, nuts and bolts, radio telescopes and refrigerators, tools and telephones, watches, wheels and winches and over 350 other terms.

This book will be a useful companion to you as you make your way through today's complex world. Use it as a dictionary or browse through it in your spare time, but be warned: once you have opened its pages, you will find it hard to put this book down!

Robin Kerrod

abacus

An abacus is a calculating machine that has been used for thousands of years. It has beads or rings which you move along wires inside a frame. It is still used in Russia, China and other Far Eastern countries.

You can count and do sums on an abacus by sliding beads along wires.

A

aeroplane

An aeroplane, or plane for short, is the commonest kind of aircraft. It has wings that support it in the air. It also has a tail, which helps it to fly straight. Planes have either jet engines or engines that turn **propellers**. Jet planes are the fastest aeroplanes. Some can travel at speeds of more than 3000 kilometres (km) per hour. See also **jet, jet engine, transport.**

This passenger plane is a Boeing 777. It can carry up to about 280 passengers, and cruises at a speed of about 890 kilometres (km) per hour.

acid rain

Acid rain is a kind of **pollution**. It is caused by gases from factory chimneys and car exhausts. The gases combine with water droplets in the air to form acid. The acid falls to the ground in rain.

Acid rain attacks the stonework of buildings, damages trees and harms water and the plants and animals that live in it.

adhesive

An adhesive is a sticky solution or mixture. You use it to join two surfaces together. Glue is an adhesive that has been used for hundreds of years. Modern adhesives include rubber solutions and plastic mixtures.

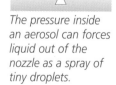

fine spray

nozzle

button

gas under pressure

liquid that turns to spray

The pressure inside an aerosol can forces liquid out of the nozzle as a spray of tiny droplets.

aerosol can

An aerosol can sprays out liquid as a fine mist. The liquid is kept inside the can under pressure. When you press a button, the liquid spurts out as a fine spray. Aerosol cans may contain liquids such as hair lacquer, furniture polish, paint and **pesticides.**

air conditioning

Air conditioning means controlling the state, or condition, of the air inside a room or building. An air conditioner can warm or cool the air, no matter what the temperature is like outside. It can also change the humidity (the amount of moisture in the air). Air conditioning can remove dirt and bad smells from the air.

aircraft

See **transport.**

air resistance

When something moves through the air, the air pushes against it and tries to hold it back. This force is called air resistance. Aircraft, cars and other vehicles are often **streamlined** to reduce air resistance.
See also **drag.**

aerial

An aerial sends out or receives radio signals. It is used in **communications**. An aerial may be a wire, a rod or a metal dish. It is sometimes called an antenna.
See also **radio.**

airship

An airship is a powered aircraft that stays up in the air because it is lighter than air. Airships were the first aircraft to carry passengers over long distances, in the early 1900s. Only a few are flying today.

An airship is really a very large balloon filled with a light gas. It is driven through the air by **propellers** that are powered by engines.

Modern airships like this one are filled with helium gas. Early ones were filled with hydrogen gas, which can easily catch fire.

alloy

An alloy is a mixture of two or more metals. The silver-coloured coins in your pocket are made from an alloy of copper and nickel, called cupronickel. Copper-coloured coins are made from an alloy of copper, tin and a little zinc. It is called bronze. Most cutlery is made of stainless steel. Stainless steel is a mixture of three main metals – iron, chromium and nickel.

Our most widely used metal, ordinary steel, is an alloy. It contains iron and tiny amounts of a non-metal called carbon.
See also **steel-making.**

alternative energy

Alternative energy is energy that we can produce without burning **fossil fuels.** Alternative energy includes geothermal power, hydroelectric power, solar power and wind and wave power.

Alternative energy has several advantages. Its sources, such as wind and energy from the Sun, will never run out. Also, they do not cause pollution like fossil fuels. There are not enough alternative energy schemes yet to supply the energy needs of all the world.
See also **geothermal power, hydroelectric power, solar power, wave power, wind power.**

Wind 'farms' use the power of the wind to supply alternative energy. This wind farm is at Altamont Pass in California, USA.

alternator

An alternator is a kind of **generator**.

antenna

See **aerial**.

aqueduct

An aqueduct is built to carry water. It may be a tunnel, a pipeline or an open channel.

arch

An arch is a curved structure that is used in building. Arches are strong because of their shape. They are widely used in building bridges and dams.

assembly line

See **making and manufacturing**.

atomic bomb

See **nuclear weapon**.

atom-smasher

An atom-smasher is a machine that breaks up atoms. (An atom is the smallest possible part of any substance.) Its correct name is particle accelerator. Atom-smashers use huge amounts of electricity and magnetism to speed up, or accelerate, beams of very tiny atomic parts called particles. Then they smash the atoms with these beams.

automation

See **making and manufacturing**.

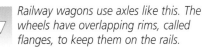
Railway wagons use axles like this. The wheels have overlapping rims, called flanges, to keep them on the rails.

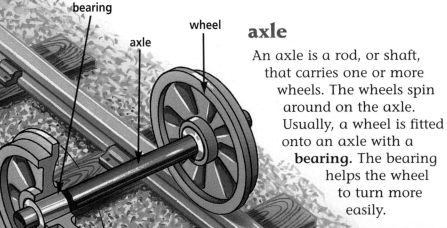

axle

An axle is a rod, or shaft, that carries one or more wheels. The wheels spin around on the axle. Usually, a wheel is fitted onto an axle with a **bearing**. The bearing helps the wheel to turn more easily.

ball-bearing

See **bearing**.

balloon

A balloon is a simple kind of aircraft. It consists of a large bag that is filled with gas. The gas needs to be lighter than air to make the balloon rise up into the air. Some balloons use hot air as the lifting gas, but others use helium gas.

ballpoint pen

A ballpoint pen uses a tiny moving ball to spread ink. When you write with a ballpoint, the ball rolls across the paper. As it rolls, it spreads the ink from a thin tube inside the pen.

bar code

Most goods that are sold in shops have a bar code. It is a pattern of black and white stripes, with a row of numbers below the stripes. The bar code on an object carries coded information about what kind of product it is. Many shops have a machine that 'reads' bar codes. It sends information about a product to a computer, which tells salespeople the product's price and how many of it are in stock.

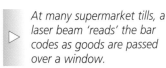
At many supermarket tills, a laser beam 'reads' the bar codes as goods are passed over a window.

battery

A battery produces electricity. It is used to make things like torches and radios work. The battery in a car helps to start the engine and keep it running. The commonest battery is the dry battery, or dry cell. It has a zinc case filled with a chemical paste. There is a carbon rod in the middle of the battery. All these materials react together to produce electricity. The batteries in cars contain lead plates that are dipped in acid.

beam

A beam is a straight piece of wood, metal or other material. It is designed to carry a load. Metal beams called girders are used in many buildings, including bridges and skyscrapers.

bearing

A bearing is used in a machine which has moving parts. Bearings do two main things. They support the moving parts. They also reduce the **friction** (rubbing) between the moving and fixed parts. Bearings are found, for example, in the hub (centre) of bicycle wheels. They support the wheel **axle** and let it turn freely in the hub.

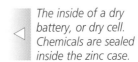

cap (terminal)

plastic cover

chemical paste

zinc case

chemicals

carbon rod

base (terminal)

The inside of a dry battery, or dry cell. Chemicals are sealed inside the zinc case.

bicycle

A bicycle, or bike for short, has two wheels that are held in a frame. When you pedal, a system of toothed **cog wheels** and a chain make the back wheel turn and move you forwards. You steer the bike by moving the handlebars, which turn the front wheel. Most bikes have several gears, which let you change your speed. The bike is one of the most popular forms of transport in the world.

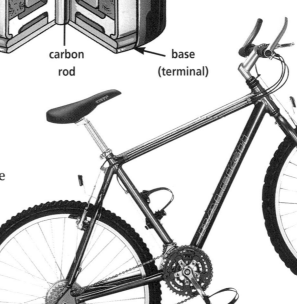

This mountain bike has many gears to help the rider climb steep slopes.

binoculars

You look through a pair of binoculars to see distant objects more clearly. Binoculars are a type of double telescope to use with both eyes. They have pieces of glass called lenses. The lenses produce bigger images (pictures) of distant objects.

bionics

Bionics is a short name for biological electronics. Bionic engineers develop electronic systems that work like real systems in living things. Some artificial limbs are bionic. They work by using tiny electrical currents that are produced by muscles in the human body.

biotechnology

In biotechnology, scientists make products by using tiny living things called organisms. The organisms are mostly so tiny that you need a microscope to see them. That is why they are called micro-organisms. Biotechnologists use micro-organisms such as bacteria and moulds, for example, to make some kinds of drugs. See also **genetic engineering.**

bit

A bit is the smallest piece of information that a computer can handle. Bit is short for binary digit. There are just two binary digits, 0 and 1. Computers handle information in groups of bits called bytes.

blast furnace

A blast furnace uses heat to help separate, or extract, metals from their **ores**. This process is called smelting. Air is blasted into the furnace to make the fuel inside it burn fiercely. Iron is the most important metal produced in blast furnaces.

In a blast furnace, iron forms when a mixture of iron ore, coke and limestone is heated to a temperature of about 1500 degrees Celsius (°C).

valve

loading skip

air blasted in here

slag (waste)

iron

furnace lining

hot air in

waste gases out

block and tackle

A block and tackle is a group of **pulleys.** It is used to lift heavy loads. Garage mechanics may use a block and tackle to lift the engine out of a car.

blueprint

See **plans.**

bolt

A bolt is a metal pin with a head at one end and a screw thread at the other. It is used with a nut to join together pieces of metal and other materials. A nut has a matching thread, and screws onto the bolt. You use a spanner to turn the bolt head and nut.

brake

A brake slows down or stops moving vehicles or other moving things. Many brakes work by **friction** (rubbing). They are forced against moving parts, and the rubbing action causes the parts to slow down. Cars have this kind of brake on all four wheels. The space shuttle uses rockets to brake before it returns to Earth and a parachute after it has landed.

The space shuttle uses a parachute as a brake to help it slow down quickly once it has landed.

brazing

Brazing is a method of joining metal parts using a metal called brass. The brass is heated until it becomes liquid, and it is then dripped onto the parts to be joined. When the brass cools, it hardens and forms a strong joint. Bicycle frames are made by brazing.

brick

Bricks have been one of the most common building materials for thousands of years. They are very hard blocks of clay that have been strongly heated, or fired, inside a special oven called a kiln. In house-building, a kind of concrete called mortar is placed between layers of bricks to bond them strongly together. In some countries with a hot climate, bricks may be made from mud and dried in the sun.
See also **materials**.

Cables help to strengthen the middle part of this long beam bridge at St Petersburg in Florida, USA.

bridge

A bridge carries a road or railway across a river, a valley or another obstacle. The simplest bridge is a **beam** that is supported at each end by pillars. Beam bridges cannot stretch across wide gaps, so other kinds must be used, such as arch bridges and suspension bridges. In a suspension bridge, the road hangs from wire cables.

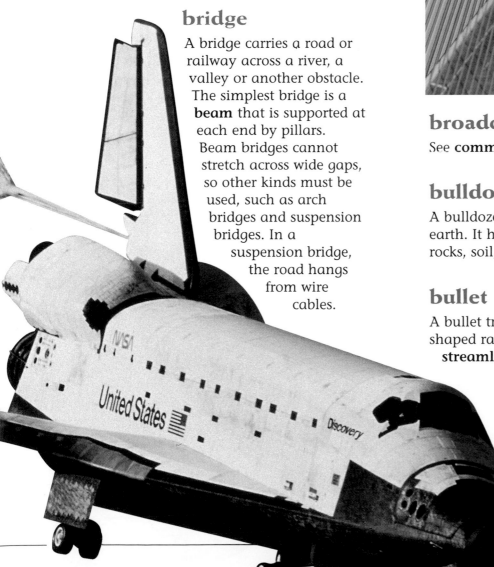

broadcasting

See **communications**.

bulldozer

A bulldozer is a powerful machine for moving earth. It has a steel blade at the front to move rocks, soil, tree stumps and other obstacles.

bullet train

A bullet train is a high-speed train that is shaped rather like a bullet. Bullet trains are **streamlined** so that they can travel faster.

bus

A bus is a vehicle that carries passengers over short distances. Bus is short for omnibus. A bus that is built to travel over quite long distances is usually called a coach.
See also **transport**.

CAD

See **design**.

calculator

You use a calculator to do sums. An **abacus** is a simple calculator. Calculating machines with gears were used in the 1600s. Most calculators today are electronic. They are simple computers.

camcorder

A camcorder is a combined video camera and videocassette recorder. The latest ones are small, light and easy to use. People use them to make their own video recordings.
See also **videocassette recorder**.

camera

You use a camera to take photographs. A simple camera is a lightproof box. It has a piece of film at one end and a hole, called the aperture, at the other. When you press a button, a blind, or shutter, in front of the aperture opens briefly to let in the light. A lens focuses the light onto the film, which records an image (picture).

In many cameras, you can change the speed of the shutter and the size of the aperture. The lens can be moved in and out to focus on objects at different distances.
See also **cine camera**.

A look inside a compact camera. The speed of the shutter and the aperture size are set automatically to take the best picture.

canal

A canal is an artificial waterway. Most canals are built to carry boats and ships. Some carry water for irrigation (watering farmland) and water supplies to towns. Two famous canals are the Suez Canal in Egypt and the Panama Canal in Central America. They carry ocean-going ships.

A cassette tape used for recording sound. Tapes like this are played in personal stereos, for example.

canning

See **food technology**.

car

See **motor car**.

cassette

A cassette is a sealed case that contains a reel of film or tape. Audio (sound) and video tapes come in cassettes that you simply slot into recording machines.
See also **videocassette recorder**.

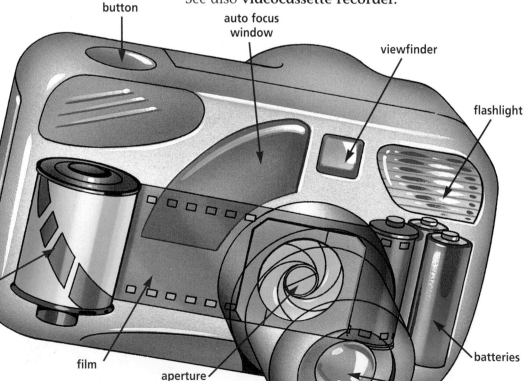

reels

protective case

magnetic tape

shutter release button

auto focus window

viewfinder

flashlight

film cassette

film

aperture

batteries

lens

casting

Casting is a method of shaping objects by pouring a hot liquid into a mould. The main part of a car engine is made by pouring hot liquid iron into a shaped mould. When the iron cools and turns solid, it has the same shape as the mould.

A casting is the shaped metal object that is made by the method of casting.
See also **moulding.**

catalytic converter

A catalytic converter can be fitted to the exhaust pipe of a car. It contains a chemical called a catalyst. The catalyst changes, or converts, harmful gases from the car engine into harmless ones.
See also **motor car.**

cathode-ray tube

A cathode-ray tube (CRT) changes electrical signals into pictures. It forms the main part of a television set. In a CRT, beams of tiny particles, called electrons, are fired at a screen and make it glow. The beams build up a picture as they travel quickly backwards and forwards across the screen in a series of lines.
See also **television.**

This compact disc is used to record music. It measures just 12 centimetres (cm) across.

Inside the cathode-ray tube, an electron gun fires beams of electrons at the screen. The focusing coil bends the beams so that they move backwards and forwards across the screen.

electron gun

electron beams

cathode-ray tube

focusing coil

mask

electron beams

coating on back of screen

screen

CD

A CD, or compact disc, is a small, round piece of plastic and metal. It is used to record music and other sounds. Sound signals are recorded on a CD in code, in a pattern of tiny pits (sunken areas). When you play the disc, a **laser** beam inside the CD player reads the coded pattern. The code is changed back into sound signals, which then go to **loudspeakers.**

Other CDs can record words, photographs and movies as well as sound.
See also **CD-ROM.**

CD-ROM

A CD-ROM is a compact disc that stores many different kinds of information. This information may be words, photographs, video, pictures or sound. You can play back the disc through a computer or a television set. A single CD-ROM can hold all the words and pictures of a large encyclopedia.
See also **multimedia.**

cement

Cement is a grey powder. It is made by roasting a mixture of iron ore, limestone and clay in a **kiln.**
Cement is mixed with sand, gravel and water to make concrete, one of our most useful building materials.
See also **materials.**

central heating

Central heating is a heating system for buildings. The heat is produced in one place and then distributed to the various rooms. Oil or gas is usually burned to heat up water in a boiler. The hot water is then pumped through pipes to the rooms. There, it passes through tubes inside the radiators, which give out the heat.

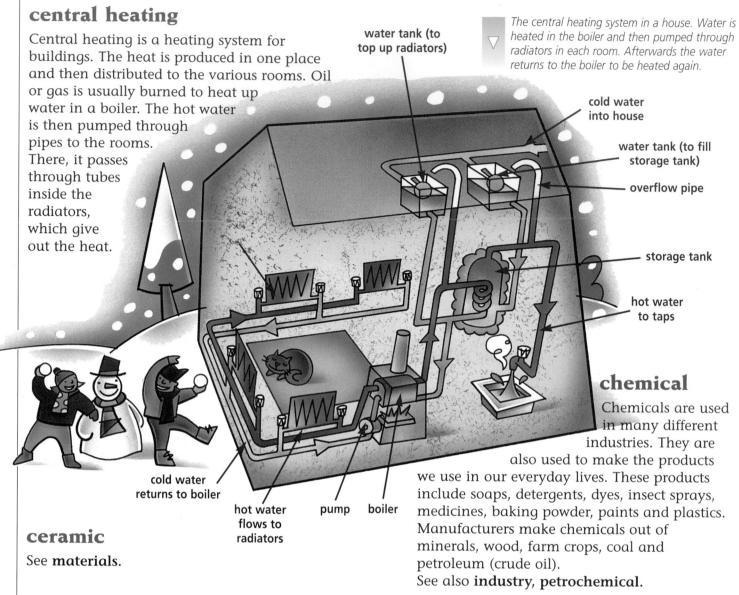

water tank (to top up radiators)

The central heating system in a house. Water is heated in the boiler and then pumped through radiators in each room. Afterwards the water returns to the boiler to be heated again.

cold water into house

water tank (to fill storage tank)

overflow pipe

storage tank

hot water to taps

cold water returns to boiler

hot water flows to radiators

pump   boiler

ceramic

See **materials**.

CFC

CFCs are liquid mixtures that contain the **chemicals** chlorine, fluorine and carbon. Their full name is chlorofluorocarbons. They were once widely used in refrigerators and aerosol spray cans, and to make foam products. They are used less now because scientists think that they can cause **pollution**.

chain

A chain is a series of rings that are joined together. These rings, or links, are usually made of metal. Chains are used in machines to move, or transfer, power from one place to another. In a bicycle, a chain transfers pedal power to the back wheel.

chemical

Chemicals are used in many different industries. They are also used to make the products we use in our everyday lives. These products include soaps, detergents, dyes, insect sprays, medicines, baking powder, paints and plastics. Manufacturers make chemicals out of minerals, wood, farm crops, coal and petroleum (crude oil).
See also **industry**, **petrochemical**.

chisel

See **tool**.

cine camera

People use a cine camera to make movies, or motion pictures. It takes a series of pictures quickly, one after the other. The camera has a shutter, a lens and a film like an ordinary camera. A motor moves the film through the camera. The film stops for a tiny part of a second while each picture is taken.
See also **camera**, **movie**.

cinema

See **movie**.

clock

A clock measures time. For thousands of years people have used shadow clocks to tell the time. These clocks use the movement of the shadow produced by the Sun. Sundials are shadow clocks.

Mechanical clocks have a device called a regulator, which moves at a steady rate. It turns the hands of the clock through a system of **gear** wheels. Electronic clocks are controlled by the tiny movements of crystals of quartz.
See also **watch**.

In this transparent (see-through) clock, you can see the system of gear wheels that turns the hands.

coach

See **bus**.

coal

Coal is a quite hard, black substance that we burn. It is a **fossil fuel.** It is mined throughout the world. Coal is made up mainly of carbon, with water and dirt. The best coal is anthracite, which is nearly all carbon. When coal is heated strongly without air, it turns into coke. This is used as fuel in **blast furnaces.**

cog wheel

A cog wheel has tiny teeth, or cogs, around its outside edge. Cog wheels are used in **gear** systems and, with chains, for passing on power.

Cog wheels pass on motion (movement) to one another when their teeth lock together.

combine harvester

A combine harvester is a farm machine. It is used to harvest cereal crops, such as wheat and barley. It is so called because it combines the actions of cutting the crop and then beating the grain from it.

commercial vehicle

A commercial vehicle is a road vehicle that is used for work. The most common one is the lorry. Other commercial vehicles include buses, dustcarts, fire engines and tip-up trucks.
See also **lorry**.

A combine harvester has a rotating reel at the front to help collect the cut crop into the machine.

Communications

Communications are ways in which we keep in touch with people, share information and find out what is happening in the world around us. We communicate mainly by speaking and by writing and reading. With the help of modern technology, we can now communicate with each other over long distances, for example by telephone, fax or e-mail.

The electric telegraph was the first reliable method of 'instant' long-distance communications. It was developed in the 1830s, in Britain and in the United States. Messages were sent along wires in the form of electrical signals. The signals stood for words and numbers in a code, usually the **Morse code**. The telephone was invented in 1876 by Alexander Graham Bell in the United States. Fax machines have become popular only in recent years. An even more modern method of communication is electronic mail, or e-mail for short, which uses computers to send messages.

This communications satellite far out in space receives and sends out radio signals from countries all over the world.

The telephone, fax and e-mail are ways of sending personal communications between a small number of people. Other forms of communications, such as printing and broadcasting, reach millions of people. They are examples of mass communications.

Millions of people read printed newspapers and tune in to radio and television programmes every day.

communications satellite

A communications satellite is a spacecraft that passes on, or relays, communications signals. These signals may be telephone calls, television programmes, fax messages or computer information.

With a mobile phone, you can keep in touch with people while moving from place to place.

This is a picture of Alexander Graham Bell in 1892, speaking on one of his telephones.

e-mail

E-mail is short for electronic mail. It is a method of sending letters using computers and a communications network like the Internet. You write a letter on your computer and, using a code, address it to the person you want to contact. You can then send the letter, using the telephone line, directly to that person's computer. If the person's computer is switched off, your electronic letter is 'dropped in the mailbox', or put in the memory of a central computer. The person can use a password to open the mailbox and pick up the letter.

▷ *A fax machine is connected to a telephone line. You press the number buttons to contact the person who will receive the fax. Then you press the green button to send the fax.*

fax

A fax machine sends written messages, documents and pictures along telephone lines. The word 'fax' is short for facsimile, which means an exact copy. A fax machine changes words and pictures into signals. These travel along telephone lines to another fax machine, which reads the signals and then prints out the original words and pictures.

Internet

The Internet is an international communications network. It joins together millions of computer users around the world. Through the network, you can send letters to other users by e-mail. You can also reach huge stores of information, on all kinds of subjects, that are provided by individual people and by organizations.

telephone

The telephone has been the most popular method of personal communications for over 100 years. Today, more than 600 million phones are in use across the world. Many people carry a mobile phone when they move around. Mobile phones are connected to the ordinary telephone network by **radio**. With a videophone, you can see the person you are calling at the same time as you hear them.

telex

The telex is a modern version of the electric telegraph. It sends written messages in the form of electrical signals.

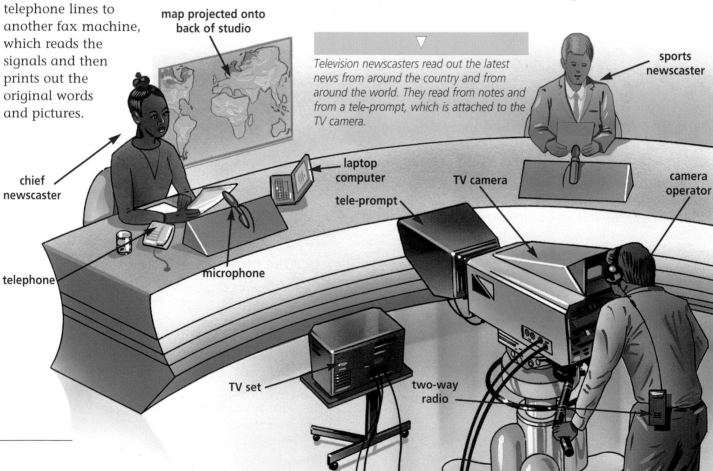

map projected onto back of studio

Television newscasters read out the latest news from around the country and from around the world. They read from notes and from a tele-prompt, which is attached to the TV camera.

sports newscaster

chief newscaster

laptop computer

tele-prompt

TV camera

camera operator

telephone

microphone

TV set

two-way radio

computer

A computer is an electronic device that handles all kinds of information. Computers are used in every part of our lives – in homes, schools, businesses, shops, science, industry and transport. We use them to play games, draw graphs, send electronic mail, keep records of goods, forecast the weather, run chemical plants, fly aeroplanes and much more. They are a central part of **information technology.**

The data stored in the memory and the program of instructions form part of the computer's software.

You feed data into a computer in the form of words and numbers. The computer automatically changes the words and numbers into a code made up of sets of 0s and 1s, or **bits.**
See also **communications, disk, word processing.**

- visual display unit (VDU)
- disk drive
- keyboard
- speaker
- CD-ROM drive
- mouse
- printer
- modem
- CD-ROM
- floppy disks

The keyboard and mouse are 'input' devices (for putting information into the computer). The VDU, printer and modem are 'output' devices (for taking information from the computer).

A computer stores information, or data, in its memory. It then handles, or processes, the data by following a set of instructions, called a program. The part of the computer that carries out the instructions is called the processor, or central processing unit (CPU).

The memory and CPU are made up of **microchips.** They are part of the computer's hardware. Other items of hardware include a keyboard, a mouse, a computer screen, or visual display unit (VDU), a disk drive, a printer and a **modem.**

concrete

See **materials.**

conservation

Conservation means taking care of, or preserving, something. The conservation of resources, such as minerals and fossil fuels, and the conservation of wildlife are very important in the modern world. If we carry on using up resources too quickly, there will be none left for the future.
See also **fossil fuel, materials, recycling.**

conveyor

A conveyor carries, or conveys, objects or materials. A conveyor belt is an endless band of material that is looped around a set of **pulleys.** In a roller conveyor, objects move over a row of rotating (turning) rollers. Both kinds of conveyor are used widely in factories.

△ *A worker inspects newly made pasta as it passes by on a conveyor belt.*

cracking

Cracking is one of the most important chemical processes that takes place at an **oil refinery**. It breaks down thick oils into more useful products, such as petrol and chemicals for use in industry.

crane

A crane is a machine for lifting and moving heavy loads. The load is carried by a hook at the end of a wire rope, or cable. The cable is let out and wound back by a power-driven **winch.**

crude oil

See **petroleum.**

jib

cable

pulley

cable

winch

counterweight

trolley

pulley

winch

dam

A dam is a thick strong wall built to hold back water. The artificial lake trapped behind the dam is called a reservoir. Dams are built of concrete or a mixture of earth and rock. Very thick dams are called gravity dams because their weight holds back the water. Slimmer concrete dams have an arch shape to hold back the water.
See also **hydroelectric power.**

▷

This is the Hoover Dam on the Colorado River in the western United States. It is an arch dam made of concrete, and is 221 metres (m) high.

data

Data means information. Computers handle, or process, data, for example sorting and updating records. A database is a huge store of information about a particular subject, such as airline timetables. See also **computer.**

◁ *In a jib crane (near left), the cable hangs from an arm (jib) that can move up and down and from side to side. In a tower crane (far left), the cable hangs from a trolley that travels along a horizontal arm.*

design

To design something means to draw up a plan of it. Every object, from a pencil to an ocean liner, has to be designed before it can be made or built.

In technology, a design must be practical and suitable for its planned use. A jug, for example, must be designed so that it pours without dripping, and has a handle that you can hold easily. Designers try to design the jug so that it looks attractive. They must also choose a suitable material to make it.

Even when a design works well, looks good and is made of the right material, it may cost so much to make that people will not be able to afford to buy it.

Designers draw sketches of their designs and often build models to show exactly what the designs will look like. Sometimes they test the models to find out how well they work. Aircraft designers, for example, test their designs in huge **wind tunnels**.

Hot liquid plastic is shaped into a tube as it is forced through the hole in a die.

pellets of plastic

heater

die

turning screw

liquid plastic

plastic tube

desk-top publishing

Desk-top publishing, or DTP for short, means producing printed material with a computer and a printer. Many companies and individuals now use DTP to print and publish their own reports, newsletters and booklets. They prepare the words on the computer using a word-processing program. They plan, or lay out, the pages on the computer's screen using a DTP program. The pages, with their pictures, are then printed by the printer.
See also **computer, word processing**.

developing

See **film**.

die

A die is a kind of mould. It is used to shape metals and other materials. Hot metal or plastic is forced through a die to make tubing, for example.
See also **moulding**.

diesel engine

A diesel engine is an engine that burns a light oil called diesel as fuel. Many cars, trains and ships and most lorries and buses have diesel engines.

A diesel engine works in a similar way to a **petrol engine**. Unlike petrol engines, diesel engines do not need an electric spark to burn the fuel. The air in the cylinders becomes so hot that the fuel burns straight away when it meets the hot air. It then produces hot gases that move the **pistons**.
See also **engine, internal combustion engine**.

Many manufacturers now use computers to help them design new products. This is known as computer-aided design, or CAD for short.

disk

Computer data and programs are usually stored on disks. The disks are magnetic. Disks that are built into the computer are called hard disks. Floppy disks are portable and bendy. They fit into a slot at the front of the computer called a disk drive.
See also **computer**.

doorbell

An ordinary doorbell uses electricity to make it ring. The electric bell works by using batteries. The main part of the bell is an **electromagnet**. When you press the doorbell button, electricity flows through the electromagnet. It makes a metal clapper hit the bell.

drag

Drag is a force that slows down an object when it moves through a liquid or a gas. It is a kind of **friction**. The drag of the air slows down cars and aeroplanes, and the drag of the water slows down boats.
See also **air resistance, streamlined.**

drill

See **tool**.

drilling rig

Engineers use a drilling rig to drill holes in the ground or seabed when searching for oil. The rig is a tall steel tower with lifting equipment to raise a series of pipes, called the drill pipe. A cutting tool, called a drill bit, is fitted to the bottom of the drill pipe.
See also **petroleum.**

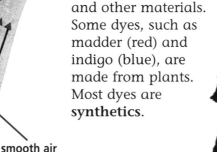

object not streamlined

unsteady air flow causes drag

smooth air flow

streamlined object

drug

A drug is a substance that is used in medicine to treat or prevent illnesses and to reduce pain. Some drugs are made from plants. Morphine, which is a powerful painkiller, is made from certain poppies. Aspirin is a milder painkiller. Like most drugs, it is made from chemicals. Antibiotic drugs are made from tiny living things such as moulds.

Chunky objects (top) experience a lot more drag than smooth, streamlined ones (bottom) when they travel through air or water.

dye

A dye adds colour to textiles, hair, food and other materials. Some dyes, such as madder (red) and indigo (blue), are made from plants. Most dyes are **synthetics**.

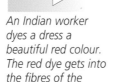

An Indian worker dyes a dress a beautiful red colour. The red dye gets into the fibres of the dress fabric.

dynamo

A dynamo is a kind of **generator**.

echo-sounder

Boats and ships use an echo-sounder to measure the depth of water below them. The instrument works by **sonar**. It sends sound waves down to the seabed, and picks up the echoes that come back. The depth of the water is calculated by measuring the time it takes for the sound waves to reach the seabed and be reflected back to the surface.

electric cell

An electric cell produces electricity. The ordinary dry batteries that we use in torches and radios are electric cells.
See also **battery, photocell, solar cell.**

electric generator

See **generator.**

electricity supply

The electricity supply comes into our homes from power stations far away. It travels to us through a huge network of overhead wires, called transmission lines, and underground cables. Tall towers called pylons carry the lines from the power stations to smaller substations all around the country. The substations then pass on the electricity through cables to nearby homes and factories.

electric light

See **fluorescent lamp, light bulb, neon light.**

electric motor

Electric motors power all kinds of machines, from electric toothbrushes and vacuum cleaners to submarines and locomotives. An electric motor is made up of two main parts. One is a rotating part called the rotor. The other is a fixed, or stationary, part called the stator. The stator is a magnet. The rotor carries many coils of wire. It rotates when electricity is passed through the coils.

E

echo

sonar equipment

sound wave

The echo-sounder on a boat sends out sound waves. The waves are reflected back by the seabed and anything on it.

A simple electric motor. The rotor spins round when electricity from the battery passes through its coils.

electromagnet

An electromagnet is a kind of magnet that only becomes magnetic when electric current passes through it. Most electromagnets are made of a piece of iron with coils of wire wrapped around the iron.

electronics

When you switch on a torch, electricity from a battery flows through a light bulb and makes it glow. The electricity is being carried by millions of tiny parts, or particles. We call them electrons.

Electronics studies the flow of electrons in materials. Engineers have developed various parts, or components, to control electrons. They group these components together to build up electronic circuits. Such circuits are found in radios, television sets, computers, calculators, digital watches, CD players, automatic cameras and many other devices.

Thousands of tiny components and circuits can be built up on one tiny piece, or chip, of a material called silicon. This produces a **microchip.** Microchips are so small and powerful that they have made it possible to build electronic devices such as the personal computer (PC).

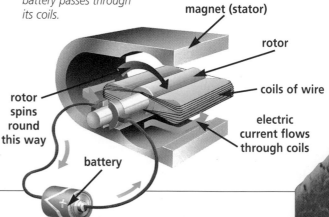

magnet (stator)

rotor

coils of wire

electric current flows through coils

rotor spins round this way

battery

electron microscope

An electron microscope uses beams of electrons (tiny particles that carry electricity) to magnify things. It contains **electromagnets** that bend the electron beams. Electron microscopes can magnify things by up to one million times, which is much more than ordinary light microscopes can. See also **microscope**.

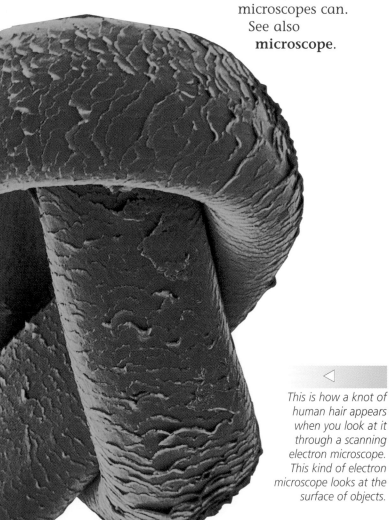

This is how a knot of human hair appears when you look at it through a scanning electron microscope. This kind of electron microscope looks at the surface of objects.

electroplating

Electroplating is a process that uses electricity to cover, or coat, one metal with another. Many car parts are plated with a metal called chromium. Some cutlery is silver plated.

e-mail

See **communications**.

endoscope

An endoscope is an instrument that doctors use to see inside the human body. It is made of bendy glass fibres, and can pass through narrow places and around corners.

engine

An engine is a machine that produces power to drive other machines. Steam engines, **petrol engines** and **diesel engines** use heat to produce power. **Turbines** are engines with rotating wheels. The wheels are spun round by a liquid, such as water, steam or a gas. See also **internal combustion engine, jet engine, steam engine**.

engineering

In engineering, science is put to work. Civil engineers design and build roads, bridges, dams and tunnels. Mechanical engineers design and build machines. Chemical engineers design and build chemical plants.

escalator

An escalator is a moving staircase. The steps are carried on an endless belt. They fold flat at the top and bottom to let people get on and off more easily.

An endless belt carries the steps of an escalator. Another endless belt acts as a handrail for passengers.

handrail

step

electric motor

drive wheel

drive belt

returning steps

excavator

An excavator is a machine for digging into the ground. Some large excavators dig up soil by dragging huge buckets across the ground.

explosive

An explosive is a chemical that explodes violently. When it is set off, large amounts of heat and gas are produced. The gas expands quickly and causes a big blast, which can shatter things. Dynamite and TNT are two very powerful kinds of explosive.

factory

See **making and manufacturing**.

fax

See **communications**.

This ferry carries passengers between Manhattan and Staten Island, in the harbour of New York City, USA.

ferry

A ferry is a boat or ship that carries passengers and cargo on journeys across water. A ferry may be an ordinary ship, a **hovercraft** or a **hydrofoil**.

fibre

See **materials**.

fibreglass

Fibreglass is a common material that is used to make items such as sailing boats and fireproof clothing. It is made of plastic that is strengthened with tiny threads, or fibres, of glass.

file

See **tool**.

film

In photography, the pictures taken by a camera are recorded on a film. The film is a ribbon of clear plastic. It is coated with chemicals which are affected by light. When a pattern of light falls on the film, the chemicals are changed. They form a kind of invisible image, or picture, on the film. When the film is developed, it is treated with certain chemicals. The invisible image then becomes visible.
See also **camera, movie**.

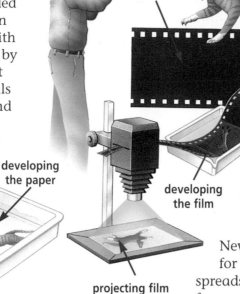

taking a picture

invisible image on film

developing the paper

developing the film

projecting film image onto photographic paper

final photographic print

Various stages of developing and printing are needed to turn a film into photographs.

flash gun

A flash gun produces a flash of very bright light. It is used in photography when the natural light is not bright enough to take pictures.
See also **camera**.

floppy disk

See **disk**.

fluorescent lamp

A fluorescent lamp is a kind of electric light. It has a glass tube that glows and gives out light. The tube is filled with gas. When electricity passes through the gas, it gives off invisible rays. These rays strike a white coating inside the tube and it gives out white light.

food technology

Food technology is all the processes that the food industry uses to produce the foods we eat. Some processes in food technology have changed little over the years. Bread and dairy products, for example, are still an important part of the diet in many countries. Bread is made from flour, which is produced by grinding grains of wheat. Butter and cheese are made by processing milk.

Newer food technologies have introduced, for example, margarines and low-fat spreads to replace butter. They are made not from milk but from other fats and oils, such as sunflower oil. Plant oils are also used for cooking. They are obtained from seeds by crushing them.

Another aspect of food technology is food preservation. This means preventing food from rotting. Early ways of preserving food, such as drying it or smoking it over a fire, are still used as well as modern methods, like canning and freezing. In canning, we seal food in cans to keep out the air and germs. In freezing, we keep foods at low temperatures to stop the processes that rot them.

Cheese-making is an old food technology. Workers make cheese by curdling milk, which involves treating the milk so that it becomes a solid called curd.

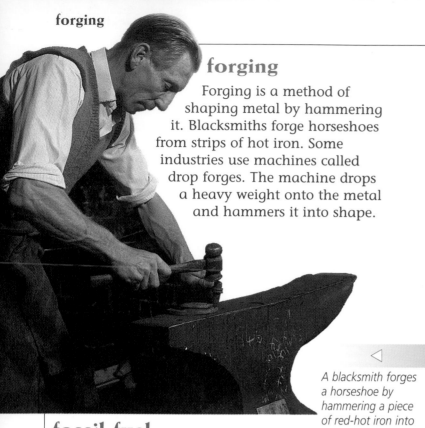

forging

Forging is a method of shaping metal by hammering it. Blacksmiths forge horseshoes from strips of hot iron. Some industries use machines called drop forges. The machine drops a heavy weight onto the metal and hammers it into shape.

A blacksmith forges a horseshoe by hammering a piece of red-hot iron into shape on an anvil.

fossil fuel

The fossil fuels are coal, petroleum (crude oil) and natural gas. They are the remains of living things. Coal is the remains of huge trees and ferns that grew up to 300 million years ago. Petroleum and natural gas are the remains of tiny living things from ancient seas.
See also **coal**, **natural gas**, **petroleum**.

foundations

The foundations are at the very bottom of a building or other structure. They support the weight of the building and stop it sinking into the ground. Most foundations are built underground and are made from concrete.

The foundations of some buildings rest on concrete columns, called piles. These go deep into the ground.

raft of concrete

concrete pile

four-stroke cycle

See **petrol engine**.

freezing

See **food technology**.

friction

Friction is a force that acts when two surfaces rub together. It tries to stop them moving. It also produces heat. Oil is added to the moving parts of machines to reduce friction.
See also **bearing**, **brake**.

fuel

Fuels are burned to produce heat. Wood has been an important fuel for thousands of years. Today, coal, petroleum (crude oil) and natural gas are our most important fuels.
See also **fossil fuel**, **nuclear energy**.

fuel cell

A fuel cell is a kind of battery. It produces electricity directly from fuel gases without burning. The space shuttle uses fuel cells to produce electricity.

furnace

A furnace burns fuel to produce heat. In the home, small furnaces heat water in a boiler for the hot-water and central heating systems. Large furnaces are used in industry, particularly for smelting metals.
See also **blast furnace**, **central heating**.

galvanizing

Galvanizing means coating steel with a thin layer of zinc. The layer of zinc stops the steel underneath from rusting.

gas

See **natural gas.**

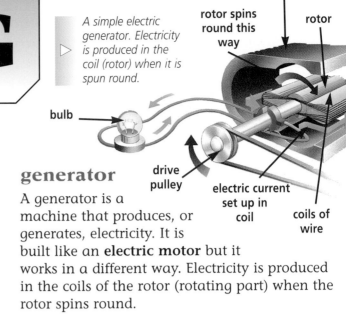

A simple electric generator. Electricity is produced in the coil (rotor) when it is spun round.

magnet (stator)

rotor spins round this way

rotor

bulb

drive pulley

electric current set up in coil

coils of wire

generator

A generator is a machine that produces, or generates, electricity. It is built like an **electric motor** but it works in a different way. Electricity is produced in the coils of the rotor (rotating part) when the rotor spins round.

genetic engineering

Genetic engineering means changing the make-up of living things, or organisms. Genetic engineers alter an organism's genes, which are the tiny parts that control what it is like. In this way they produce better medicines and crops. See also **biotechnology.**

This motorist is using a pressure gauge to check the pressure of the air in his car tyres.

gauge

A gauge is used to measure things.

The gauge of a wire or tube means its width, or diameter.

The gauge of a railway track is the distance between its rails.

geothermal power

Geothermal power is produced by using the heat inside the Earth. It is a kind of **alternative energy.** Most geothermal power stations are built near volcanic areas, where the underground rocks are hot. When water trickles into the hot rocks, it heats up and turns to steam. The steam is piped to power stations.

girder

See **beam.**

glass

See **materials.**

gear

Gears are used in machines to pass on, or transmit, power and movement from one part of the machine to another. A gear is usually a set of wheels with teeth around the outside edges. The teeth of one wheel fit into the teeth of another wheel. So when one wheel turns, it makes the other turn too. If the second wheel has a different number of teeth from the first, it will be driven round at a different speed. See also **cog wheel.**

glider

A glider is an aeroplane without an engine. It flies by 'riding' on currents of air. Another name for glider is sailplane. Gliders are launched from the ground by a powerful **winch,** or towed into the air by an aeroplane powered by an engine.

global warming

Global warming is the gradual heating-up of the Earth's climate. Scientists think that global warming is being caused by an increase in the **greenhouse effect.**

glue

Glue is a liquid used for sticking things together. It is one kind of **adhesive.** Glues are made out of natural materials such as fish bones and animal bones and hides (skins).

gramophone

See **record player.**

greenhouse effect

The layers of air around the Earth trap some of the heat we receive from the Sun. We call this process the greenhouse effect. These layers, known as the atmosphere, trap the heat like a garden greenhouse. Scientists think that the greenhouse effect is increasing because heavy gases are building up in the atmosphere. This increases the temperature of the Earth. See also **global warming.**

▷ Aircraft and ships use gyrocompasses like this one to find directions. This gyrocompass works by means of a gyroscope.

gyroscope

A gyroscope is a spinning wheel set inside a frame. When it spins, a gyroscope wheel always points in the same direction. For this reason it is used in compasses to show directions.

half-tone process

The half-tone process is used to print copies of paintings and photographs. It breaks up the painting or photograph into a pattern of tiny dots. This pattern is then copied onto printing plates.
See also **printing.**

hammer

See **tool.**

hardware

See **computer.**

helicopter

A helicopter is an aircraft that can fly in any direction. It can also hover in the air like a hummingbird. There is a set of rotating blades, called the rotor, on top of the helicopter. When the rotor blades spin round, they produce forces that lift the helicopter in the air and move it.

Helicopters also have a small rotor at the back, or tail. The tail rotor stops the helicopter from spinning round when the main rotor turns.

hi-fi

Hi-fi is short for high-fidelity. A hi-fi sound system, such as a record player or tape recorder, reproduces sound that is almost as good as the original sound.

hologram

A hologram is a picture made by a **laser** beam. It does not look flat like an ordinary picture. We call a hologram a three-dimensional (3D) picture because it seems to have depth.

hot-air balloon

See **balloon.**

propellers

rudder

engines

lift fan

air cushion

hovercraft

A hovercraft is a vehicle that glides over the surface of land or water on a cushion of air. It is sometimes called an air-cushion vehicle (ACV). A powerful fan forces air under the hovercraft to produce the cushion. Hovercraft are driven forwards by **propellers**.

△

A hydroelectric power station in California, USA. The water stored behind the dam is used to turn the generators that produce electricity.

hydroelectric power

Hydroelectric power (HEP) is electricity that is produced by using the energy in flowing water. In a typical hydroelectric power station, water from a reservoir is pumped to water **turbines**. It turns the turbines. They drive electric **generators** to make electricity.
See also **power station**.

hydraulic power

Hydraulic power is the force that is carried by a liquid, usually an oil. The foot brake in a motor car works by hydraulic power. When the driver presses down the brake pedal, liquids in pipes carry the pressure to the brakes.

▽

A hovercraft that travels over the sea has a 'skirt' to trap the air underneath. This makes a deeper cushion of air.

hydrofoil

A hydrofoil is a boat that skims across the surface of the water. It is fitted with underwater wings called foils. When the foils move through water, they lift the body, or hull, of the hydrofoil above the surface. It can now travel much faster because it is free from the resistance of the water.
See also **drag.**

air in

water flows over front foil

skirt

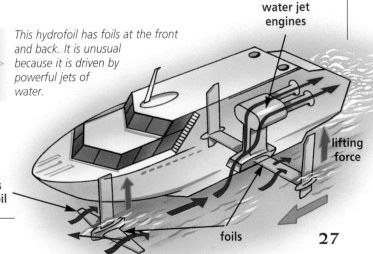

water jet engines

This hydrofoil has foils at the front and back. It is unusual because it is driven by powerful jets of water.

lifting force

foils

27

Industrial Revolution

The Industrial Revolution is a period of history when people first worked in factories. At this time, they began to use machines to produce goods. At first the machines were driven by water power, and then later by steam engines. The Industrial Revolution began in Britain in the mid-1700s and soon spread to other countries.

industry

Industry is organized working. Mining is an industry which takes raw materials out of the ground. Some industries make these raw materials into other materials, such as steel or chemicals. Other industries may take steel and chemicals and make them into different materials for other industries, or into finished goods to sell.
See also **making and manufacturing.**

information technology

Information technology (IT) is the handling of information by computer systems. It includes **word processing** and **desk-top publishing.** In banks, shops and businesses, IT is used to move sums of money from one place to another. This activity is known as electronic funds transfer (EFT).
See also **communications, computer.**

internal combustion engine

An internal combustion engine burns fuel inside the engine itself. Petrol engines and diesel engines are examples of internal combustion engines. Steam engines are external combustion engines because they burn fuel outside the engine.
See also **diesel engine, petrol engine.**

Internet

See **communications.**

invention

An invention is a completely new object or idea. Usually it refers to a new machine or other device. One of the greatest inventions ever was the wheel, which was invented in about 3500 BC.

Many inventions, such as television and the motor car, come about gradually as the result of many people's work. Other inventions are the work of just one person, for example Alexander Graham Bell's telephone and Edwin Land's Polaroid 'instant' camera.
See also **communications.**

iron and steel

See **blast furnace, steel-making.**

◁

Information technology helps you to collect money from a cashpoint machine. The machine is connected to your bank so that you can take money out of your bank account.

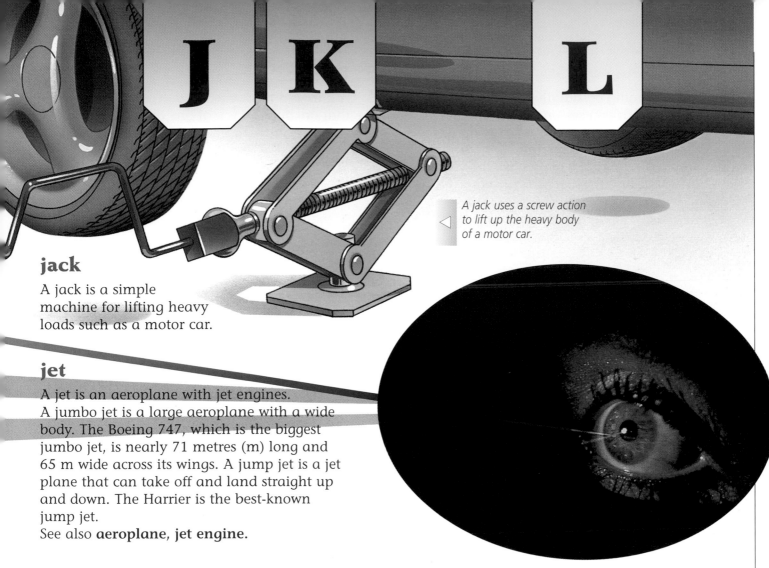

J K L

A jack uses a screw action to lift up the heavy body of a motor car.

jack

A jack is a simple machine for lifting heavy loads such as a motor car.

jet

A jet is an aeroplane with jet engines. A jumbo jet is a large aeroplane with a wide body. The Boeing 747, which is the biggest jumbo jet, is nearly 71 metres (m) long and 65 m wide across its wings. A jump jet is a jet plane that can take off and land straight up and down. The Harrier is the best-known jump jet.
See also **aeroplane**, **jet engine**.

jet engine

A jet engine is an engine that produces a stream, or jet, of gases. Most aircraft are now powered by jet engines. The jets of gases move, or propel, the aircraft through the air.

The simplest kind of jet engine is called a turbojet. It has three main parts – a compressor, a combustion chamber and a **turbine**. The compressor takes in air and forces it into the combustion chamber. Fuel is burned in the chamber. This produces hot gases which spin the turbine. The gases then escape as a jet out of the back of the engine.

key

See **lock**.

kiln

A kiln is a kind of oven. Pottery is baked hard, or 'fired', in a kiln. **Cement** is made in kilns.

Surgeons sometimes use laser beams to carry out delicate operations on people's eyes.

laser

A laser is an electronic device that produces a powerful beam of light. The beam is very narrow and does not spread out like an ordinary beam of light. Some laser beams are powerful enough to melt and to cut metal. They can be used for **welding**.
See also **CD**.

lathe

A lathe cuts and shapes metal parts. It is one of the commonest **machine tools** in industrial workshops. A sharp cutting tool is forced against a piece of metal to be shaped while it is being turned, or rotated. This process is called turning.

LCD

LCD stands for liquid crystal display. It is the kind of display that you see on digital watches and pocket calculators. An LCD is made up of strips that contain a liquid crystal. This is a kind of liquid plastic that behaves like a crystal. When electricity passes through the strips, the liquid crystal stops light from passing through, so the strips look black.

This pocket organizer has an LCD screen. The letters and numbers on the screen are made up of different arrangements of tiny black strips.

lever

A lever is a very simple machine. It is a **beam**, which rests and turns on a fixed point. This point is called the pivot or fulcrum. A see-saw is a simple lever with the pivot in the middle. A crowbar is a lever with the pivot close to one end. You pull on the handle with a certain force (your effort) to move a heavy load at the end.

life-support system

See **space technology**.

lift

A lift carries people and goods up and down, usually inside tall buildings. It moves inside a space called a shaft. The passenger car usually hangs from a wire rope that goes around a **pulley** at the top of the shaft. A heavy weight is fixed to the other end of the rope. The pulley is driven round by an electric motor.

light bulb

The electric light bulb is our main source of artificial light. It is a glass bulb that is filled with gas. Inside the bulb is a thin coil of wire called the filament.

liner

A liner is a passenger ship. It has many decks that are built on top of one another.

lock

You use a lock to fasten a door. An ordinary lock has a key. When you insert the right key in the lock, it moves the levers or pins inside the lock so that the key can turn. When the key turns, it moves a bolt forwards to lock the door or backwards to unlock it.

Safes and bank vaults are usually fitted with a combination lock. You have to dial the right set, or combination, of numbers to open it.

base

When electricity flows through the filament inside a light bulb, it becomes white-hot and gives off light.

glass bulb

electricity flows through wire

supports

locomotive

A locomotive pulls trains on the railways. Most modern locomotives have diesel engines or are powered by electricity. Early locomotives had steam engines. See also **transport**.

filament of coiled wire

gas

A close-up view of a loom. The threads that you can see are the warp threads. The woven cloth is on the left.

machine

Machines do work for us. They help us to carry out all kinds of jobs more easily. They manufacture goods, carry us around and do simple jobs such as opening cans. Simple machines include the **lever** and the **pulley**.

loom

A loom is a machine for weaving cloth. One set of threads (called the weft) is threaded under and over another set of threads (the warp). The warp threads are stretched lengthways on the loom.

lorry

A lorry is a vehicle that carries goods and materials. Lorries are often called trucks. Most lorries have **diesel engines**. Ordinary lorries are built with an all-in-one frame, or chassis. Different kinds of body can be built on this chassis.

machine tool

A machine tool cuts and shapes metal parts. All machine tools have powerful electric motors. The **lathe** is a common machine tool. See also **making and manufacturing.**

maglev

The word 'maglev' is short for magnetic levitation. It is a way of using magnetism to lift an object above a surface. Maglev trains can travel very fast because they are not slowed down by **friction** with the track.

magnetic tape

A magnetic tape is a plastic tape that is coated with magnetic material. It is the kind of tape used in tape recorders and videocassette recorders. Sounds or pictures are recorded on the tape in the form of a magnetic pattern. See also **cassette.**

loudspeaker

A loudspeaker, or speaker for short, is a device that gives out sounds. It turns electrical signals into sound. Speakers are part of sound reproduction equipment, such as tape recorders, record players and radios.

A maglev train in Japan. Magnetism lifts the train a few centimetres above the track.

lubrication

Lubrication usually means oiling. The lubrication system in a car engine supplies oil to the moving parts. The oil helps to reduce **friction**.

MITSUKOSHI HSST

Making and manufacturing

In our daily lives, we buy and use many different things, such as pens and pencils, socks and shirts, pots and pans, bicycles and cars, radios and computers. All these goods have been made in workshops or factories.

Making goods in factories is known as manufacturing. The word 'manufacturing' means making by hand. But in most factories the goods are made by workers using machines.

The different stages of building a motor car. First, the car is designed with the help of computers. Then it is put together, piece by piece, on an assembly line.

People have been making things for many thousands of years. The first materials that people used were wood and stone. They used these materials to make tools and weapons. Later, people learned how to bake clay into pottery and smelt minerals into metals. They learned how to mould the clay and cast the metals into shape.

When making a product, first we decide on a suitable design. Then we work out how to make it. Usually, we build it up by joining together, or assembling, simpler parts called components. Then we select suitable materials for the components and suitable tools to shape them. If the product is to be made in a factory, we also have to work out which machines and people will be needed to produce it.

assembly line

In many factories, workers assemble products from a number of different parts on an assembly line. They stand or sit in line beside a moving **conveyor**. As the product slowly passes by on the conveyor, they add the parts one by one. At the end of the assembly line, the product is complete. The US car maker Henry Ford introduced the moving assembly line in 1913.

More fittings are added to the inside of the car.

Robots spray the body with several coats of paint.

Robots weld together steel panels to make the body.

Workers fit other body parts, such as the doors.

automation

Automation is the use of automatic machines to produce goods or handle industrial processes such as painting or welding. The machines are controlled by computers.

factory

A factory is a place where workers make goods, nearly always by using machines. Work in a factory is very organized. It is split into different jobs, which are carried out by different workers. For example, in a car factory each worker builds only part of a car. Then all the various parts are put together, usually on an assembly line. Because each worker has only one kind of job to do, he or she can learn to do it quickly. This helps to speed up production.

finishing

When something is made in a workshop or a factory, it usually needs finishing in some way before it can be sold or used. For example, a wooden table needs to be varnished or painted. This treatment protects the wood and makes the table look better.

joining

The parts of a product can be joined together in different ways. Wooden parts can be fitted together with the help of carefully cut joints, such as dove tails. They can also be glued, nailed or screwed together. Metal parts can be joined by nuts and bolts. They can be joined more permanently by **soldering** and **welding.**

A Chinese worker finishes a newly made vase by painting a beautiful design on it.

mass production

Mass production means making large amounts of goods in factories. It is possible because factories use machines and efficient methods of working, such as the assembly line.

The final fittings, such as seats and wheels, are added.

shaping

Workers in workshops and factories use various processes to shape the parts or products they make. Cutting is a common process. Carpenters use tools such as knives, chisels and saws to cut wood. Metalworkers use power-driven **machine tools**, which carry out processes such as drilling and milling.

Metalworkers also shape metal by a hammering process called forging. They shape hot liquid metal by **casting** it in moulds. Moulding is a common way of shaping plastics and pottery too. Many pieces of pottery are shaped by hand on a rotating potter's wheel.

The engine and wheel axles are fixed to the body.

The car is now complete and ready to be driven away.

Materials

How many different things can you see around you? Maybe a table, a cup, a telephone, a window and, through the window, a car. All these things are made from different materials. The table is made of wood, the cup of baked clay, the telephone of plastic, the window of glass and the car of metal. Wood, clay, plastic, glass and metal are some of the most important materials that we use to make things.

When we make something, we must choose a material with the right qualities, or properties. We make a window out of glass because we can see through glass. It is transparent. We make a car out of metal because metal is strong. We make many objects out of plastic because it is cheap and easy to shape.

ceramic

A ceramic is a material that is made by baking clay and other substances taken out of the ground. Pottery, bricks and tiles are common ceramics. Special ceramics are used for making cooking equipment and cooker hobs. Like many other ceramics, they do not crack or break when you heat them.

concrete

Concrete is a very important building material. It is made by adding water to a mixture of cement, sand and stones. As the mixture dries, it sets hard. Steel bars are sometimes put in concrete to give it extra strength. Then we call it reinforced concrete.

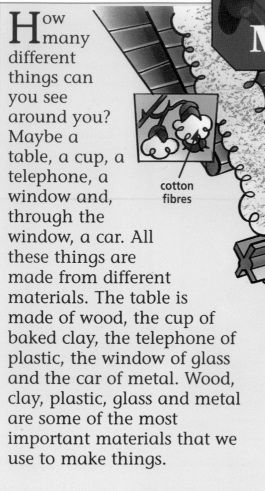

cotton fibres

loose cotton

cotton is washed and beaten

mat of cotton fibres

cotton is combed

fibre

A fibre is a thin thread. Fibres from plants and animals are used to make cloth and other textiles. Cotton from the cotton plant and wool from sheep are the most widely used natural fibres. **Synthetic fibres** are made from chemicals. They are also widely used in textiles and to make strong materials such as **fibreglass**.

glass

Glass is a hard, transparent (see-through) material. It is cheap to make and easy to shape. It is made by heating sand, limestone and other substances in a **furnace**. The mixture melts into a liquid, which forms glass when it cools.

Liquid glass can easily be shaped into flat sheets for windows. Glass is also shaped into bottles, jars, drinking glasses and other objects. It can be shaped into fine fibres too.

cotton rope

cotton spinner

finished cotton thread

◁

Cotton fibres have to be cleaned and combed straight before they can be made into thread. The thread is used for weaving into cloth to make clothes such as T-shirts.

metal

Most of the metals we use are shiny, hard and strong. Iron, aluminium and copper are our most important metals. We use more iron than all the other metals put together. Iron is used mainly in the form of its **alloy**, steel. Aluminium is useful because it is so light. Copper is used to make electrical wire because it passes on, or conducts, electricity well.

A few metals, such as platinum, gold and silver, are found as metals in the ground. We call them native metals. But most metals are made from minerals.

mineral

A mineral is a chemical substance that makes up rocks. We use many minerals as raw materials. For example, we use limestone to make cement, and sand to manufacture glass. The most important minerals are **ores**, from which we make metals. We can make copper from a mineral called cuprite. It is a copper ore.

plastic

A plastic is a material that can be shaped easily. Plastics are **synthetics**. Most plastics are made from chemicals obtained from petroleum. In general, plastics are light and tough. They do not rust or rot, and they do not conduct electricity.

Common plastics include polythene (polyethene), **PVC** and Teflon. Polythene is used to make bottles, bowls and bags. PVC is used to make floor tiles, guttering and rainwear. Teflon is heat-resistant and is used for the non-stick coating on kitchen pans. Some plastics can be filled with air bubbles to make foams.

Plastic objects like these teaspoons are cheap and easy to make. Also, they can be brightly coloured.

raw material

Raw materials are the basic substances we use to make things. Some of the most important raw materials are minerals, petroleum, wood, and fibres from plants and animals.

wood

Wood from trees has been used for tens of thousands of years, and is still widely used today. We call pieces of wood 'timber'. Most timber is used in buildings to make roofs, floors, doors and so on. Large amounts of wood are used to make paper. See also **paper**.

Wood is still the best material for making some musical instruments, such as guitars.

35

memory

See **computer**.

metal

See **materials**.

metal fatigue

Metal fatigue can weaken a metal. It happens when the metal has been bent, twisted or stretched over and over again.

metallurgy

Metallurgy deals with metals. It includes the removal, or extraction, of metals from their ores, and how the metals are then refined and shaped. **Casting**, **forging** and **rolling** are different methods of shaping metals.

meter

A meter is a measuring instrument. It refers especially to instruments that make electrical measurements, such as an ammeter which measures electrical current.

microchip

A microchip is a tiny thin piece of a hard substance called silicon. It is sometimes called a silicon chip. It contains thousands of miniature electronic pathways, or circuits. The circuits can be seen only under a microscope.
See also **computer**.

▷

This magnified picture of a microchip shows its different circuits. Microchips are used in computers, calculators, robots and many other machines.

microfilm

Microfilm is a piece of photographic film. It contains tiny images (pictures) of documents, records, newspapers and so on. Many libraries have microfilm readers. These produce a bigger, or magnified, image of the film on a screen.

microphone

A microphone is used to record or broadcast sounds. It turns the sounds into electrical signals. Sound waves enter a microphone and make a thin metal plate shake backwards and forwards, or vibrate. The vibrations are then changed into electrical signals. These signals can be broadcast by radio or television, or recorded on magnetic tape or on a CD.

metal plate

coil of wire

magnet

A cutaway view of a microphone. When you speak or sing into it, the sound of your voice makes the metal plate vibrate. These vibrations set up tiny electrical signals that carry the pattern of your sound. ◁

36

△ The letters of the alphabet in the international Morse code.

microscope

A microscope is an instrument that makes tiny objects look much bigger. It uses glass lenses to magnify an object placed on a glass slide. A compound microscope has two lenses – one near the object (the objective) and one near your eye (the eyepiece). You change the position of the two lenses until you can see a clear picture.
See also **electron microscope**.

eyepiece

focusing knob

body tube

objective lenses

slide

mirror

stage

stand

With a compound microscope, you look through the eyepiece and the objective at an object on the slide. You turn the focusing knob until you can see the object clearly. △

microwave oven

A microwave oven cooks food by using microwaves. These waves are similar to radio waves. The microwaves make tiny drops of water in the food move quickly backwards and forwards, or vibrate. This causes the food to heat up.

mineral

See **materials**.

mining

Mining means digging out coal, metals and minerals from the ground. Gravel and rock are dug out of a **quarry**. Mines on the surface are called opencast mines. In underground mines, vertical shafts and horizontal tunnels have to be dug to reach the coal, metals or minerals.

missile

A missile is any object that is thrown. In warfare, a missile is a weapon with a **rocket motor**. It flies towards its target. Most missiles are guided to their target. Some missiles may be attracted to a target by its heat. Some fly along a **laser** beam. Other missiles follow a detailed map inside the memory in the missile's computer.

modem

A modem is an electronic device that can be fitted to a computer. It allows the computer to send and receive information, or data. The modem changes the computer signals into suitable electrical signals that can travel along telephone lines.
See also **computer**.

monorail

A monorail is a kind of railway. It has just one rail, instead of the usual two. Monorail trains run on top of the track or hang beneath it.

Morse code

The Morse code is used to send messages over long distances. Dots and dashes in the code stand for letters of the alphabet and numbers. They are arranged into coded messages. An American, Samuel Morse, invented the code to send messages on the telegraph, which he also invented.
See also **communications**.

motion picture
See **movie**.

motor

A motor is a machine that changes energy into movement, or motion.
See also **electric motor, engine, rocket motor**.

▷ *Here is a message in Morse code. What does it say? (The answer is at the bottom of the page.)*

Answer: TAKE ME TO YOUR LEADER

start here

motor car

The motor car is our most common means of transport. There are over 400 million cars throughout the world, more than half of them in the United States. The car is one of the most complicated machines we come across in our daily lives. It has up to 14 000 separate parts.

Most cars are powered by a **petrol engine**, but some have a **diesel engine**. The transmission system carries, or transmits, the power from the engine to the wheels that drive the car.

The driver chooses different gears in the gearbox. This allows the engine to drive the wheels at different speeds. The clutch disconnects the engine from the gearbox while the driver changes gear. The driver operates the clutch with a foot pedal.

Two other foot pedals are used to control the car. One is the accelerator, which controls the speed of the engine. The other is the brake pedal, which the driver presses to put on the brakes. The driver changes direction by turning the steering wheel, which turns the front wheels.

motorcycle

A motorcycle, or motorbike, is a two-wheeled vehicle. It is driven by a **petrol engine**. In most motorbikes, a chain connects the engine with the back wheel and drives it round. In a few motorbikes, the engine drives the back wheel by a rod, or shaft.

motorway

A motorway is a main road that is specially built for high-speed motor vehicles. It has two sets of lanes that are separated by a central barrier. The barrier keeps apart the traffic travelling in opposite directions. A motorway has no crossroads, roundabouts or traffic lights. Other roads must cross either over or under it.

Some of the main parts of a motor car. The suspension helps to cushion the driver and passengers from bumps in the road. The battery supplies electricity to the engine. The radiator is part of the system that cools the engine.

gear-lever · engine · battery · exhaust pipe · rear suspension · rear brake · fuel tank · silencer · handbrake · catalytic converter · front suspension · front brake · gearbox · steering gears · cooling radiator

moulding

Moulding is a way of shaping materials by pouring or forcing them into moulds. Most plastics are forced into a mould when they are soft or liquid. When they cool and harden, they take the shape of the mould. Plastic bottles are blown into shape in moulds. Plastic bowls are made by injecting melted plastic, under pressure, into moulds. See also **casting**.

mouse

See **computer**.

A piece of film from a movie. Each picture has been taken a tiny part of a second after the picture before it.

movie

A movie is a moving picture like the one you watch in a cinema. It is also called a motion picture or a film. In fact, the pictures in a movie do not move. At the cinema, a **projector** throws a series of still pictures onto the screen. In each picture, anything moving has changed its position slightly. When you look at the cinema screen, all the different pictures blend together in your eyes. You think that the action you see is part of one moving picture.
See also **cine camera**.

multimedia

Multimedia refers to the many different ways of handling and presenting information using a computer. It is a part of **information technology**. A **CD-ROM** is one kind of multimedia device.

natural gas

Natural gas is one of our most important fuels. It is a **fossil fuel**. It is a mixture of methane and a number of other gases.

neon light

Neon lights produce a very bright, red-orange light. They are widely used in advertising signs. The light is a glass tube that contains neon gas. The gas glows when electricity passes through it.

Vivid neon lights brighten up the streets of Hong Kong at night.

nuclear energy

Nuclear energy is a kind of energy that is locked up inside the centre, or nucleus, of atoms.

Scientists can obtain, or extract, this energy from certain atoms, such as atoms of uranium. A uranium atom gives off huge amounts of energy when its nucleus is split apart. The energy is given off mainly as heat and **radiation**. This process is called fission.

Nuclear energy is also released in another way. This other process is called fusion. In fusion, atoms come together to form a heavier atom. The process of fusion takes place in the Sun and in the stars. It provides the energy to keep them shining.

In a nuclear power station, heat from the fission process inside the reactor turns water into steam. The steam is then fed to turbines, which drive generators to produce electricity.

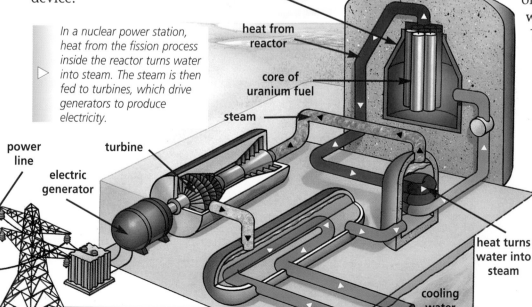

concrete shield
nuclear reactor
heat from reactor
core of uranium fuel
steam
power line
turbine
electric generator
heat turns water into steam
cooling water

nuclear weapon

A nuclear weapon uses nuclear energy to cause very powerful explosions. An atomic bomb is one kind of nuclear weapon. It uses the nuclear energy that is given off when atoms are split. Another kind of nuclear weapon is the hydrogen bomb. It uses the nuclear energy that is given off when atoms of hydrogen join together.
See also **nuclear energy.**

You put oil on metal hinges to let them move easily and to stop them from squeaking.

nut

See **bolt.**

nylon

Nylon is a well-known plastic. It is widely used as a fibre. Nylon was the very first **synthetic fibre.** It was first made in the early 1930s.
See also **materials.**

This scientist is holding an optical fibre. It is carrying a beam of green laser light. Most of the light stays inside the fibre.

offset-litho

See **printing.**

oil

An oil is a greasy liquid that does not mix with water. One kind of oil comes from the ground. We call it crude oil, or petroleum. Other kinds of oil come from animals and plants, for example cod-liver oil and sunflower oil.
See also **petroleum.**

oil refinery

An oil refinery is a place where crude oil is processed. Crude oil, or petroleum, is a mixture of many chemicals. These chemicals are separated out at the refinery. Some of the main products from a refinery are fuels such as petrol, diesel and heating oil, and **petrochemicals.**
See also **cracking, refining.**

oil well

See **petroleum.**

optical fibre

An optical fibre is a thin thread of very pure glass. It can carry a beam of light without the light escaping from the sides. Optical fibres are used to make telephone cables. These cables are now replacing copper wires in telephone and other communications systems. They carry electrical signals in the form of **laser** light.
See also **endoscope.**

ore

An ore is a kind of rock. Ores are minerals that contain metal. Magnetite, for example, is a mineral that contains iron. It is a common iron ore. The metals are separated from most ores by **smelting.**
See also **materials.**

organism

An organism is a living thing. Animals, plants, fungi and bacteria are the main kinds of organism. Bacteria are so tiny that you need a microscope to see them. They are called micro-organisms.

P

pacemaker

A pacemaker is a device that is used in medicine. It helps a patient's heart to beat regularly.

paper

Paper is the material on which this book is printed. Most paper is made from wood pulp, which is really a mass of wood fibres. The wood pulp is mixed with water and other materials and is then beaten by machines. The watery pulp flows onto a net of wire, and the water drains away. The thin layer of fibres that remains is dried and then rolled into a smooth sheet of paper.

This X-ray picture shows a pacemaker inside a patient's chest. It sends tiny electrical shocks to the heart muscles.

Paper comes off the paper-making machine as an endless sheet. It is then wound onto a huge reel.

petrochemical

A petrochemical is a chemical that comes from petroleum (crude oil). Petrochemicals are produced in an oil refinery. Many products, such as plastics, paints and dyes, are made from petrochemicals.

petrol

Petrol is a kind of fuel. It is made from petroleum in an oil refinery. Petrol is burned as a fuel in petrol engines.
See also **oil refinery, petrol engine.**

petrol engine

A petrol engine burns petrol as fuel. Most motor cars and motorcycles have petrol engines.
The main part of the engine is a metal block containing a number of round sleeves, called cylinders. Inside each cylinder is a **piston**. A mixture of petrol and air is sucked into each cylinder, one after the other, and burned by an electric spark. The burning produces hot gases that force the pistons down the cylinders.

The pistons are connected to a shaft and make it turn. In a motor vehicle, this turning movement is then passed on to the driving wheels.
See also **internal combustion engine.**

pesticide

A pesticide is a kind of chemical. It kills insects, fungi and other living things that harm crops. The main kinds of pesticides are insecticides (which kill insects), fungicides (which kill fungal diseases) and herbicides (which kill weeds). Herbicides are often called weedkillers. Unfortunately, many pesticides can harm wildlife, and so they must be used with care.

In a petrol engine, each movement of the piston is called a stroke. We say that the engine works on a four-stroke cycle.

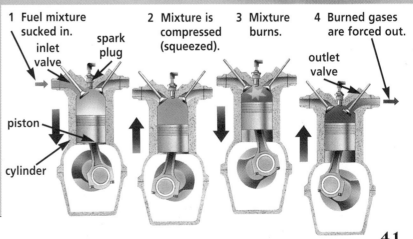

1 Fuel mixture sucked in.
inlet valve
spark plug

2 Mixture is compressed (squeezed).

3 Mixture burns.

4 Burned gases are forced out.
outlet valve

piston

cylinder

petroleum

Petroleum is oil we take out of the ground or from under the sea. We often call it crude oil. It has become the world's most important fuel.

Petroleum is a **fossil fuel**. It is the remains of tiny organisms that lived many millions of years ago. When these organisms died, their bodies rotted and formed a slimy liquid. Over the years, this liquid changed into petroleum. In places, pools of petroleum have become trapped in the layers of rocks. Oil engineers try to find these pools and drill holes down to them. If they find one, the hole becomes an oil well.
See also **drilling rig**.

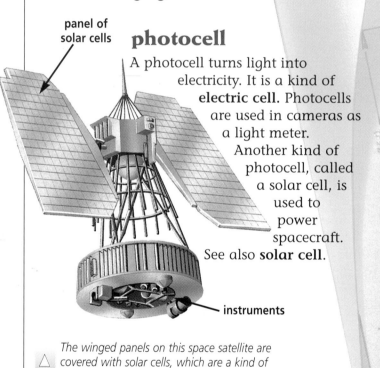

panel of solar cells

instruments

photocell

A photocell turns light into electricity. It is a kind of **electric cell**. Photocells are used in cameras as a light meter. Another kind of photocell, called a solar cell, is used to power spacecraft.
See also **solar cell**.

△ The winged panels on this space satellite are covered with solar cells, which are a kind of photocell. They turn sunlight into electricity.

photocopier

A photocopier is a machine that makes copies of pictures and of printed or written words. In a photocopier, the words or pictures on a page are changed into an electrical picture, or image, on a drum. A special ink powder is attracted to this image. The ink is then transferred onto a sheet of clean paper and set by heat.

photography

Photography means taking pictures with a camera.
See also **camera, cine camera, film**.

piston

A piston is part of an engine. It moves backwards and forwards inside a sleeve, or cylinder. Pistons in cylinders are the most important parts of petrol engines, diesel engines and steam engines. Hot gases or steam force the pistons down the cylinders to produce power.
See also **diesel engine, petrol engine, steam engine**.

plane

See **tool**.

plans

Plans are a set of drawings that show how something is to be made or built. Sometimes plans show where something is to be positioned. Usually they are drawn to scale. This means that all the things shown in the plans are the right size in relation to one another. In some plans, the lines of the drawings are reproduced as blue lines. These plans are called blueprints.
See also **design**.

plastic

See **materials**.

pliers

See **tool**.

▷ The plans for a house show what the building will look like. They also give details about how the house will be built.

plough

A plough is a farm tool that turns over, or tills, the soil. It is pulled by a tractor. Ploughs break up the soil and bury the weeds. They are used to prepare the soil for sowing and planting.

pollution

Pollution means poisoning or causing some kind of harm to our surroundings. The gases that are given out by car engines and factory chimneys cause air pollution. Oil spills from ships can cause pollution of the seas. **Pesticides** can pollute farmland and harm wildlife.
See also **acid rain**, **greenhouse effect**.

On a plough, curved blades cut into the soil and turn it over.

polymer

A polymer is a kind of material. The word 'polymer' means many parts. Usually, polymer refers to a plastic. Plastics are built up by joining together many groups of atoms, called molecules. So a plastic is a material built up of many parts. Some natural materials are made up of polymers too. For example, wood and cotton are made up of a natural polymer called cellulose.
See also **materials.**

polythene

Polythene is a well-known plastic. Its correct chemical name is polyethene. It is made by heating a gas called ethene (ethylene), which is produced in an **oil refinery**.
See also **materials.**

pottery

Pottery is any object that is made of baked clay. Making pottery is one of the oldest human activities. Since about 5000 years ago, potters have shaped their pottery on a rotating wheel. The three main kinds of pottery are earthenware, stoneware and porcelain. They are made from different clays and are baked, or 'fired', at different temperatures.
See also **kiln, making and manufacturing, materials.**

A potter shapes wet clay into a vase while the clay spins round on a rotating wheel.

power station

A power station is a place where huge amounts of electricity are produced. Hydroelectric power stations produce electricity by using the energy in flowing water. Nuclear power stations use **nuclear energy.** Most power stations use the energy in fuels, such as coal, oil and natural gas. They burn fuels to produce heat, which changes water into steam. The steam is fed to **turbines,** which spin generators to produce electricity.
See also **electricity supply, hydroelectric power.**

pressure cooker

A pressure cooker is a container in which food can be cooked quickly. In an open pan, food cooks at the temperature of boiling water (100 degrees Celsius, or 100°C). When food and water are heated in a pressure cooker, the water reaches a temperature of about 130°C before it boils. The food therefore cooks faster than in an open pan.

printer

A printer is a machine that prints out onto paper the words and pictures from computers. A dot-matrix printer prints letters or numbers as a pattern of dots. An ink-jet printer squirts ink onto the paper from tiny nozzles. A laser printer uses a fine laser beam to form the printed letters and numbers.
See also **computer**.

printing

Printing is the process of making copies of words and pictures, usually on paper. The most common method of printing books and magazines is called offset-litho. In this method printing is done from a flat surface. The type area on the printing plate is treated in a certain way so that it is the only part that attracts printing ink.

probe

See **space technology**.

program

See **computer**.

A worker checks a sheet of paper from a printing press. Both sides of the sheet are printed. Later, the sheets will be cut up and folded to make the pages of a book.

projector

A projector is used to throw, or project, a picture onto a screen. Projectors have two main parts – a powerful light and a lens. The lens is used to enlarge, or magnify, the picture.
See also **movie**.

propeller

A propeller is used to move an aeroplane or a ship forwards. It is a device with curved blades. It is often called a screw, because it turns round rather like a screw as it travels through the air or water.
See also **screw**.

This is a slide projector for showing colour slides, or transparencies. Its powerful light shines through a slide and throws a large picture onto the screen.

screen →

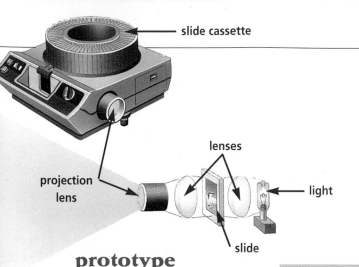

slide cassette

lenses

projection lens

light

slide

quarry

A quarry is a place where rock, stone and gravel are dug out of the ground. Gravel is dug out in huge quantities and is mixed with cement to make concrete.

prototype

A prototype is an early working example of a machine or some other object. It is usually made in order to test the machine. Aircraft manufacturers, for example, carry out many tests on prototypes to make sure that their designs work well. See also **design**.

pulley

A pulley is a simple lifting machine. Pulleys make it easier to lift heavy loads. A simple pulley consists of a grooved wheel with a rope passing over it.

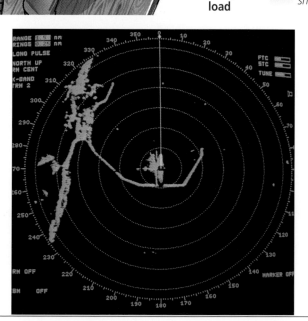

By using a rope and pulleys, you can move heavy loads more easily.

grooved wheel

pulleys

rope

heavy load

pump

A pump is used to move liquids and gases. A bicycle pump uses a **piston** to push air into a tyre. In a car, a pump with turning **gears** moves oil through the engine.

PVC

PVC is a common plastic. It is short for polyvinyl chloride. PVC is used to make things such as waterproof clothing, drainpipes, beach balls and the covering, or insulation, around electrical wires.

radar

Radar is a method of using radio waves to find out where objects are. Air traffic controllers use radar to mark the position of aircraft in the skies. Ships at sea use radar to spot other ships.

In a radar system, an **aerial** sends out beams of very short radio waves, called microwaves. Any object in the path of these waves reflects them back to the aerial as a kind of echo. This echo is displayed on a screen, which shows exactly where the object is.

A ship's radar screen. The screen shows up the coastline and any ships in the area.

radiation

Radiation means rays. Certain objects give off energy in the form of radiation. Light rays, X-rays and radio waves are some of the many different kinds of radiation. See also **X-ray machine**.

radio

Radio is a way of communicating over long distances. It uses radio waves, which are one kind of **radiation**. The waves can carry electrical signals. These signals may stand for the sounds in radio broadcasting, or the sounds and pictures in television broadcasting.
See also **microphone**.

radio telescope

A radio telescope collects radio signals from outer space. From these signals, astronomers produce pictures of the heavens. Most radio telescopes have a huge metal dish that picks up the signals.

railway

See **transport**.

R & D

R & D stands for research and development. It means thinking up ideas for new products or how to improve existing ones. Many manufacturers have an R & D department. The people who work in it look into, or research, new processes and new materials. If they find something that works well, they may design and build a **prototype**.
See also **making and manufacturing, materials**.

raw material

See **materials**.

recording

See **cassette, CD, record player, tape recorder, videocassette recorder**.

This group of dish aerials in New Mexico, USA, makes up one of the world's largest radio telescopes.

record player

A record player plays back the sound from a thin plastic disc. The disc is called a record. Sounds are recorded on it in a spiral groove.

To play back the sounds, the record is spun round on a turntable. A needle is placed on the record and it moves quickly backwards and forwards, or vibrates, as it follows the groove. The vibrations are changed into electrical signals. These pass to a loudspeaker, which turns them into sounds. A record player is also called a gramophone. Records are no longer so common. They have mostly been replaced by **CDs**.

recycling

Recycling means re-using waste materials. Glass, steel, aluminium, paper and plastics are now recycled in large amounts. Recycling saves materials as well as the energy that is needed to make the materials in the first place.

refining

Refining means making pure. Metals need to be refined after **smelting** because they contain many unwanted substances. Petroleum (crude oil) refining has to take place before the petroleum becomes useful.
See also **oil refinery**.

refractory

A refractory is a material that stands up to, or resists, heat well. Refractories are used, for example, to line furnaces.

refrigerator

A refrigerator is a machine that keeps foods and drinks cool. It uses the scientific idea that something takes in heat when it turns from a liquid into a gas.

In a refrigerator, a cooling liquid flows through pipes around the food compartment. Inside these pipes it changes from a liquid to a gas and takes in heat from the food. The gas then flows to a kind of pump called a compressor. This helps turn the gas back to a liquid. You hear a refrigerator make a noise when the compressor is working.

reservoir

See **dam**.

riveting

Riveting is a way of joining together pieces of metal. It is used in shipbuilding and other construction work. A rivet is a metal pin with a head at one end. The tail end is pushed through holes in the metal pieces to be joined. Then it is hammered to form another head. The metal pieces are firmly held between the two heads.

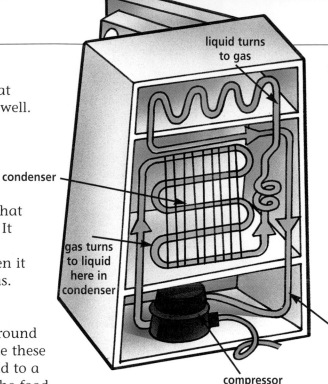

liquid turns to gas

condenser

gas turns to liquid here in condenser

compressor

gas returns to compressor

A look inside a refrigerator, showing the parts that make it work. The cooling substance takes in heat from inside the refrigerator as it changes from a liquid to a gas.

road

Roads are built to carry people and vehicles from place to place. Two main kinds of roads are built today. One has a concrete surface, and the other has a tarmac surface. Tarmac is a mixture of tar and crushed stone. Both kinds of roads have **foundations** of crushed stone.
See also **materials, motorway**.

robot

A robot is a machine that is built to do the work of humans. Some robots even look like humans. They are called androids. The robots used in industry have mechanical arms and hands, but they do not look at all like humans. They are now widely used on factory production lines.
See also **making and manufacturing**.

rocket motor

A rocket motor drives a missile or a space rocket forwards. It burns fuel to produce a stream of gases. The gases shoot backwards out of a nozzle at the back of the motor. As the gases shoot out backwards, the rocket is pushed, or propelled, forwards.

Rocket motors can work in space, where there is no oxygen. They carry the oxygen that is needed to burn the fuel. Jet engines take the oxygen they need from the air around them, so they do not work in space.
See also **jet engine, space technology**.

rolling

Rolling is a way of shaping metal. Thick pieces of metal are first heated and then squeezed between heavy rollers.

rivet

Rivets hold together the handle of this knife. Each rivet has two heads that keep the handle firmly in place.

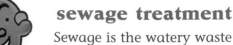

S

satellite

See **space technology**.

scales

Scales are used to weigh objects. A balance is a pair of scales that weighs very accurately. It is used in chemical laboratories. In some scales the weight of the object moves a lever or stretches a spring. Modern electronic scales have a device called a strain gauge. The object being weighed stretches a wire inside the gauge.

This is a pair of electronic scales. It measures the weight of the apples by using a strain gauge.

screw

A screw is a metal pin that fastens things together. The pin has a spiral groove, or thread. Nuts and bolts also have screw threads.

A screw is a simple machine. A **jack**, for example, uses a screw and a lever to lift up a motor car. An aeroplane or boat **propeller** is another kind of screw.
See also **bolt**.

When you turn a screw, the thread digs into the material you want to fasten.

— thread

sewage treatment

Sewage is the watery waste that comes from homes and other buildings. It contains detergents and dirt as well as human waste from lavatories.

Sewage must be cleaned and made safe before it can be allowed back into the environment. It is piped to sewage treatment plants. There the solid matter is separated from the waste and the liquid part is passed through filter beds. In these beds, tiny **organisms** feed on the waste and so help to clean the water. Chemicals may also be added.

shaping

See **making and manufacturing**.

ship

See **transport**.

silicon chip

See **microchip**.

simulator

A simulator is a machine or device that copies, or simulates, another one. Pilots train in a flight simulator. It behaves like a real aeroplane but it never leaves the ground. The inside of the simulator is built to look exactly like the flight deck of an aeroplane. It has the same controls and instruments, but its 'windows' are large computer screens. Astronauts use simulators of spacecraft for training.

seaplane

A seaplane is an aeroplane that takes off from and lands on water. A flying boat is a seaplane with a hull that is shaped like a boat. A float plane has floats instead of wheels.

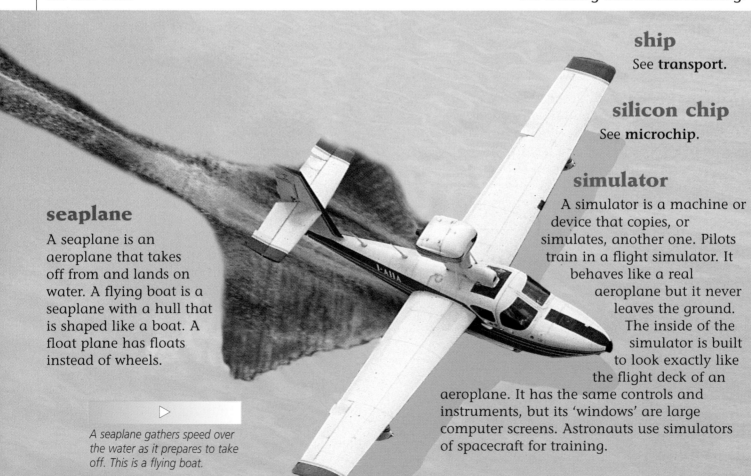

A seaplane gathers speed over the water as it prepares to take off. This is a flying boat.

skyscraper

A skyscraper is a very tall building. It is built with very firm **foundations** to support its heavy weight. Skyscrapers have a very strong frame that is made of steel beams, or girders. The walls 'hang' from this frame. Skyscraper walls do not carry any weight, unlike the walls in ordinary houses. Skyscrapers are made mostly of metal, concrete and glass.

smart card

A smart card is a plastic card, rather like a credit card. It carries a large amount of information. This information is in a **microchip**, which is set in the plastic. Special card readers can read the information that is stored in the microchip.

smelting

Smelting is a process that uses heat to take out, or extract, a metal from its **ore**. Metal is produced when the ore is heated strongly with a substance such as coke. Iron ore, for example, is smelted in a **blast furnace**.

software

See **computer**.

solar cell

A solar cell turns sunlight into electricity. It is a kind of **electric cell**. Most satellites are powered by solar panels that carry thousands of cells. The cells are made of thin slices of a hard substance called silicon.

▷

Tall skyscrapers like these are found in modern cities throughout the world. The tallest skyscraper in the world is the Sears Tower in Chicago, USA, which stands 443 metres (m) high.

solar power

Solar power is produced by using energy from the Sun. This energy is called solar energy. Houses can be heated by solar power. Solar panels on roofs trap the Sun's energy rather like a greenhouse does.

soldering

Soldering is a way of joining metal parts. It uses an **alloy** called solder, which is made of tin and lead and melts easily. In use, the solder is melted and dropped on the parts to be joined. It quickly cools and hardens.

▷

Solar power supplies electricity for this phone box in the desert. The electricity is produced by a panel of solar cells.

sonar

Ships and submarines use sonar to find objects underwater. It is a method of navigation (sailing in the right direction) that uses sound waves. Sonar equipment works in much the same way as **radar**. See also **echo-sounder**.

49

Space technology

The Earth we live on is surrounded by layers of air. We call these layers the atmosphere. The atmosphere is not very thick. About 200 kilometres (km) above the Earth's surface there is hardly any air left at all. This is the beginning of space.

Scientists started launching craft into space in 1957, beginning with the artificial satellite *Sputnik 1*. It was launched on 4 October 1957. They used rockets to launch these craft because **rocket motors** are the only engines that can work in space. *Sputnik* and other early spacecraft moved around the Earth along a path known as an orbit. They were Earth satellites. Later, scientists launched space probes that went beyond the Earth and travelled to the Moon, other planets and comets.

In 1961, humans began travelling in space. The first person was a Russian, Yuri Gagarin. The first American was John Glenn, early in 1962. Since then, many men and women have been launched into space. Space travellers are called astronauts, but Russian ones are known as cosmonauts.

ESA

ESA stands for the European Space Agency. It organizes space activities in countries in Europe.

life-support system

All spacecraft that carry astronauts and cosmonauts have a life-support system. This keeps them alive while they are in space. The system supplies the spacecraft's cabin with air, keeps it at a comfortable temperature and removes stale air and smells.

The space shuttle blasts off from the launch pad at the Kennedy Space Center in Florida, USA. In less than 15 minutes, it will be travelling in space.

NASA

NASA stands for the National Aeronautics and Space Administration. It organizes space activities in the United States of America.

probe

A probe is a spacecraft that travels beyond the Earth. Probes visit the Moon and distant planets and comets. They take pictures and collect data (information) and send them back to Earth. Probes have now visited all the planets in the Solar System, except Pluto.

helmet visor

jet-propelled backpack

controls

satellite

A satellite is a spacecraft that circles around the Earth in space. As many as 100 satellites are launched every year. Communications satellites pass on, or relay, telephone, radio and television signals from country to country. Weather satellites keep a watch on the world's weather. Astronomy satellites look into outer space to study stars and galaxies.

spacesuit

A spacesuit protects astronauts when they walk in space. It gives them oxygen to breathe and protects them from heat and cold, and from dangerous rays.

Spacelab

Spacelab is a space laboratory that is carried into space by the space shuttle. It was built by the ESA. Both American and European scientists fly on Spacelab missions. They carry out all kinds of experiments, such as finding out how substances and people are affected by being in space.

spacesuit

△

This astronaut is ready to go spacewalking. A jet-propelled backpack helps the astronaut to move around outside the spacecraft.

spacewalking

We say that astronauts go spacewalking when they work outside their spacecraft. The proper name for spacewalking is extra-vehicular activity (EVA).

space shuttle

The space shuttle is the main spacecraft that NASA uses to send astronauts into space. It is made up of three parts. The main part, called the orbiter, carries the astronauts. The external tank holds fuel for the orbiter's engines. The solid rocket boosters, or SRBs for short, provide extra power at lift-off. Both the orbiter and the SRBs are used again and again. The four orbiters in the shuttle fleet are *Columbia, Discovery, Atlantis* and *Endeavour*.

weightlessness

In space, astronauts seem to have no weight. We call this condition weightlessness. It affects everything that the astronauts do, such as eating, sleeping and moving about.

◁

Astronauts on board one of the space shuttles took this picture of Russia's space station Mir. It is made up of several units that have been joined together.

space station

A space station is a large spacecraft. Astronauts live and work inside it for months at a time. The Russians have a space station called *Mir*. NASA is planning to build an international space station called *Alpha*.

▷ *American astronauts and Russian cosmonauts meet inside the Mir space station in 1995. Mir was launched into orbit in 1986, and people have been living in it ever since.*

spanner

See **tool**.

speaker

See **loudspeaker**.

spinning machine

A spinning machine makes thread by twisting together lots of fibres (tiny threads). The thread, or yarn, is used to make cloth. The first simple spinning machine was the spinning wheel, which came into use in the 1300s. In the 1700s, better spinning machines were invented. They helped to make the textile industry the first great industry. All spinning machines do two things. They take masses of short fibres and gather them into a loose rope. Then they draw out and twist this rope into a fine thread. The twist gives the thread extra strength. See also **loom**.

spring

A spring is a machine part that can be bent, pulled or pushed. Afterwards it returns to its original state. Metal coil springs are often used in the suspension system of motor cars.

sprinkler system

A sprinkler system is fitted inside a building so that it sprays water if a fire breaks out. It consists of water pipes and nozzles. The holes in the nozzles are filled with an **alloy**, which melts at a low temperature. The heat from a fire melts the alloy and allows water to spray out.

clockwork spring

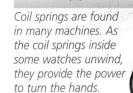

Coil springs are found in many machines. As the coil springs inside some watches unwind, they provide the power to turn the hands.

expanded spring

compressed spring

stealth plane

A stealth plane is a military aeroplane that is difficult to find in the air. It is specially designed so that it is almost invisible to **radar**. The plane has an unusual shape, with many flat surfaces. Its engine exhausts give off very little heat. This helps the plane to avoid missiles that find their target by looking for heat.

steam engine

A steam engine produces power to drive machinery. Steam engines were the first successful engines. They were the main power source in industry in the 1700s and 1800s, and also on the railways until the middle of this century.

In a steam engine, steam from a boiler forces a **piston** along a sleeve-like cylinder. A connecting rod passes on this movement to the machinery that needs to be driven.

steel-making

Making steel is one of the most important processes in industry. Steel is made from iron, which is our most important metal. It is an **alloy** of iron, small amounts of carbon and other metals. The iron, which comes from **blast furnaces**, has to be refined to make steel. Unwanted substances in the iron are burned out with a jet of oxygen. Some steel is made in electric furnaces.

stereo system

A stereo system is a sound system that reproduces life-like sounds. It often consists of a radio, a **CD** player and a cassette player. Stereo is short for stereophonic, which means sound in depth. We hear sounds in depth because we have a right ear and a left ear. Each ear picks up slightly different sounds, and this provides depth. Stereo systems produce a stereo effect by using right and left **loudspeakers** (or headphones) that give out slightly different sounds.

This stealth plane is called the F-117A. Its odd shape makes it almost invisible on radar. This allows the plane to get close to its target without being spotted.

streamlined

A fish can swim through the water easily because it has a streamlined shape. Aircraft, cars and ships are streamlined so that they can travel through the air or water more easily. Streamlining of cars and aeroplanes reduces the **air resistance** on them, so that they can travel faster and use less fuel.

The body of a shark is smooth and streamlined. It slips easily through the water.

structure

A structure is something that has been built, or constructed. Bridges and skyscrapers are structures.

Structure also means the way that something is made or put together. Scientists examine the structure of the Earth, for example.

submarine

A submarine is a kind of ship that can travel underwater. The body, or hull, of a submarine has tanks that can be flooded with water. This makes the submarine sink. The tanks can also be filled with air, to make the submarine rise to the surface again.

Submarines have **propellers**. They are driven by diesel engines on the surface, and by electric motors under water. Other submarines are powered by **nuclear energy**. Their propellers are driven by steam **turbines**.

submersible

A submersible is a small submarine.

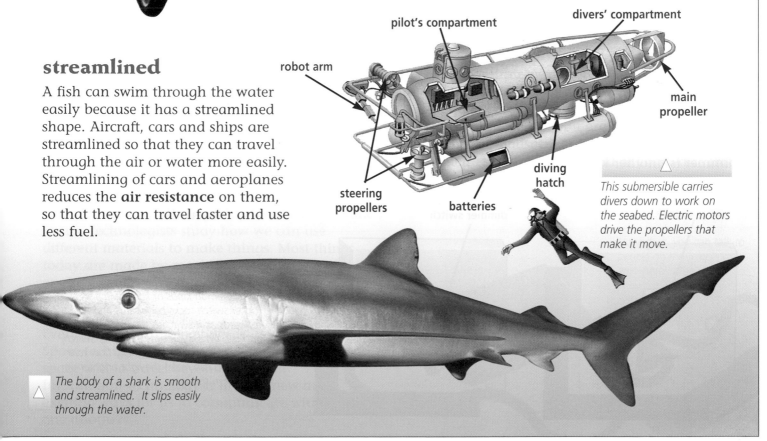

pilot's compartment · divers' compartment · robot arm · main propeller · steering propellers · batteries · diving hatch

This submersible carries divers down to work on the seabed. Electric motors drive the propellers that make it move.

telescope

A telescope is an instrument for looking at faraway objects. It uses lenses or mirrors to collect light and to produce a bigger, or magnified, picture of the distant object.

teletext

See **videotex**.

television

Television is a way of bringing pictures and sounds from faraway places into our homes. It sends, or transmits, these sounds and pictures by using **radio** waves.

A television camera takes pictures of a scene. Inside the camera, the pattern of light in the pictures is changed into a pattern of electrical signals. These picture signals and sound signals are added to a radio wave and then transmitted. At home, an aerial picks up the radio wave and feeds it to a television set. The television signals are changed into pictures on a screen and sounds from the television's loudspeakers.
See also **cathode-ray tube**, **communications**.

textiles

Textiles are fabrics and other materials made from thin threads, or fibres. Textiles include felt, rugs, carpets and sacks. Natural fibres such as cotton and wool have been used to make textiles for thousands of years. Today, **synthetic fibres** are also widely used.
See also **loom**, **spinning machine**.

TGV

A TGV is a very fast French train. TGV stands for *Train à Grande Vitesse*, which is French for high-speed train.
     See also **transport**.

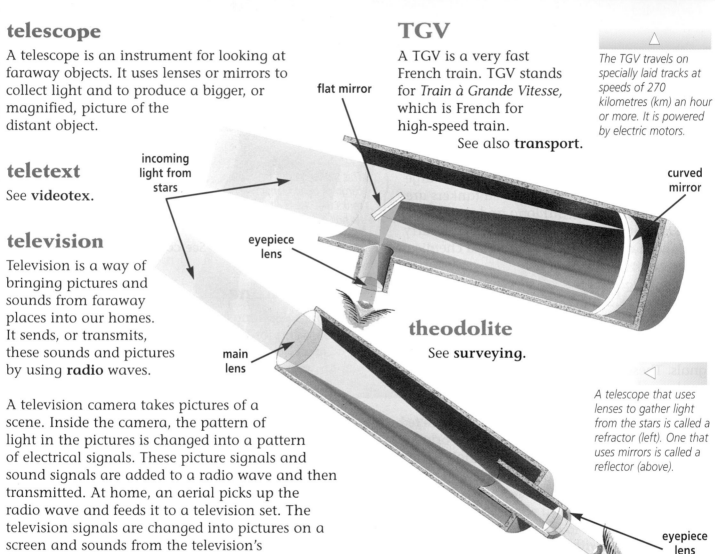

The TGV travels on specially laid tracks at speeds of 270 kilometres (km) an hour or more. It is powered by electric motors.

theodolite

See **surveying**.

A telescope that uses lenses to gather light from the stars is called a refractor (left). One that uses mirrors is called a reflector (above).

tidal power

Tidal power is produced by using the energy in the tides of seas and oceans. In some parts of the world, the difference between high and low tides can be 10 metres (m) or more. The energy of the water as it flows backwards and forwards with the tides can be used to spin water **turbines.** They turn electricity generators.

56

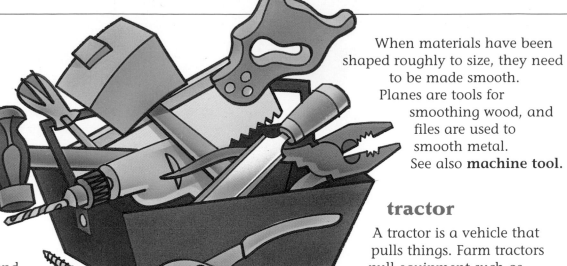

When materials have been
shaped roughly to size, they need
to be made smooth.
Planes are tools for
smoothing wood, and
files are used to
smooth metal.
See also **machine tool.**

tool

We use different
tools to help us cut
and shape materials,
and to fasten and mend
things. Most of these
tools are hand
tools, which we
hold and move
with our hands.
Some are powered by electric motors. Factories
use powerful tools called machine tools.

Some of the most common hand tools are
cutting tools. They include knives, scissors, saws
and chisels. Knives and scissors have a straight
cutting edge. Saws have a cutting edge made
up of sharp teeth. Large scissors are called
shears. Chisels have the cutting edge at
one end.

Drills cut holes in materials. They work
by a turning, or rotary, action.
You may need to drill a
hole for a screw or bolt.
You tighten a screw
with a screwdriver,
and use a spanner to
fasten a nut onto a
bolt. Pliers are a
useful gripping and
cutting tool.

tractor

A tractor is a vehicle that
pulls things. Farm tractors
pull equipment such as
ploughs. Lorry tractor units
pull trailers for
transporting goods.
Most tractors have a
diesel engine.

train

A train is a vehicle that travels on the railways.
It is made up of a **locomotive** and a number of
passenger carriages or goods wagons. The
locomotive provides the power to pull the train.

tram

A tram is a passenger vehicle that travels on
rails in city streets. It is powered by electricity
from overhead wires. A trolley-bus is powered
in the same way as a tram. It has wheels like
a bus.

transmitter

A transmitter is part of a
communications system. It is
an electronic device that sends
out messages or signals. In a
telephone, the transmitter is
the microphone inside the
mouthpiece. Radio and
television transmitters produce
radio waves that carry sound
and picture signals. These
signals are then sent out from
tall transmitting aerials.
See also **telephone, television.**

Transport

Cars, buses, lorries, trains, ships and aeroplanes are our main means of transport by land, sea and air. They carry people, materials and goods from place to place.

Transport by land depends on wheels. The first wheeled wagons, drawn by oxen, came into use about 5500 years ago. Horse-drawn carriages were the main form of transport until the early 1800s. By the late 1800s, people began travelling on roads in 'horseless carriages'. These were powered by **petrol engines**. The age of the motor car had begun.

Transport by sea also began about 5500 years ago. People put to sea in sailing ships that used the power of the wind. Today, most ships are powered by **diesel engines** or steam **turbines**.

Planes get ready to depart from London's Gatwick Airport. Almost 23 million passengers pass through the airport every year.

Transport by air began in the early 1900s. In 1900, Count von Zeppelin in Germany began building huge airships. The Wright brothers in the United States built and flew the first aeroplane three years later. In the late 1930s, new kinds of aircraft began to appear in the skies. They included the helicopter and the jet.

aircraft

Aircraft are vehicles that fly in the air. The most common one is the aeroplane. Other aircraft include the **glider** and the helicopter. All these aircraft are heavier than air. Balloons and airships are lighter than air.

airport

An airport is a place where aircraft take off and land. Tens of millions of passengers pass through international airports across the world every year. At busy airports, aircraft take off and land every few minutes.

Among the many activities that take place at an airport are checking in passengers, handling baggage, refuelling the planes and servicing the engines. In a control tower at or near the airport, air-traffic controllers use **radar** to find the positions of all aircraft on the ground, taking off and coming in to land.

container

A container is a large box that contains different kinds of goods. It can be carried by road, railway or sea. Special handling equipment is used at container terminals to move the containers between lorries, railway wagons and container ships.

▷ A container ship carries goods in containers that are stacked on its flat deck.

mass transit

Mass transit is a transport system that can carry large numbers of passengers. It transports them over short distances in a short time. Mass transit systems are used in cities, where the roads often become blocked with traffic. A mass transit system may include buses, trams, an underground railway and a surface railway.

Many cities now have mass transit railways. The tracks run on the surface, underground and above ground level.

railway

A railway is a transport system in which trains run on steel rails. On most railways, the track consists of two rails which are placed exactly 143.5 centimetres (cm) apart. This is called the standard gauge. Tracks with rails which are closer together are known as narrow gauge.

The United States has the world's biggest railway network, with over 350 000 kilometres (km) of track. Britain has about 16 000 km of railway track, on which there are around 2600 stations.

▽ Railway tracks are made up of steel rails that are welded together in long lengths. The rails are supported by shorter cross-pieces called sleepers.

◁ Concorde is the world's fastest airliner. It travels at speeds of up to 2350 kilometres (km) an hour, which is twice the speed of sound.

port

A port is a place where ships load and unload passengers and cargo. Ports are built in natural or artificial harbours, where the waters are calmer. They have facilities for ships to dock, and equipment such as cranes for lifting cargo. Some ports have dry docks for repairing ships. A dry dock is a basin from which the water can be drained out.

ship

A ship sails on the seas. Most ships are driven by **propellers.** They are powered by **diesel engines** or steam **turbines.** Ships are a slow form of transport. This is because **friction** slows them down. Liners and ferries are ships that carry passengers. Freighters carry cargo. Special kinds of freighters include container ships and oil tankers.

truck

A truck is another name for a lorry.

tunnelling

Tunnelling means digging a hole under the ground. Tunnels are dug, or bored, in mines. They are also used to carry water supplies. The biggest tunnels are bored to carry roads and railways. Many road tunnels have been bored through the Alps in Europe. They were made through the hard rock using explosives.

turbine

A turbine is an engine with wheels that spin round. The wheels are spun round by liquids or gases. Water turbines are used to drive the generators in **hydroelectric power** stations. In other power stations, steam turbines are used to spin the generators. Jet engines contain gas turbines.
See also **jet engine**.

two-stroke engine

Some motorbikes have a two-stroke engine. It produces power once in every two movements, or strokes, of its **pistons**.
See also **motorcycle**, **petrol engine**.

typesetting

Typesetting is putting together letters and words in lines ready for printing. Today, most letters, or type, are formed by computers that use fine **laser** beams. Less modern typesetting is done by arranging bits of metal that are shaped as individual letters.

typewriter

A typewriter is a small printing machine. It prints words on paper, one letter, or character, at a time. A typist taps a key, for example b, on a keyboard. Levers push a piece of type with a b on it against an inked ribbon and onto the paper.

U

Machines like this were used to bore the Channel Tunnel under the English Channel. The front part of the machine rotates and slowly grinds away the rock.

flow of steam

casing

blades

rotor

turbine wheels

The rotor in a steam turbine spins round when steam rushes through the blades of the turbine wheels.

underground railway

An underground railway travels in tunnels below the surface. It is sometimes called a subway or a metro. Underground railways are useful in busy cities because they are not affected by traffic jams on the streets above. The London Underground (opened in 1863) was the first underground railway and is still the biggest in the world.
See also **transport**.

uranium

Uranium is a kind of metal. It is used as fuel in nuclear power stations. Atoms of uranium can be made to split. When they do, enormous amounts of **nuclear energy** are given out as heat.

V

valve

A valve controls the flow of a liquid or a gas. A water tap is a kind of valve that you can open and close. Tyres have one-way valves. They let you pump air in, but the valve stops the air from escaping. Valves inside **petrol engines** let fuel and air into the cylinders, and allow burned gases to pass out.

VDU

VDU is short for video display unit. It is the name for a computer screen. See also **computer**.

Velcro

Velcro is a kind of fastener. It is made of tiny plastic hooks and loops. Velcro is often used instead of a zip fastener to join together pieces of fabric.

hooks

loops

vice

A vice is a device for holding something firmly. When you work on a piece of wood with a tool, for example, you place the wood in a vice to hold it steady.

videocassette recorder

A videocassette recorder, or VCR for short, is a machine on which you can record and play back television programmes. You can also play back recorded films. The programmes and films are recorded on a wide **magnetic tape** called a videotape. It is enclosed inside a **cassette**. The machine is also called a videotape recorder, or a video recorder.

A soldier uses virtual reality to help him work out how to fight battles. By looking in different directions he gets different views of what is happening.

videotex

Videotex is the name of the systems that call up information on a television screen. There are two main systems, called teletext and viewdata. They both use information, or data, that is stored in a powerful computer.

In a teletext system, the information is broadcast with television programmes. In the United Kingdom, Ceefax and Oracle are examples of teletext systems. In a viewdata system, the information travels to the television set along telephone lines.

Velcro fasteners are used, for example, in clothing, sports shoes, and cushion and duvet covers.

viewdata

See **videotex**.

virtual reality

Virtual reality is the use of computers to create an imaginary world that appears like the real world. To explore this world, you wear a special helmet with a built-in screen. You see different views on the screen as you turn your head. You can wear a special glove that lets you 'touch' objects in the imaginary world.
See also **simulator**.

VTOL

VTOL is short for vertical take-off and landing. A VTOL aircraft, for example a helicopter, takes off directly upwards.

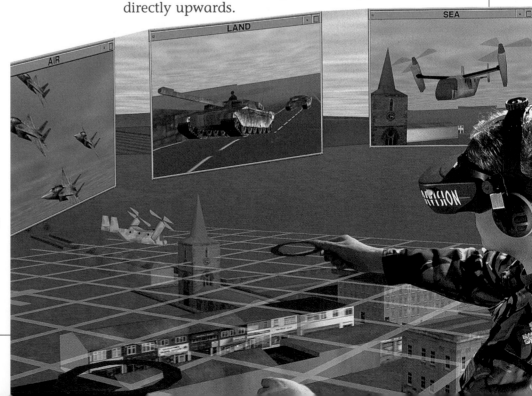

W

waste disposal

Waste disposal means getting rid of waste materials. On average, people in Europe and the United States throw away more than 2 kilograms (kg) of rubbish every day. This rubbish includes cans, paper, cardboard, bottles and plastics.

Some people send waste materials to be recycled. But most waste is put in the dustbin and then taken from our homes. It is either burned or buried in huge pits. Rubbish in pits is known as 'land-fill'. This method of waste disposal is a great waste of materials and land. See also **recycling, sewage treatment**.

watch

A watch is a small clock that you wear on your wrist. Some watches work mechanically. Their hands are turned by a system of tiny **gear** wheels, which are driven round by a spring. Digital watches have no hands. The time is shown by numbers, or digits. Digital watches are powered by a tiny battery. They are often called quartz watches because they measure time by counting the very quick movements of crystals of quartz. Some quartz watches have hands to show the time.

The insides of a mechanical watch (right). The rocking movement of a balance wheel is used to measure time. This movement lets the gear wheels move slowly, to turn the hands. A digital watch (left) uses a quartz crystal to measure time.

digital display (LCD)

balance wheel

gear wheels

jewel bearings

water power

See **hydroelectric power, tidal power, wave power**.

water supply

The water supply is the water that comes into our homes, factories, schools and businesses through pipes. The water often starts its journey in a distant river or lake. It is piped first to waterworks, where it is treated so that it is fit to drink. Chemicals such as chlorine are added to the water to kill any germs. The water is then filtered to make it crystal clear. Finally, the water is piped to our homes and to other buildings.

wave power

Wave power is produced by using the energy of the waves in seas and oceans. It is a kind of **alternative energy**. Several ways of using wave energy have been invented. None of them is suitable yet for large-scale use.

weaving

See **loom**.

weightlessness

See **space technology**.

Waves contain a huge amount of of power when they rise to be several metres high. They can give surfers an exciting ride.

water closet

A water closet (WC) is another name for a toilet or lavatory. It gets rid of human waste into the sewage system. A stream of water flushes the waste away. It leaves the WC through a bent pipe. Water trapped in the bend stops smells from rising up through the sewage pipes.

wheel and axle

See **winch**.

winch

A winch is used to lift heavy loads. It is an example of a simple machine called the wheel and **axle**. A simple hand winch has a drum with a rope wound around it. It is called a windlass. When the handle is turned, the drum turns round and winds up the rope. Cranes use winches that are driven by engines.

Some of the many kinds of wheels used on different vehicles and in various machines.

wind power

Wind power is the use of the energy blowing in the wind. It can be used to generate electricity. The windmill was the first machine to use the wind's energy. Today, windmills have been replaced by wind **turbines.** Most of them have huge **propellers,** which spin round when the wind blows. The propellers turn generators to produce electricity. In places, groups of wind turbines have been built to create wind 'farms'. See also **alternative energy.**

welding

Welding is a very common method of joining pieces of metal. The pieces are held together and then heated strongly where they touch. The metal there melts and mixes. When it cools, it forms a strong joint between the pieces. Extra metal may be added to the joint during welding. Burning gas or electricity may be used to produce the high temperatures that are needed for welding.

Sparks fly as a welder uses an electric welding torch to make a metal joint.

wheel

The wheel is one of the most important inventions ever made. One of its first uses, in about 3500 BC, was as a potter's wheel to make pottery. But people soon discovered how to make wheeled carts, which became the main way of transporting goods. Without the wheel, there would be no cars, bicycles or trains. There would be few machines or engines. Most of them use wheels of some kind, particularly **gear** wheels.

wind tunnel

A wind tunnel is a structure through which air is blown or sucked. Aircraft and vehicle designers use wind tunnels to test new aircraft and vehicles. They can find out how well their designs 'slip' through the air. They try to make their designs as **streamlined** as possible to reduce **air resistance.** Other engineers use wind tunnels to test the effects of the wind on structures such as bridges.

X Z

wing

The wings of an aircraft keep it up in the air. They are made in a special shape, which is called an aerofoil. When the wings move through the air, the air pressure above them drops slightly. The air underneath tries to force the wings upwards. When an aeroplane travels fast enough, the lifting force on its wings becomes so strong that the aeroplane lifts off the ground and flies.
See also **aeroplane**, **hydrofoil**.

wire

Wire is a thin thread of metal. It is made by pulling a metal rod through smaller and smaller holes in special pieces of equipment called **dies**.

wood

See **materials**.

Using a word processor, it is quick and easy to set out and print letters and other documents.

word processing

Word processing means preparing and printing out words by using some kind of computer. A simple word processor is like a typewriter with a small screen. It has a small memory which can store words and sentences that you use regularly.

More powerful word processors have a large memory and a bigger screen. They can store many different instructions for moving and arranging the words that are typed in. Word-processing programs for computers do the same things. For example, they let you alter the text you have typed, move around paragraphs, check the spelling, change the size and style of the type, and so on. You only need to print out the text when you are completely happy with it.

Zip fasteners have been in use for more than 100 years.

xerox

A xerox is another word for a photocopy. The word comes from xerography, which is the name for the process that most photocopiers use.

Xerox is also the name of one make of photocopier. See also **photocopier**.

X-ray machine

Doctors use an X-ray machine to look inside the human body. An X-ray machine produces invisible waves called X-rays. They are a kind of **radiation**.

When an X-ray is taken, the rays pass through your body and are recorded on a piece of film. They pass easily through your flesh, but not through the bones. The X-ray photograph shows whether any of your bones are broken. X-ray machines are also used at airports to detect dangerous metal objects, such as guns and knives, on passengers or in their luggage.

zip fastener

A zip fastener is a fastening device for clothes. It has two tapes with rows of tiny teeth. The teeth are made of metal or hard plastic. When you do up a zip, a clip joins the teeth so that they lock firmly together.
See also **Velcro**.